Conversations wi

Literary Conversations Series

Peggy Whitman Prenshaw
General Editor

Conversations with Saul Bellow

Edited by
Gloria L. Cronin and Ben Siegel

University Press of Mississippi
Jackson

Books by Saul Bellow

Dangling Man. New York: Vanguard, 1944.
The Victim. New York: Vanguard, 1947.
The Adventures of Augie March. New York: Viking, 1953.
Seize the Day. New York: Viking, 1956.
Henderson the Rain King. New York: Viking, 1959.
Herzog. New York: Viking, 1964.
The Last Analysis. New York: Viking, 1965.
Mosby's Memoirs. New York: Viking, 1968.
Mr. Sammler's Planet. New York: Viking, 1970.
Humboldt's Gift. New York: Viking, 1975.
To Jerusalem and Back. New York: Viking, 1976.
The Dean's December. New York: Harper, 1982.
Him with His Foot in His Mouth and Other Stories. New York: Harper, 1984.
More Die of Heartbreak. New York: Morrow, 1987.
A Theft. New York: Penguin, 1989.
The Bellarosa Connection. New York: Penguin, 1989.
Something To Remember Me By: Three Tales. New York: Signet, 1991.
It All Adds Up: From the Dim Past to the Uncertain Future. New York: Viking, 1994.

Copyright © 1994 by the University Press of Mississippi
All rights reserved
Manufactured in the United States of America

97 96 95 94   4 3 2 1

The paper in this book meets the guidelines for permanence and durability of the Committee on Production Guidelines for Book Longevity of the Council on Library Resources.

Library of Congress Cataloging-in-Publication Data
Bellow, Saul.
    Conversations with Saul Bellow / edited by Gloria L. Cronin and Ben Siegel.
        p.   cm.—(Literary conversations series)
    Includes index.
    ISBN 0-87805-717-X (cloth : alk. paper).—ISBN 0-87805-718-8 (paper : alk. paper)
        1. Bellow, Saul—Interviews. 2. Authors, American—20th century—Biography. I. Cronin, Gloria L., 1947– . II. Siegel, Ben, 1925– . III. Title. IV. Series
PS3503.E4488Z55 1994
813'.52—dc20
    [B]   94-19474
                                                                          CIP

British Library Cataloging-in-Publication data available

Contents

Introduction

Saul Bellow has been writing fiction for a half-century and is
generally recognized to be the preeminent American novelist of the
second half of the twentieth century. Curiously, he has managed to
appear both the most public and private of writers. He is not
given to public displays or to being seen frequently on television
talk shows. Hence, he is not well known to the general public.
Most Americans do not recognize his name, much less his face. Yet
those who read Bellow's fiction cannot help feeling they know
him intimately. He is a strongly autobiographical fictionist whose
probings of the self help explain his strong reliance on monologue.
Indeed, Bellow's monologists usually share many of their creator's
views, traits, and personal experiences. Those who know Bellow
personally easily recognize themselves or other members of his
circle of relatives and friends.

Bellow also has made himself known intellectually to his readers.
He has done so not only by his novels and stories, but also by his
essays, lectures, and interviews. Most commentators find his intel-
lect impressive. Nowhere have this intelligence and far-reaching
play-of-mind revealed themselves more clearly or succinctly than in
his interviews. Bellow has granted approximately seventy interviews, most of them to newspaper or magazine staffers. But those
interviews given to television reporters also have found their way
into print or transcript. On occasion, Bellow has responded pa-
tiently to questions posed by a young academic at work on a
thesis or dissertation. Generally, however, his interviews have been
keyed to his novels—that is, each novel's appearance has been
followed by a cluster of related interviews. Often the questioners
have veered from Bellow's new book to his writing habits or
opinions of other writers (past and present), his personal beliefs
(religious, political, and cultural), and his life experiences. Collec-
tively, the interviews form a telling intellectual account or portrait
of a penetrating, comprehensive mind. In fact, Bellow's sound grasp

of diverse individuals, events, and issues becomes evident in almost any one of the interviews included here. What also becomes clear here is that Saul Bellow is an observer of the human scene on whom, as Henry James once stated, "nothing is lost."

Bellow published his first novel, *Dangling Man,* in 1944. Almost unbelievably, his first interview did not appear in a significant publication until nine years later. Yet *Dangling Man* had been reviewed by such prominent critics as Diana Trilling, Irving Kristol, Delmore Schwartz, and Edmund Wilson. Still, there were no interviews. In 1947, he published *The Victim,* a novel that received even more critical attention from reviewers like Mordecai Richler, Alan Downer, Leslie Fiedler, Elizabeth Hardwick, and (again) Diana Trilling. But there were no interviews. Bellow may have opted not to be interviewed. Perhaps he had not felt "ready" to respond to reporters' questions. Some years later he would complain that he disliked interviews, especially television interviews. He felt no connection, he explained, with "those long-isolated writers who yearn to become part of the cultural furniture of the scene, emerging all too ready into the arms of the jet set like King Kong meeting the Monster from 20 fathoms." It was only when, in 1953, *The Adventures of Augie March* resounded like a thunderclap on the American literary scene, that a major reviewer, Harvey Breit, sat down for a direct conversation with Bellow. Making adroit use of the occasion, Bellow here outlined his educational background, described the ease with which he had written his big novel, and, perhaps even more significantly, put on record his thoughts on the contemporary novel.

Bellow granted only one more interview in the 1950s. The next decade, however, was very different. By the time he sat for Bruce Cook's "profile" in 1963, Bellow had published five novels, with a sixth, *Herzog,* soon to come off the press. He had become an important writer in the intervening years and a favorite with journalists and academics. Seemingly, he also had experienced a change of attitude toward his interviewers. He would now *use* the interview more openly—to explain his work, to make certain he was not misunderstood, to respond to his critics, and to express his views on a wide range of cultural and societal issues. Bellow lamented repeatedly that too often reviewers, especially the academic ones, misread his work and distorted his intentions. (He would prove especially unhappy, even years later, that most professional readers had missed the humor in *Herzog*.) His change of heart resulted in his being interrogated in print at least sixteen times between 1963 and 1969.

Always confident and candid, Bellow was now even more outspoken about his need for privacy and creative independence. "Nothing irritates me more," he informed Cook, "than to be taken for a piece of cultural furniture." He then added: "I detest Culture, because it belongs to the department of public iconolatry." He himself harbored no wish to be a cultural or media darling, nor to be placed in competition with other writers. Later in the interview Cook asked him to respond to the question that resonates both in his first novel and throughout his later fiction: "What can a good man do?" Bellow did not hesitate: "I'd say you have to struggle with the evil in life. Not with the abstract, but with evil as you see it and feel it around you. If you abdicate to it—and that's so easy to do—then you succumb to the common life, the unenlightened, unillumined life. Everyone pretends to praise the common life, but everyone is secretly bewildered by it. Some even loathe it—as they should."

In 1970, immediately following publication of *Mr. Sammler's Planet*, Bellow allowed Jane Howard of *Life* magazine to observe an encounter he had with a group of Yale University students in the creative-writing class of his friend Robert Penn Warren. In his new novel Bellow had come down hard on the Radical Left, especially the politicized university young. One student got straight to the point: What did the eminent visitor think of "campus revolutionaries"? Bellow did not hesitate: "The trouble with the destroyers is that they're just as phony as what they've come to destroy. Maybe civilization is dying, but it still exists, and meanwhile we have our choice: we can either rain more blows on it, or try to redeem it." The students responded by leaving. Later, Bellow took aim at one of his favorite targets, America's so-called intellectuals. "Ten years ago," Bellow informed Howard, "all the intellectuals expressed nothing but horror of mass media." Since then they have reversed themselves, for "now, just as violently, that's what they're embracing. This reflects their faddishness, not to say

their sneakiness and cowardice." As a result he held a special
distrust of those fellow academics and intellectuals who assume
"defiant, radical, independent points of view" for the wrong
reasons. "A radical stance," Bellow insisted, "is the ultimate
luxury for those who already have everything else."

He then expressed his particular annoyance with those intellectuals of his own generation who succumb to the American myth
that "the intellectual life is somehow not virile. Artists and professors, like clergymen and librarians, are thought to be female. Our
populist tradition requires the artist to represent himself as a man
of the people, and to conceal his real concern with thought.
Maybe that's why we don't have more novels of ideas." As for the
recently published *Mr. Sammler's Planet,* noted Bellow, that was
his own "first thoroughly nonapologetic venture into ideas." In
Henderson the Rain King and *Herzog,* he added, "I was kidding
my way to Jesus, but here I'm baring myself nakedly." Asked his
views on the feminist movement, Bellow again did not hesitate:
"I'm all for freedom, short of degeneracy. As John Stuart Mill
foresaw, women today show all the characteristics of slaves in
revolt. They're prone to the excesses of the lately servile, the newly
freed. I'd like to see their increased freedom accompanied by
human development. Gentleness and generosity, which used to be
considered feminine qualities, are certainly not contemptible—
are they?"

Bellow seems to have sustained that angry mood for the rest of
the decade. For eleven years and twenty-five more interviews
later, he struck the same notes of social irritation and concern. In a
lengthy 1981 interview with Michiko Kakutani, he made clear his
views had not changed. Appearing on the front page of the *New
York Times* their discussion marked publication of his angry
political novel *The Dean's December.* Kakutani spiced her piece
with quotes from earlier interviews and essays, but these statements differed little in tone or stance from Bellow's direct responses
to her questions. Reaffirming his own credentials as a social
observer, Bellow declared the modern novelist to be "an imaginative historian, who is able to get closer to contemporary facts than
social scientists possibly can." He had set out to prove this in *The
Dean's December* where, he pointed out, he dealt with political

oppression behind the Iron Curtain, the terrible living conditions of
the American "underclass," college-student radicalism and militancy,
and the progressive deterioration of American urban life. Indeed,
this novel represented a departure: "I had never really attempted
anything of this sort before, though I've been all my life an amateur
student of history and politics. It became clear to me that no
imagination whatsoever had been applied to the problems of demoralized cities. All the approaches have been technical, financial
and bureaucratic, and no one has been able to take into account the
sense of these lives. I thought I had to cut loose with this book."

Bellow also took occasion here to deal with an earlier charge
leveled at him in *Partisan Review* by Richard Poirier. The latter
had accused him of propagating "a kind of cultural conservatism"
in *Herzog* and *Mr. Sammler's Planet*. Bellow now rejected the charge.
"People who stick labels on you are in the gumming business," he
declared angrily. "What good are these categories? They mean
very little, especially when the people who apply them haven't had
a new thought since they were undergraduates." Having warmed
to the occasion, Bellow vented his long-suppressed resentment at
the unfair ethnic criticism meted out to him early in his career.
He referred specifically to the anti-Semitic backlash by a few
members of the WASP literary establishment when he received
the 1953 National Book Award for *Augie March*. "It came at a
strange point when I think the WASP establishment was losing
confidence in itself," he stated, "and it felt it was being challenged
by Jews, blacks and ethnics." So desperate did some people
become that they insisted "there was a Jewish mafia, and other
people, who should have had more sense, spoke of—well, they
didn't use the word conspiracy, but they saw it as an unwelcome
eruption." Bellow then seized the chance to dismiss the related
label of "Jewish writer," an appellation that also had long irritated
him. "I think of myself as an American of Jewish heritage," he
declared, not for the first time. "When most people call someone a
'Jewish writer,' it's a way of setting you aside. They don't talk
about the powers of the 'Jewish writers' who wrote the Old Testament; they say to write novels you need to know something about
manners, which is something you have to be raised in the South to
know. I felt many writers [during the 50s and early 60s] treated

their Jewish colleagues with unpardonable shabbiness." What made
all this hostility doubly sad was that, as he saw it, "anti-Semitism
after the Holocaust is absolutely unforgivable."

At that point Bellow shifted rather unexpectedly to the institution
where he has spent his entire adult life: the university. Bellow's
ambivalence toward the academy has always been pronounced.
Here he could declare unequivocally that "it's in the university
and only in the university that Americans can have a higher life."
But, at the same time, he has found professors to be "so eager to
live the life of society like everybody else that they're not always
intellectually or spiritually as rigorous as they should be." He then
catalogued quickly, in Kakutani's paraphrase, a few of academe's
other notable misdeeds. "By institutionalizing the avant-garde
magazines and giving writers the security of tenure," he stated,
"universities effectively destroyed the independent literary culture
that once existed in this country." Despite his mixed views of
academe, Bellow had spent the past three decades at the University of Chicago, relocating only recently to Boston University. He
had explained repeatedly his need to live in his home city of
Chicago. There he not only could keep close contact with relatives
and old friends, but he also encountered a rich cross-section of
humanity. Many Chicagoans, naturally enough, have worked their
way into his fiction. "You meet people," he explained. "They
reveal or conceal themselves, and you read them or try. They
struggle with their souls or don't. They either generate interest or
not. It forms a picture for you. The people who interest me the
most do concern themselves with the formation of a soul. The
others are what Hollywood used to call the cast of thousands."

Bellow launched the nineties with a lengthy two-part dialogue in
Bostonia magazine. It proved not only the longest interview by far
that he had granted but also the most intellectually ambitious. Here
Bellow related a childhood experience he had used in his fiction.
When he was eight, he was hospitalized for about a half-year in the
Children's Ward of Montreal's very Protestant Royal Victoria
Hospital. With children dying about him, young Solomon Bellows
(his birth name) decided his own survival was a near-miracle. He
was convinced he "was privileged" and that there was some form
"of bookkeeping going on." Doing his "own mental bookkeeping,"

the youthful Solomon decided he "owed something to some entity
for the privilege of surviving." In other words, he believed he
had "better make it worth the while of whoever it was that authorized all this." In short, he has nurtured always the possibility he had
"gotten away with something but that it had been by permission of
some high authority." He felt obliged to strengthen himself both
physically and mentally. Certainly he had numerous opportunities
to exercise his mind. Political issues were the topic of choice in
the Bellow home. His Russian-emigré parents followed avidly the
Russian Revolution's ebb and flow. "Their parents and brothers
and sisters were still there," said Bellow. "I was born in 1915.
Before I was three the Russian Revolution was fully under way. . . .
I knew all about Lenin and Trotsky," despite not grasping precisely
"what the Revolution as such meant." But when he was nine, his
family moved from Montreal to Chicago, and Bellow's political
ideas now were fed by that city's newspapers which, he recalled,
were very important. "There was no radio of course. Everybody
took positions based on the paper he read, whether it was the
Hearst paper or the McCormick paper in Chicago." In the early
Twenties these papers were hardly lacking in "daily drama,"
noted Bellow, what with such colorful figures and vivid events as
"Clarence Darrow and the Leopold and Loeb murder."

But more important to his family than murders and killers, said
Bellow, "was Americanization and assimilation." These were
immediate issues that literally "divided" the household. "My eldest
brother pulled for total Americanization; he was ashamed of being
an immigrant." His father, too, "was all for Americanism," Bellow
remembered. "At the table he would tell us, this really is the land of
opportunity; you're free to do whatever you like, within the law,
and you're free either to run yourself into the ground or improve
your chances." Clearly, the novelist has integrated into his fiction
many of the lessons he learned at the kitchen table. "For Jewish
immigrants, especially the children," he added, life in America
"was a strange mixture, not an easily blending one. Let's say you
went to an American school, you played baseball in cinderlots, and
then you went to Hebrew school at three in the afternoon. Until
five, you were studying the first five books of Moses and learning to
write Yiddish in Hebrew characters—and all the rest of it. So

there it was. I didn't go to a parochial school, but the religious vein
was very strong and lasted until I was old enough to make a
choice between Jewish life and street life. The power of street life
made itself felt.''

As for his vaunted street life, young Saul Bellow spent much of it
in the public library. He was always a voracious reader. ''By the
time I was in high school I was reading Dreiser, Sherwood Anderson, Mencken. Dreiser was fresh stuff, active and of the moment,
right up to date.'' He also read Jack London and Upton Sinclair.
''Those two socialist apostles . . . were also at the same time
Darwinists.'' The two of them ''taught the struggle for survival.
Victory to the strong.'' Lest he be misunderstood, Bellow was
quick to point out that a considerable ''amount of junk'' from the
pages of the *Saturday Evening Post* and *Collier's* was brought
into the family home by his ''Americanizing brother.'' Yet despite
all his readings, said Bellow, he never thought of himself as an
intellectual: ''I was just a pair of eyes.'' When he did think of his
mind in those early years, he perceived it as a ''melange.'' It was,
he suggested, ''as if the head of a modern person were sawed open
and things were tumbling in from every direction. So you had the
Bible and the Patriarchs cheek by jowl with Russian novelists and
German philosophers and revolutionary activists and all the rest.
Your mind was very much like the barrel of books at Walgreens
where you could pick up a classic for 19¢.''

But more powerful than the books he read, Bellow now thought,
was his ''inner conviction that we were all here on a very strange
contingency plan, that we didn't know how we had gotten here, nor
what meaning our being here really had.'' With all his reading he
had hoped to make ''some discovery of truth about these persistent
intimations. At bottom the feeling was always very strange and
would never be anything but strange. All of the explanations you
got failed to account for the strangeness. The systems fall away
one by one and you tick them off as you pass them. *Au revoir*.
Existentialism. But you never actually finish with this demand that
you account for your being here.'' What he has repeatedly tried to
convey, he explained, ''is that we've been misled by our education into believing there are no mysteries.'' However, he himself,
he insisted, was not misled. He supposed this was because he

"had a radical Jewish skepticism about all of the claims that were made." He began early to have grave doubts, for example, about the very anthropology scholars whose books he had to read. He realized "they had no literary abilities. They wrote books, but they were not real writers. They were deficient in trained sensibilities. They brought what they called 'science' to human matters, matters of human judgment, but their 'science' could never replace a trained sensibility." For Bellow there was no way of acquiring such a sensibility without first taking "certain masterpieces into yourself as if they were communion wafers." He had become convinced that "If you don't give literature a decisive part to play in your existence, then you haven't got anything but a show of culture." Any claimed culture devoid of literature "has no reality whatever." Bellow has laid down the gauntlet to the would-be educated. "It's an acceptable challenge," he declared, "to internalize all of these great things, all of this marvelous poetry. When you've done that, you've been shaped from within by these books and these writers." Certainly few lovers of modern fiction, including those who read these interviews, will deny that Saul Bellow not only has internalized much of Western literature but also has done his best to share his findings.

This collection makes clear that Saul Bellow grasped quickly the lesson learned by many of his literary colleagues: to use the interview form as a means of responding to critics (literary and personal) and of clarifying aspects of his own thought and fiction he felt had been misinterpreted. Some critics have argued that writers should not be held as responsible for their interviews as they are for their writings. Whatever the validity of this claim, it seems clear that the bringing together of a writer's ideas and words expressed on numerous occasions over many years inevitably provides important insights into that individual's character and work. Indeed, such a cumulative "index" should enable not only the interested reader but also the bemused writer to look back and discern patterns in his or her own life and thought not realized at the time. Let it also be said that in a gathering of interviews granted over four decades, some repetition is inevitable. Indeed, a basic consistency of thought and outlook is to be welcomed. Still, readers here should avoid the temptation to skip over subjects

discussed in other interviews. Bellow is given to offering new
details and perspectives each time he returns to familiar ideas or
events. Following Literary Conversations Series procedure, we
have reprinted the interviews uncut and in their original form—and,
whenever possible, arranged them by the date the interview was
given. In a few pieces there are periods suggesting ellipses, but
these are reproduced from the original versions. Occasionally, however, we have silently corrected typographical errors, supplied
omitted words, added in italics the full titles of works, and
provided needed punctuation marks.

   We would like to thank William H. Davenport, Professor Emeri-
tus at Harvey Mudd College (Claremont, California), for his
thoughtful editorial suggestions. At Brigham Young University, we
are indebted to Blaine H. Hall, the Humanities Librarian, for his
untiring cooperation, to Daryl Carr for his relentless combing of the
files and library stacks tracking down needed materials, and to Lynne
Facer for her expert editorial assistance.

GLC
BS
April 1994

Chronology

1915	Saul Bellow born Solomon Bellows 10 July in Lachine, Canada, the fourth child of Abraham Bellows and Liza Bellows, who have emigrated from St. Petersburg, Russia in 1913
1919	Bellow takes Hebrew lessons and memorizes large passages of the Old Testament.
1923	Hospitalized for tuberculosis for nearly six months in the children's ward of Montreal's Royal Victoria Hospital
1924	Bellows family moves to Chicago and lives in the tenements of Humboldt Park. Saul (Solly) attends Lafayette School, Columbus Elementary School, Sabin Junior High, and Tuley High. Liza Bellows dies.
1933	Graduates from Tuley High School (on Chicago's Northwest Side) and enters University of Chicago
1935	Transfers to Northwestern University; works under Melville J. Herskovits in anthropology.
1937	B.A. from Northwestern (honors in sociology and anthropology); goes to Madison to study at the University of Wisconsin. Leaves before year's end.
1938	Marries Anita Goshkin; returns to Chicago; works on WPA Writers' Project.
1939	Supports himself by teaching, odd jobs, and working on the Index (*Synopticon*) of *Great Books* series; generally leads a bohemian existence; teaches at Pestalozzi-Froebel Teacher's College.
1940	Enters Merchant Marine Maritime Camp at Sheepshead Bay, Long Island
1941	"Two Morning Monologues"
1942	"The Mexican General"

1943   "Notes of a Dangling Man"

1944   *Dangling Man,* first novel; first son, Gregory, born.

1945   Lives on Pineapple Street in Brooklyn Heights, writing
            book reviews and reading for newly formed Penguin
            Books; works on *The Victim.*

1946–48   Teaches at the University of Minnesota in Minneapolis

1947   *The Victim*

1948   Guggenheim Fellowship

1948–50   Writes and lives in Paris; travels in Europe; begins work
            on *The Adventures of Augie March* and publishes segments
            in various magazines.

1949   "Dora"; "Sermon by Dr. Pep."

1950   "The Trip To Galena"; returns to U. S. A. for the next
            ten years and lives in New York City and Dutchess
            County, New York; teaches evening courses at New York
            University, Washington Square; reviews books, writes
            articles; works on novels and short stories.

1951   "Looking for Mr. Green"; "By the Rock Wall"; "Ad-
            dress by Gooley MacDowell to the Hasbeens Club
            of Chicago."

1952   National Institute of Arts and Letters Award; Creative
            Writing Fellow, Princeton University.

1953   Professor of American Literature, Bard College; *The
            Adventures of Augie March*: National Book Award;
            translates Isaac Bashevis Singer's "Gimpel the Fool"
            from the Yiddish.

1956   *Seize the Day;* "The Gonzaga Manuscripts"; marries
            Alexandra Tsachacbasov.

1957   Second child, Adam, born

1958   "Leaving the Yellow House"; Ford Foundation grant.

1959   *Henderson the Rain King;* leaves his wife, embarks on
            European lecture tour in Poland and West Germany.

1960–62   Coedits *The Noble Savage;* Friends of Literature Fiction
            Award.

1961   Marries Susan Alexandra Glassman, his third wife

1962   Honorary Doctor of Letters, Northwestern University;
        joins Committee on Social Thought at the University of
        Chicago; "Scenes from Humanitis," an early version of
        the play *The Last Analysis;* third child, Daniel, is born.

1963   Edits *Great Jewish Short Stories;* Honorary Doctor of
        Letters, Bard College; returns to Chicago in the fall.

1964   *Herzog;* James L. Dow Award; National Book Award;
        Fomentor Award; *The Last Analysis* opens on Broad-
        way and closes within two weeks.

1965   International Prize for *Herzog;* three one-act plays, "Out
        from Under," "Orange Souffle," "A Wen," staged in
        April off-Broadway by Nancy Walker for a private show-
        ing at the Loft; *The Last Analysis* published with revi-
        sions.

1967   Reports on the Israeli Six-Day War for *Newsday* maga-
        zine, then published by Bill Moyers; accepts permanent
        position at University of Chicago and returns from New
        York to furnished rooms in South Chicago.

1968   "Mosby's Memoirs"; "The Old System"; *Mosby's Mem-
        oirs and Other Stories;* Jewish Heritage Award from
        B'nai B'rith; French Croix de Chevalier des Arts et
        Lettres; begins work on *Mr. Sammler's Planet.*

1969   Early version of *Mr. Sammler's Planet* appears in the *At-
        lantic*

1970   *Mr. Sammler's Planet;* booed and catcalled off the stage
        at San Francisco State College.

1971   National Book Award for *Mr. Sammler's Planet; Last
        Analysis* performed again at the off-Broadway theater, Cir-
        cle in the Square, closes five weeks later.

1974   "Zetland: By a Character Witness;" "Burdens of a
        Lone Survivor."

1975   *Humboldt's Gift;* meets Owen Barfield; marries Alexan-
        dra Ionescu Tulcea.

1976   *To Jerusalem and Back: A Personal Account;* Nobel Prize
        for Literature; visits Bucharest.

Conversations with Saul Bellow

A Talk with Saul Bellow

Harvey Breit / 1953

From the *New York Times Book Review*, 20 September 1953, 22.
Reprinted in *The Writer Observed* (Cleveland: World Publishers,
1956), 271–74. © 1953 by New York Times Company. Reprinted
by permission.

It was of Dostoevsky that Andre Gide once said all factions could
find something in him to support their claims but no one faction
could claim him exclusively. Some of this holds true for Saul
Bellow. He came up as a writer out of the tough, tight literary
magazines, established his beachhead, as it were, and is now
successfully fanning out into the broader and brighter domains:
his talents, valued from the start by the severer critics, have
gradually begun to be noticed by greater numbers of ordinary,
intelligent vintage. Mr. Bellow's work contains innumerably diverse
elements. It has variousness and is against the grain. His readers,
therefore, are to be found anywhere and everywhere and they can
be anyone at all.

Mr. Bellow's face has variousness too: sharply etched, the structure conveys scientific coldness, but the texture is bold, lyric,
poetic. And similarly with his manner, he will talk on the most
abstruse or delicate or complex subjects in a matter-of-fact, even
breezy, colloquial. What he renders unto Caesar is public, what he
renders unto God is a strictly private matter.

His first leap into the swaddling banded world was in 1915 in
Quebec. His father, living in Petrograd, had been importing
Egyptian onions. He decided to migrate to Canada because his
sister was living there. In telling it, Mr. Bellow said in an aside
that his father was a fascinating character. Since *The Adventures of
Augie March* was a big novel, one wondered whether his father
was in it? "No," Mr. Bellow said laughingly, "I've saved him."

[Bellow moved] From Canada to Chicago at the age of 9, and
there the youthful Bellow remained for quite a while. Two years
at the U of Chicago brought him around to the conclusion that the
study of literature was not the best way to become a writer. He

decided to become an anthropologist and he buried himself in the
stacks of Northwestern U, working under the famed Professor
Herskovits (who wanted to make a pianist out of him). He next got
a scholarship at Wisconsin, where he plugged at his master's
thesis in anthropology. There Dr. Goldenweiser assured him he
wasn't cut out for science. His papers had too much style. "It
was a nice way of easing me out of the field," Mr. Bellow said.

"Goldenweiser played Chopin and wept. He was very Chekhov-
ian. The old boy's heart was really in literature. Every time I
worked on my thesis, it turned out to be a story. I disappeared for
the Christmas holidays and I never came back." Mr. Bellow
laughed a little, and then said, "This is my way of making a change.
Disappearing from something and never coming back."

And so at this juncture began "The Adventures of Saul Bellow"
because at this point he started to write. Between then and *Augie
March,* Mr. Bellow had written two novels, *Dangling Man* and *The
Victim.* Mr. Bellow nodded but contradicted, "This is the third
published novel. I threw two novels away because they were too
sad."

Mr. Bellow has written steadily all the while: short stories,
essays, literary articles. He won a Guggenheim Fellowship and a
National Institute of Arts and Letters Award. Along the way he
taught at the University of Minnesota and at Princeton. He has
taken a job on the English staff of Bard College, which brings our
author up to the immediate present. Except for *Augie.* Would Mr.
Bellow tell us what he could?

He thought a bit and then said, "I started *Augie* in Paris. I wrote
it in trains and cafes. I got used to writing on the roll. I hunted for
the right cafe in Rome, and when I found it, I worked there all the
time. After I was there about a month, the waiter told me it was
where D'Annunzio used to come to write. But," Mr. Bellow added
dryly, "I don't expect to get into politics."

Had he had any trouble getting so right a name as Augie March?
Mr. Bellow shook his head negatively, almost sleepily. "It just
came to me," he said. "The great pleasure of the book was that it
came easily. All I had to do was be there with buckets to catch it.
That's why the form is loose."

Then it had just flowed easily and loosely and there was no

literary principle back of the looseness. "Something like that," Mr. Bellow replied. "But I do think that the novel has imitated poetry far too much recently." How had it done that? "In its severity and style and devotion to exact form. In the great period of the novel, the novelist didn't care—there was a great mass of sand and gravel, there was diversity of scene, a large number of characters. One of the reasons the novel has diminished is that a great many people, writers, find it difficult to write dramatic scenes.

"After all, the novel grew out of daily events, out of newspapers. Today, the novelist thinks too much of immortality and he tries to create form. He tries to make his work durable through form. But you have to take your chances on mortality, on perishability. That's what I felt. I kicked over the traces, wrote catch-as-catch-can, picaresque. I took my chance."

Mr. Bellow shrugged, smiled and made his momentous novel seem casual. It was, we were convinced, what he wanted and needed to do. Obviously, Mr. Bellow was against the over-solemn, the too-pious manner, the inflated ego. Who could be against Mr. Bellow for that?

Saul Bellow: A Mood of Protest
Bruce Cook / 1963

From *Perspectives on Ideas and the Arts,* 12 February 1963, 46–50.

"Nothing irritates me more than to be taken for a piece of cultural furniture." Belligerent words from a reasonable man—Saul Bellow. In his office at the University of Chicago, he leaned back in his chair, collar open and tie askew, hands clasped behind his head, with a smile on his face. "I detest Culture, because it belongs to the department of public iconolatry." The smile widened into a grin with the last word; he was obviously pleased with it.

"This is one of the few advantages a writer has here in America— he can fade out. In Europe, everyone has this *cher maitre* attitude toward writers and artists. And something like it is developing over here—like it, but not the same. A whole new class of literate, well-to-do people have become interested in reading about writers. What they've done is to encourage a new breed of clowns among writers—you can supply the names—who have created a new branch of the entertainment industry." He shrugged, and again came the grin. "But it's all right with me. I'm entertained, too."

For the interest and edification of this new, literate, well-to-do class, the *New York Times Book Review* recently printed answers from six American critics to the question, "Whom do you see on the horizon who may in time take the places of Hemingway and Faulkner as the internationally recognized greats of American letters?" To their credit, the critics hedged artfully; most of them hinted that the question was a rather silly one. But in the end, all but one named names, and between them the critics compiled a list of 25 writers. For what it's worth, the writer mentioned most often was Saul Bellow.

Despite his distaste for them, Bellow always places high in such literary beauty contests. When, as is their wont, critics draw up lists of the "Ten Greatest Living American Novelists" or "Five Fiction Prophets of the Post-Atomic Era," he is always up there—

win, place, or show. This is mildly paradoxical, for Bellow feels he is competing with no wish to square off a la Hemingway with his contemporaries, much less with Tolstoy or Stendhal. "I find that every book I write seems different from the last. I would be glad if I could find a consistency in myself."

Yet it should surprise no one, least of all Saul Bellow, that he is so often taken for a piece of cultural furniture—a lamp of course: *lux* to the modern literary *tenebris*. To ignore him would be impossible, for his five books comprise perhaps the most solid body of work yet produced by any writer since the war. His first novel, *Dangling Man* (which Edmund Wilson called "one of the most honest pieces of testimony on the psychology of a whole generation"), was published during the war, in 1944. *The Victim,* which followed in 1947, was praised by Diana Trilling as "hard to match, in recent fiction, for brilliance, skill, and originality."

While these two books established him as a writer of considerable talent and one whose intellectual credentials were in impeccable order, they did little to prepare his critics or his small public for *The Adventures of Augie March*. This novel surprised everyone with its variety and vitality; it won him wide critical acclaim, thousands of new readers, and the 1953 National Book Award. Since assuming his present, pre-eminent position with *Augie March,* he has published the short novel, *Seize the Day* ("the best single piece Bellow has written"—Richard Chase), and the wild and woolly "African" book, *Henderson the Rain King* ("Have I ever been to Africa?" echoed Bellow. "Why should I go to Africa?"). His new novel, *Herzog,* has been scheduled for spring publication, and he may have a play produced next season in New York—"if I can get it into shape by then."

In the opinion of critic Richard Chase, what Saul Bellow has written so far distinguishes him as "just about the best novelist of his generation." Some have been even more generous in their praise; others have been downright antagonistic in their criticism. Maxwell Geismar has called him the Herman Wouk of the academic quarterlies. After writing off *Augie March* as "a travelogue for timid intellectuals," Norman Mailer allowed that "his work does no obvious harm, but I think one must not be easy on art which tries for less than it can manage. . . ."

The point is simply that Saul Bellow is a writer about whom one must have an opinion. His staunchest supporters are aligned with the *Kenyon* and *Partisan Review* axis. His detractors are a motley, though often vocal, group made up of reviewers for the popular press, political partisans of the far Left and Right, and old intellectual opponents from the literary wars of New York. With so much praise and blame heaped upon him, Bellow is often exposed to the fickle attentions of journalists, literary and ordinary. And he has learned to be cautious of them.

When I called Saul Bellow to talk to him about preparing this article, I made the mistake of referring to it as a "profile." "Well," he said with a sigh audible through the telephone receiver, "I suppose I can't stop you." I assured him that while that might be true, he could make the job pretty difficult for me if he made himself unavailable. "All right then," he said at last, "come on over, and we'll talk about it."

He was still uncommitted and unenthusiastic when I arrived at his office at the University of Chicago—but not unreceptive. He is of slightly less than average height, stocky, and with a distinctly rugged quality about him. This last impression came partly from his physical appearance (blue jaw and slightly craggy features), but partly, too, from his direct (and in the beginning) almost abrupt manner.

He is handsome—though not perhaps in the most conventional way. Pictures of Bellow from the 30's and 40's show a face quite like that of the young John Garfield, sensitive and a little soft, yet with a slightly desperate look. It is probably significant that three of his five novels have had protagonists who are pointedly presented as handsome men; one of them, Tommy Wilhelm of *Seize the Day,* had even gone to Hollywood on his good looks. I learned from a friend of Bellow's that Mozart's *Don Giovanni* is one of his personal passions; he once considered retelling the story of this great lover in a novel set in contemporary America.

Bellow had been reading Wright Morris's new book, *What a Way to Go,* when I interrupted him. As he laid it aside, I noticed how few books there were in the room. That surprised me. But Bellow had been there at the University only a little over a month; he had, he told me, barely moved in.

We did as he had promised on the phone: we talked about it. He explained that when he heard "profile," he pictured himself frying in a *New Yorker* skillet or stretched out on *Time's* procrustean bed. Gradually, as we talked, he warmed to the idea (or at least reconciled himself to it), and he began to loosen up. But throughout the interview he spoke in a slow, measured way, often hesitating or stopping altogether to choose his words. At first, I thought he was purposely holding down his rate of speech to make it easier for me to take notes. But I noticed that when I laid down my pencil to listen and to talk, he continued to speak slowly and carefully as before. Words are important to him; he seems not to waste them even in conversation.

Enlarging on his objections to the role of the writer as public figure, Bellow pointed out that here in America "the writer can and should invent his own life. Only two choices are offered him by the public. He can either be a hell-raiser in the manner of Fitzgerald, or he can be a virile, proletarian writer. Beyond these, he must invent. That, I suppose, is what I am trying to do in my own mellow way, just obeying my intuitions. Mind you, I have no gripe against society for its treatment of writers. Sometimes I find it aggravating, but I have no recommendations to offer."

This was his second visit to the University of Chicago in less than a year. He had spent the 1962 Winter Term as Celebrity in Residence, teaching a course called "The Modern Novel and Its Heroes." I asked him if he would be here through the entire college year. "Yes," he said, "and maybe longer. With the arrangement here I could stay as long as five years." He stopped then, glancing distractedly out the window. After a moment, he said: "I feel I have unfinished business here in Chicago. I don't know what it is, but I'm trying to find out."

Saul Bellow, an alumnus (though not a graduate) of the University of Chicago, has returned to the Midway as a professor in the Committee on Social Thought. The Committee, founded at the University in 1942 under the encouragement of Robert M. Hutchins, is a graduate-degree-granting unit, administratively within the University's Division of the Social Sciences. Its faculty cuts across departmental and divisional lines. According to its chairman, professor John U. Nef, the Committee "has as its ultimate task to contribute, according to its modest means, to the unification of all recent discoveries in the arts and sciences."

Although Saul Bellow has put in his share of time on the college circuit (he seems to have been everywhere from Pestalozzi-Froebel to Princeton), he does not really think of himself as a teacher. "Actually, I've taught surprisingly little," he said."—and practically no writing courses at all. Just enough of the workshops to know that I want to keep away from them from now on." On the University's Committee on Social Thought, Bellow "represents" literature. Besides instructing a handful of graduate students in its "secret" ways, he is presumably expected to create a bit of it.

His present teaching obligations are actually quite light (tutorial courses), but he takes them, as he has all his teaching, seriously. A friend of Bellow's who has watched him at work in the classroom says that he is a "most conscientious teacher. It's not an obligation that he feels to the people who are paying his salary, but an obligation that he feels to his craft and to the students themselves. Some writers coast along on their names when they're teaching, but not Saul. He has a tremendous respect for anyone who asks a question. His secret is that he never talks down to people."

"In general," said Bellow, "I am here to defy the prejudice that writers are either (a) stupid, or (b) belong in the gutter." I asked him who said they belonged *there,* and he told me that while he was teaching at Princeton he had happened to meet a teacher friend in New York whom he hadn't seen for some months. *The friend was most surprised and interested when he learned that Bellow was at Princeton.* "He wanted to know how my colleagues there felt about me," Bellow remembered, " 'me' as a writer. I told him I didn't know why they should feel anything in particular. Then my academic friend told me that he thought that writers belonged down in the gutter, that they had a moral duty to live with and write about the butt end of the race." He shrugged. "Now, I've no objection to gutters—I've spent a lot of time sitting in them. But I *do* object to a ruddy-looking, well-dressed teacher assigning me to a place there. This is characteristic of an obsolete Romantic idea of the artist's role which I detest. Besides, these days it's hard to find a reasonable gutter to sit in."

Placing this incident involving the "academic friend" in the Bellow chronology, I later came to the conclusion that it had happened about fifteen years ago. And that seemed strange, for it was told with such freshness and in such detail that I had the impression the meeting had taken place no more than a few months before. This suggests one of the sources of his power as a novelist: he seems to be one of those people who never forgets anything. People who know him well say Bellow is given to long friendships and deep antagonisms. "He's always been a sensitive guy," I was told, "always easily injured."

At about this point in our conversation, he leaned forward and peered with curiosity at the book on which I had propped my writing tablet. "What's that you're reading?" he asked.

It was his friend Isaac Rosenfeld's collection of essays and reviews, *An Age of Enormity*. Bellow himself had written the preface to the volume. I held it up for him to see.

"Oh," he nodded, "Isaac's book."

Since he had been mentioned I decided to ask about Rosenfeld, whose life, in its short course, ran almost parallel to Bellow's. I said, "I notice that in a couple of places in the book and especially in the last essay on Chicago, Rosenfeld keeps referring to himself as a *luftmensch* (this is a Yiddish word incorporating the "alienated man" concept). Do you consider *yourself a luftmensch*?"

"Not in the same way, no. There is in that the same Romantic idea that the artist necessarily has to stand outside the social order and oppose accepted values. I'm sure I oppose many accepted values, but not as a matter of policy. Sometimes I scarcely see myself as an artist—just as a person who devotes himself to literature. When I write I feel like an artist. When I'm not writing I don't feel like anything at all. No," he said with an emphatic shake of his head, "I think that the real things have to do with the purity of a man's heart and not with his airs. This was true of Isaac, too. He was dedicated to the truthful course of life. It simply suited him to call himself a *luftmensch*."

All of this seems to indicate a fairly offhand, matter-of-fact attitude toward writing and the writer's role. Bellow's friends feel, however, that his deepest feelings run a bit stronger than this. One of them, David Peltz, who has known him since high school, says, "He was always single-minded about writing. I remember that by the time Saul was sixteen he had torn up two novels that he had written."

Samuel Freifeld, a Chicago attorney who has known him for more than 35 years, is sure that Bellow feels deeply the mission of the writer as prophet. "We used to take endless walks along the lake when we were in college, and we talked about this over and over again. It was Saul's contention then that it was the job of the writer to 'bear witness to life'—I think Isaac Rosenfeld picked up the phrase and used it. Saul used to say that a writer may be making scriptures for future ages and never know it."

Saul Bellow is known—and remembered—by many Chicagoans. Born in Lachine, Quebec, a suburb of Montreal, in 1915, he moved with his family to the city when he was nine, and grew up in the Humboldt Park area. This was the neighborhood described so completely and eloquently in the first section of *The Adventures of Augie March*. In the opening lines of that book, he calls Chicago "that somber city"; it has become his most quoted phrase. "Chicago was a somber city in those days," he said. "Anyone who differs with me about conditions on West Augusta Boulevard at that time had better be able to prove he's from the same neighborhood."

He entered Tuley High School the year of the stock market crash. Tuley and Humboldt Park provided the setting for a curious social phenomenon in that period. The high school and the neighborhood produced a remarkable number of scientists, mathematicians, and intellectuals of every sort. The arts predominated, however. Add to the name of Saul Bellow, Isaac Rosenfeld, Oscar Tarcov, and Sam Wanamaker, and you will have a fair sampling. I asked Bellow about columnist Sydney J. Harris. He nodded, smiling. "Yes," he said. "Sydney and I were very friendly in high school." What was left unsaid here, I later learned, was that he and Harris had run away to New York when they were about sixteen with high hopes of peddling their first novels to some publisher. They returned months later, unpublished and somewhat chastened.

It was Sam Freifeld who introduced Bellow to Isaac Rosenfeld. "He was two years younger than Saul and a year younger than I was, but brilliant," says Freifeld. "I remember that we used to go over to Saul's, and his father, who was quite a Yiddishist, would read Dostoevsky and Tolstoy to us in Yiddish." Rosenfeld and Bellow later became accomplished Yiddishists in their own right. Although Saul Bellow has translated stories of Sholom Aleichem and Isaac Bashevis Singer into English, his most impressive feats were the Yiddish translations of T. S. Eliot he used to improvise with Rosenfeld. "But that was later," says Dave Peltz, "after they got used to the idea of being Jewish. In high school, being Yiddish wasn't something you talked about in the neighborhood—unless you wanted to get involved in a street brawl."

Isaac Rosenfeld left his memorial to the old neighborhood in *Passage from Home,* a novel of west side Jewish family life, among other, larger things. And Saul Bellow left his memorial to Isaac Rosenfeld in a brief and moving obituary which he wrote for the *Partisan Review* shortly after Rosenfeld's death in 1956. One paragraph from it in particular evokes not only the spirit of Rosenfeld, the boy, but the time and place as well:

"It is late afternoon, a spring day, and the Tuley Debating Club is meeting on the second floor of the old building, since destroyed by fire. The black street doors are open, the skate wheels are buzzing on the hollow concrete and the handballs strike the walls with a taut puncturing sound. Upstairs, I hold the gavel. Isaac rises and asks for the floor. He has a round face, somewhat pale, glasses, and his light hair is combed back with earnestness and maturity. He is wearing short pants. His subject is *The World as Will and Idea,* and he speaks with perfect authority. He is very serious. He has read Schopenhauer."

In the years that followed, he and Rosenfeld became increasingly close, sort of literary Doppelgängers. "I loved him," Bellow wrote in his preface to *An Age of Enormity,* "but we were rivals."

The Tuley High School crowd was precociously political. "We were all Left-wingers back in the 30's," one of them recalls. "It was just the thing to be—that's all." Most, including Bellow, went on to the University of Chicago. "Everybody breathed, ate, and read radical politics," he remembered. "It was understandable. The foreign intellectual press was radical, the most interesting American writers of the time were radical. And it was our feeling that the American tradition was radical, too."

It wasn't all politics, though. Surrealism was also in vogue, and Rosenfeld was especially enthusiastic. Together with Oscar Tarcov, Bellow and Rosenfeld put on a couple of shows (one, "Twin Bananas," in which the three presented themselves as headless men) in the lobby of Harper Library. "We read verses," said Bellow, then added with a pained smile "—of ours."

Eventually, he left the University of Chicago and transferred to Northwestern University. In the beginning, he continued to live on the south side near the Midway, commuting to classes on the El. But he finally gave in and moved out to Evanston ("a wax museum of bourgeois horrors"). Politically, it was a far country from the University of Chicago. "I founded a Socialist Club and the University administration was appalled and a little frightened. Even then, with eight million unemployed in the country, Northwestern was shocked at the idea of radical politics on campus."

By the time he had graduated from Northwestern and had entered the University of Wisconsin, Bellow was firmly committed to the study of anthropology. Isaac Rosenfeld followed him up to Madison as a graduate student in philosophy. Eventually, Rosenfeld received his degree and left; Bellow simply left. A teacher of his, Alexander Goldenweiser, had commented on the papers Bellow had turned in. Goldenweiser advised him to leave anthropology for literature. "You have too much of a sense of style," he told him. Observed Bellow, "this just confirmed my narcissism, my natural self-love."

A long, unsure period for him followed: he was in and out of the WPA Writers Project, an occasional student at Chicago, and, for a while, an editor on the Encyclopedia Britannica. Then, finally, the war came, and with it, the situation described in *Dangling Man*. Bellow, born in Canada and technically an alien, could not enlist, nor could he be drafted until he was properly investigated. And so he dangled, waiting for months and months to be called, waiting for the war to happen to him. It was a debilitating experience, but a beautiful central metaphor for the novel which came out of it—a novel for which he has little sympathy today. "I can't read a page of it without feeling embarrassed. The ideas in it are the ideas of a very young man."

When at last he *was* called up, he was given a medical rejection.

He then left for sea training at the Maritime Camp at Sheepshead
Bay, Long Island. It was his first real taste of New York. He began
by sailing aimlessly on a training ship in the Atlantic. When this
began to seem a little foolish to him, he took a shore job with the
Maritime Commission which he kept through the war.

He decided to stay in New York. With his first novel behind him
and his second, *The Victim,* half-completed, he had, he confessed,
a desire "to take the Big Town." At that time, there was still a
certain amount of intellectual life there in the Village, the remnant
of the old literary Left Wing. "This was Village life before the
razzle-dazzle set in." He had odd jobs of all kinds—editorial,
office—and he "hacked around, reviewing books and writing articles." In book reviewing, "the important thing was to get the
book. After you had read it and written your piece, you could sell
it to a bookstore for one-third its price and have enough for
a meal."

Dangling Man was enough to establish Saul Bellow as a comer,
enough, too, to win him his first full-time teaching job at the
University of Minnesota. It was while he was there that *The Victim*
was published in 1947. He had worked on it for years. Sam
Freifeld remembers that by 1945 he already had seen it in two
versions. *The Victim* is in most ways a considerably better book
than *Dangling Man*. It is also the tightest, most conventionally
plotted, full-length novel Bellow has written.

The Victim is about anti-Semitism in the same sense that *Moby
Dick* is "about this whale." It is actually a "double" story in the
tradition of Joseph Conrad's *The Secret Sharer*. Who is the *victim*
of the title? It is hard to say. Asa Leventhal, an urban Jew living
in New York, has accidentally (or perhaps *not* accidentally) caused
an anti-Semitic Gentile, Kirby Albee, to lose his job. Albee's wife has
died, he has become a heavy drinker, and has slipped almost to the
state of a derelict when he fastens onto Leventhal and demands
that Leventhal make amends. He follows him about everywhere,
demanding, whining, complaininig, insulting, finally moving in
with him to make their identification complete. Both are victims,
both victimizers. What they share is their humanity.

The Victim was well-reviewed by the critics and well-read by a
small but influential public. It won him a Guggenheim Fellowship

to France in 1948. He went to write another novel and made a good
start at it (100,000 words). "It was a grim book," Bellow wrote
of it later, "in the spirit of the first two. But I suddenly decided,
'No.' Actually, my feeling wasn't as mild as I'm describing it. I
felt great revulsion toward what I was writing."

When Saul Bellow said no to that "grim" book, he said yes to
Augie March. "Augie was my favorite fantasy. Every time I was
depressed, I'd treat myself to a fantasy holiday with him." Finally
he decided to give in and write the book. "In *Augie,* one of my
great pleasures was in having the ideas taken away from me, as it
were, by the characters. They demanded to have their own existence."

Their demands were answered. *The Adventures of Augie March*
is rich in characters, richer than most any other American novel since
Huckleberry Finn. It has "superior men," and fine old ladies, and a
rogues gallery of schlemihls, schnorrers, and goniphs—Anna
Coblin, Einhorn, Mintouchian, Simon March, and of course, Augie
himself. It is, as the title states, Augie's story all the way—the
odyssey of a "Columbus of the near at hand," a Jewish boy from
the Chicago slums, who travels a devious route to Mexico, New
York, and on to Europe. Augie is in search of . . . what? His
identity? That of course. Happiness? Well, that too. His freedom?
Yes, that most of all.

Saul Bellow was quite willing to talk about Augie March. When
he spoke of him and his book, there was something quite like
personal affection apparent. I mentioned that I was quite taken with
the *tone* of *Augie March.* Told exuberantly by Augie in the first
person, the language of the novel has a texture and vitality that
make it as different from the usual academic novel or New Fiction
piece as it is from Bellow's first two books.

I asked him if he had consciously set about to change his tone in
writing *Augie March.* "No," he said, "there was no conscious
effort to change anything. I felt undisciplined as I was writing the
book. For me, it had the emotional quality of a resurrection. You
see, in my first two books, I yielded to emotional limits that were
very confining. And being an unruly and disobedient sort beneath
it all, I was in a mood of protest when I began to write."

Most of his critics feel that *The Adventures of Augie March* is his

best book; a few consider it the finest American novel to appear
since the war. But how does *he* feel about the book? "I make no
claims for it," Bellow said. "As a matter of fact, I've been
attacked from all sides on it. The more you write, the better you
learn that there can be little agreement on any matter under the
sun. I was both praised and attacked for the same qualities in Augie.
I was accused of having contrived a naïveté or innocence of
character which couldn't possibly exist. And let's just say this: it
was revealed to me with time that I had created a character whose
charm I might not be able to justify under contemporary conditions.
I could say, in my own defense, that I knew such people as Augie.
But such defenses are no good."

Although he was never a doctrinaire radical ("I have no orthodoxy whatever"), Saul Bellow considers himself by no means an
"ex"-radical. "I think I've made my attitudes to money and power
pretty clear," said Bellow. "Look at *Seize the Day*. It's hardly a
hymn in praise of capitalism, is it?" It isn't. In detailing the
emotional collapse of Tommy Wilhelm in *Seize the Day,* Bellow has
created something rather more like an elegy to the Great American
Success Story. Characteristically, it is only by losing his illusions
that Wilhelm gains humanity.

"And what about *Henderson the Rain King?*" Bellow asked,
pursuing the question a bit further. "I'm hardly leading cheers for the
American millionaire there, am I?" Here I felt less willing to
agree—perhaps not cheers for *the* American millionaire, but a
few qualified huzzahs for *this* American millionaire, Eugene Henderson. Everything about him is big: physical size, wealth, passions, and most of all, desires. It is the voice of desire inside him
with its chant of "*I want, I want, I want*" that drives him on to Africa
for his bizarre adventures in the interior. Henderson is an overpow-
ering character, one who is himself almost overpowered by his
own freedom.

If Saul Bellow's fiction has a single, dominant theme, it is this
one of freedom which is put so plainly in *Henderson the Rain
King* and *Augie March*—freedom, the variety of life, the choice
offered each of us. Bellow acknowledged this: "Our period has
been created by revolutions of all kinds—political, scientific, industrial. And now we have been freed by law from slavery in many of its

historical, objective forms. The next move is up to us. Each of us
has to find an inner law by which he can live. Without this, objective
freedom only destroys us. So the question that really interests me
is the question of spiritual freedom in the individual—the power
to endure our own humanity.''

There is a question which is explicitly repeated in his first novel,
Dangling Man, and implicit in all he has written since. Again and
again, throughout the book, it occurs, "What can a good man do?"
It grew late as we talked. Outside, the light dimmed until it was
almost dark there inside his office. The bells at Rockefeller Chapel
tolled. I asked a final question: What can a good man do?

"I'd say you have to struggle with the evil in life. Not with the
abstract, but with evil as *you* see it and feel it around you. If you
abdicate to it—and that's so easy to do—then you succumb to the
common life, the unenlightened, unillumined life. Everyone pretends
to praise the common life, but everyone is secretly bewildered by
it. Some even loathe it as they should." He paused, then added,
"These are simply my own feelings. They may or may not have a
bearing on what I write."

An Interview with Saul Bellow

David D. Galloway / 1963

From *Audit-Poetry* 3 (1963), 19–23.

One of America's finest contemporary novelists, Saul Bellow has amply distinguished himself in the tradition of the comic novel—a form which, in his hands as in Mark Twain's, is appropriately serious and precise. Bellow is perhaps best known for *The Adventures of Augie March* and *Henderson the Rain King;* his next novel, *Herzog,* will be published later this year, and a play, *Bummidge,* opens on Broadway in the fall. Bellow is currently a member of the Committee on Social Thought at the University of Chicago, and visited Buffalo in December, 1962 at the invitation of the Graduate Management Program of the School of Business Administration. Using Walt Whitman's *Democratic Vistas* as his point of departure, Bellow delivered a lecture on "The Writer as Moralist in American Society." Although he observed that his tongue is always "strangely coated" during interviews, Bellow generously consented to submit himself to the ritual, which was performed in the Poetry Room of the Lockwood Memorial Library. Bellow is a vigorous, engaging personality who speaks with the same combination of energy and vividness with which he writes.

Interviewer: As a member of an academic community, how do you feel about the charges often levelled against the "university" novel—charges that it is self-conscious and over-written?

  Bellow: That's true of many novels. It was certainly true of the novels of Joyce, who had no university connection. I feel he went too far out in this respect and begot many of these university types. I think the same is true of Eliot, but the university itself is hardly so bad as romantic opinion indicates. Many of the feelings which were so justifiable in the full strength and power of romanticism have now become only sources of shame and humiliation and things to tag people with. A man can make a fool of himself anywhere—in the gutter as well as in the university. I know plenty of both types, but there is a kind of persistent anti-intellectualism which also has a romantic source and which simply ignores the fact that the world has gone through tremendous transformations which are due not to the feelings of poets or revolutionaries, but to the activities of scientists and a new class of people who are reshaping our culture. To persist in hiding away from these people in the interests of literary chastity is, of course, dangerous, but I think the notion that the "university" novelist does this any more than his counterpart in other areas is simply unrealistic.

Interviewer: Do you yourself find the academic community conducive to creative effort?

Bellow: I have always put the requirements of what I was writing first—before jobs, before children, before any material or practical interest, and if I discover that anything interferes with what I'm doing, I chuck it. Perhaps this is foolish, but it has always been the case with me, and I imagine that the university is well aware of my feelings.

Interviewer: The hero of your longest novel, *Augie March,* grows up during the Depression, and this is clearly one of the major influences on his life. In American literary histories this is a significantly overlooked period. As a writer obviously interested with the 1930's, what do you think of their literary significance?

Bellow: The writers of that time were still concerned with social problems and problems of justice—a concern that fled this country with the beginning of the Second World War and has never returned to reclaim its own lost significance. As I think you were suggesting earlier, there is, of course, a danger in the artist's becoming so involved with institutions that he absorbs institutional attitudes and fails to question the power of the ruling class and matters of justice. This was certainly not the case of writers in the 1930's, but it need not be the condition of writers today, either. Many people in the social sciences whose own intuitions are conservative are being pressed continually to make radical discoveries and to announce them; perhaps their radical discoveries are more genuinely radical than those of the would-be writers of protest who don't seem to have any substance, whose hearts may be in the right place but who make no real study of the conditions they protest against.

Interviewer: Do you feel any particular sympathy for the literature of the absurd which has become prominent since the Second World War?

Bellow: I agree with Walt Whitman that there has never been any more good or evil than now. I think the world has been as absurd before or not as absurd. I don't like these fashions. They tend to carry one too far beyond his own powers as an observer. There are, of course, great cognitive influences which compel us to think we live in a rationally ordered or rationally disordered community. Our lives are expended in mental acts, and we are surrounded by mental atmospheres; I don't like to have my position confused with that of an anti-intellectual writer.

Interviewer: The inevitable question: What do you think of as the most significant influences on your own writing?

Bellow: It's extremely hard to name them all. Perhaps I'm a more dependent individual than I myself have realized, and to be sure, I've come back time and again to certain writers without knowing why—Dostoyevsky, Conrad, Hardy, Dreiser, and Lawrence.

Interviewer: Which of your books have given you the greatest satisfaction?

Bellow: The ones that engaged my feelings most are the ones I think of most affectionately, but they are not always the best. I don't consider that I have reached any of my objectives as a writer, but I do feel strongly that I made some kind of discovery in writing *Augie March* which I was unable to control. I returned to a tighter mode of control in *Seize the Day,* the writing of which gave me a great deal of satisfaction. But perhaps writing *Henderson* stirred me more than writing any of the other books. I felt the sheer pleasure of release from difficulty, and I suppose this may have something to do with my mental constitution. I have, perhaps, a slave-like constitution which is too easily restrained by bonds; it then becomes rebellious and bursts out in a comic revolution. This seems to be the way I work.

Interviewer: In terms of your own work you seem to have moved from rather bleak statements of man's spiritual condition in your early novels to a pointedly optimistic statement of man's spiritual capacities in *Henderson.* Do you feel this is an accurate view of the progression in your work?

Bellow: We must be in a rather sad position when we expect novelists to supply us with ethical statements which should properly be offered by society, by firm ideas of right and justice. But in our great need for consolation we seize upon every utterance of every writer and examine it for auguries of good or evil. The result is that a great burden is thrown upon the writer, who is asked to feel himself a prophetic personality. The responsibility is certainly too great for one who considers himself a comedian. But I suppose things have become so bad that one can state the modern crisis in a single proposition: either we want to continue living or we don't. If that's the case, curiosity if only that compels me to say that I want to continue living. As for a massive statement of affirmation, I have none to offer.

Interviewer: Do you feel that any of the writers who have come to prominence in America in recent years have made important contributions to the novel as a form or as a vehicle?

Bellow: Ralph Ellison has certainly had something to offer, and James Donleavy had made an interesting contribution. I think I myself have indicated a new direction.

Interviewer: Could you speculate on the course the novel is likely to take in the future?

Bellow: What I feel in reading new books as well as in writing them is a terrible impatience—understandable, though perhaps not entirely healthy—with all that is considered to be superficial, a desire for the essential, for the compact statement, and a boredom with the *longueur* of the nineteenth-century novel. There is a resentment of the leisurely novel as a form of self-indulgence, as though we had to transact our business faster and faster. This is, of course, not an altogether good thing, but it is a modern characteristic. Every now and then an appealing contemporary turns up under inconceivable circumstances and in an unpredictable place—like a Japanese novelist who in a recent book called *After the Banquet* did something I very much admire. Once in a while one comes across flashes of things of this sort in contemporary writers and realizes that there is a direction, that people who have no personal connection are proceeding along similar lines.

Interviewer: What do you think of the almost faddish popularity of Salinger and Golding?

Bellow: They speak to the youth of today, a new and separate class of society which transcends the old class lines. I think infinitely more of Golding than I do of Salinger; the latter is an excellent craftsman, and I never underestimate the value of craftsmanship, but I do think he has made up a Rousseauian critique of society which comes from the vatic judgment of the immature, as though civilization were something from which youth had the privilege of withdrawing and into which they have particular insights not available to others. I think what we see in Salinger is our old friend the liberal theory of education, which is our legacy from John Dewey.

Interviewer: Do you think, since there is a new class which transcends the class divisions of the past, that the novelist of the future will have an essentially different audience to write for than the novelist has in the mid-twentieth century?

Bellow: Those poor devils have all my sympathy.

Interviewer: You stated earlier and with characteristic dedication that you yourself had not accomplished what you had hoped to accomplish in your writing. What are these unrealized goals?

Bellow: I feel that the imagination has to provide something that explicit statements of belief can never provide satisfactorily. This can only come about if the imagination is authorized to enjoy its own power. Prophetically and ethically none of us have the strength Hamlet wanted in this world out of joint—the strength to set things right. We are not Prometheans, and those dreams have to be abandoned as impractical romantic glories. What we do have is the power provided by the imagination, by our own skill and integrity of heart, and these elements no longer seem to be under my control. Things will have to work themselves out as they will.

Talk with Saul Bellow
Robert Gutwillig / 1964

From the *New York Times Book Review*, 20 September 1964, 40–41. © 1964 by The New York Times Company. Reprinted by permission.

He came off the stage of the Belasco Theater, a cord jacket in one hand, an umbrella in the other, looking for all the world as wilted and dapper as that actor-philosopher Moses Herzog. We exchanged damp jokes about New York—a tropical paradise—he asked after my health (failing fast), and I asked after the Bellow family. Right on cue, he led me into a dressing room and introduced me to his young son.

I followed him into another dressing room that was bare of all amenities except for a hat tree from which dangled odd pieces of clothing (but no hats) and two chairs without backs. We dropped onto them. Shouted dialogue wafted over to us from the stage. A fellow came in and either took something from or put something on the hat rack. It seemed unaffected.

I had not seen Saul Bellow for four or five years, and meeting him again after all that time was a distinct shock, just as reading *Herzog* after not having read him since 1959 came as a real revelation. He is now 49 years old and he has grown almost alarmingly handsome. He has kept most of his hair and it has gone gray-white. His features—eyes, nose, mouth—are all large and full. This is an expressive face, and it expresses all the life he has seen and understood.

He roused me out of my glum study of his physiognomy (here's a guy who's got more talent than everyone else in the country, and now he's running for Robert Frost, too), and out of the room, the theater and into the street. I spotted the Blue Ribbon down the block and made for it, telling Bellow on the way that several writers had already called me after reading advance copies of the book and that he was making them feel pretty envious, pretty sick.

24

He laughed. "No, I'm doing them good. They do me good. Next time they'll make me feel sick."

Inside, it was cool and dark. There was no television. There was German beer on tap.

I said I thought *Herzog* was his best book, and Bellow said he thought so, too.

"Which makes it," I said, "better than everything else."

He smiled and ducked his head down.

A drunk at the end of the bar said. "That's the most confused (unprintable) in the whole damn country."

"Wow," said Bellow. "That's pretty confused."

Saul Bellow takes a compliment better than any writer I know. And if you don't think that takes talent, just try complimenting a writer sometime. He submitted to a seemingly endless monologue about why *Herzog* was his best book, replete with copious references to *The Dangling Man, The Victim, The Adventures of Augie March, Seize the Day* and *Henderson the Rain King,* analyses of trends and developments, explication of recurent themes, and said finally, "I think you're right about me." Any man who can and will lie so well after listening to that kind of thing can't be all bad.

New York is going to be a Bellow festival this fall. His first play, *The Last Analysis,* starring Sam Levene, is opening Sept. 29th, eight days after the publication of *Herzog.* The play is a comedy about an aging comedian who is on his way down and out, partly because he feels he has a responsibility to tell people things. "I wanted to bring rhetoric back to the theater," Bellow said, "and I did. But I brought too much. About eight hours too much," he added, pretty much summarizing what rehearsals must have been like so far.

I said life must be pretty hectic between rehearsals and pre-publication duties, and Bellow said it was calm compared to last spring in Chicago when "I was trying to finish the book—again, and trying to finish the play—again, and teaching two courses and my wife was having a baby. I gave up sleeping." He said that starting with *Seize the Day* he has been re-writing heavily. "There must be fifteen drafts of *Herzog.*

"In every generation there's a lunatic . . ." the drunk announced.

"We'd better not ask him who it is," Bellow said. "It might be me."

I said, "What do you want me to say about all the similarities between the life and hard times of Saul Bellow and Moses Herzog? Everyone's going to want to know about that. I mean, you're an artist. There aren't any accidents in your books. You don't find any surprises when you go back and look at them, do you?"

Bellow said he didn't go back to his old books, only to little pieces of *Henderson*. "Say," he said, "when a writer runs out of other people to write about there's no reason why he can't use himself."

"Okay," I said.

After the opening here, Bellow is going back to Chicago to teach, and it looks as if he will continue to make Chicago his home base and go on teaching. We agreed that being attached to a university was not necessarily the fatal disease for writers that so many people seem to think. Bellow compared universities favorably to some of the other ways writers are making do these days, but said he had to teach in a large city. "At Princeton, it was the first time I was socially inferior to my students. But that was good too," he said, although he didn't say what was good about it.

Bellow told me about life in Chicago. Like Augie March and Moses Herzog, he is interested in all sorts of strange things (at one moment he was telling me something about the British Industrial Revolution, the next about an establishment called The Shamrock). He is certainly interested in other writers and their writing, and talked about the literary magazine, *The Noble Savage,* he'd help run, and several young writers we both knew. I mentioned one who'd been having a hard time, and Bellow said, "That reminds me of what Samuel Butler once said. I've been having a lot of fun reading old Sam. Young people, I believe he said, should be careful about their aspirations. They might live to achieve them."

I thought about this and said at last that he was the only American writer I could think of who was getting better after 40. All the others in this century, anyway, seem to fall away. Bellow said it was something about American society, for in Europe writers were just beginning to hit their strides when they reached middle age. We talked a while about just what it was about American life that seemed so destructive. No conclusions.

Then it was time to go, back to rehearsals, back to his little boy. As we walked back to the Belasco, I was suddenly overcome by the emotion of this brief encounter and thought I probably wouldn't see him again for another four or five years. I remembered a sentence on Page 340 of the new book, after Moses Herzog had spent 339 pages suffering. "I am pretty well satisfied to be, to be just as it is willed, and for as long as I may remain in occupancy." It seemed to fit them both.

I said a friend of mine named Herzog was kind of upset and figured he was in for a few months of bad jokes.

Bellow stopped at the gate of the stage entrance and smiled his smile. "Tell him not to worry," he said. "Hey, what's he got to worry about? Suppose his name was Bellow!"

Successor to Faulkner?
Nina Steers / 1964

From *Show*, September 1964, 36–38.

According to Frederick W. Dupee, Professor of English at
Columbia University, "If there is any successor to Faulkner—it is Saul Bellow. Like Faulkner, he is a craftsman of
the novel in this day of mad spontaneity. His subject matter
is large and his talent, aside from the interest his individual
works may have, has shown itself capable of developing
over a long period of time."

Bellow is one of the least publicized of major writers. He
has so avoided the press conference that the only statement
that can be made about him in any certainty is that he was
born June 10, 1915 in Lachine, Quebec. All other facts are
in doubt.

He has written six novels: *Dangling Man* (1944); *The
Victim* (1947); *The Adventures of Augie March* (1953); *Seize
the Day* (1956); *Henderson, the Rain King* (1959) and *Herzog,* which is being published this month by The Viking
Press. His first produced play, *Bummidge,* is now in re-
hearsal for a Broadway opening this fall.

I read somewhere that you abandoned your work for an M.A. in
anthropology to become a writer and went to work for the WPA.
Why were you first interested in anthropology?

Anthropology students were the farthest out in the 1930s. They
seemed to be preparing to criticize society from its roots. Radicalism was implied by the study of anthropology, especially sexual
radicalism—the study of the sexual life of savages was gratifying to
radicals. It indicated that human life was much broader than the
present. It gave young Jews a greater sense of freedom from the
surrounding restrictions.

Why did the study of anthropology especially appeal to young
Jews?

It was a rejection of snobbery. They were seeking an immunity

from Anglo-Saxon custom: being accepted or rejected by a society
of Christian gentlemen. I never had any academic interests.

What kind of work did you do for the WPA?
There were two kinds of projects for the WPA: the useful and the
playful. The useful were the guidebooks—but if you had a kind-
hearted supervisor, he allowed you to do something of your own. I
did little biographies of Midwestern novelists and poets. Sherwood Anderson was one of them.

What made you decide to become a writer?
Well, I was really too young to know. I was born into a medieval
ghetto in French Canada (Lachine, Quebec). My childhood was
in ancient times which was true of all orthodox Jews. Every child
was immersed in the Old Testament as soon as he could understand anything, so that you began life by knowing Genesis in
Hebrew by heart at the age of four. You never got to distinguish
between that and the outer world. Later on there were translations:
I grew up with four languages, English, Hebrew, Yiddish and
French . . . It was a verbal environment. Writing was really just a
continuation of something I had always done.

What did your parents think of your choice of a career?
My mother lived strictly in the 19th Century and her sole ambition
was for me to become a Talmudic scholar like everyone else in
her family. She was a figure from the Middle Ages. In family
pictures, her scholarly brothers looked as if they could have lived
in the 13th Century. Those bearded portraits were her idea of what
a man should be.
My father was brought up in the same tradition, but he cast all
this off to become a sort of modern type: he was a sharpie circa
1905 in Russia. He left the seminary at the age of 17 or 18 and went
to St. Petersburg and got involved in importing Egyptian onions,
a great delicacy in Czarist Russia. He thought I should be a
professional man or a moneymaker. Then he thought I was an
idiot or worse, a moon-faced ideologist. With that, he about washed
his hands of me. A more interesting question is: Once a writer,
what do you do to become something else?
That question implies the attitude of an athlete toward himself:

How should I live to keep fit and play better basketball? I believe people survive intuitively. They do what they need to do or what they have to do in order to survive as writers. They also do what they need to do in order to destroy themselves. I have seen people undergo elaborate preparations to insure success as writers. They organized lives of Bohemian purity in the Village: smoked tea, made love to Smith girls, protected themselves from marriage and children but failed in their main objective.

To treat yourself exclusively as an artist is a poor idea today; you can only estrange yourself further from reality. The people who develop the manners and adopt the conduct of an artist are the interior decorators and dress designers. The less creative people behave like artists. They adopt manners that passed out 60 years ago. They are much more interested in playing a social role than in surviving for the sake of their talent.

I gather you do not feel that an academic life would fail to qualify as experience or a "real" life?

For a long time, writers have been coming from the well-educated middle classes in Europe. There has been a feeling in this country that education removes one from the ordinary life. But that has always seemed to me unjustifiably romantic.

American writers invent, often, a false radicalism because it is required by romantic tradition. Often they have no clear idea of what it is they are opposing or upholding as radicals. It's more a matter of style than substance in them. Very often they have the feeling of being Promethean when they're only having a tantrum.

You are quoted as saying that you started your third novel, *Augie March,* as comic relief from a more somber novel you were working on.

Well, I am a melancholic—a depressive temperament. But I long ago stopped enjoying melancholy—I got heartily sick of my own character about 15 years ago. Sometimes I think that these comic outbursts are directed against my own depressive tendencies. When I was a little boy, I loved a comic strip called "Desperate Ambrose"—a little boy who paced the floor, hands clasped behind his back, saying, "much too tame, much too tame." I must have taken "Desperate Ambrose" to heart.

Do you write every day?

I am in the habit of writing every day, when I have something to write about and I am feeling keen about it. So I usually do, now that my life is fairly settled.

Any particular time?

I used to get up early when I wasn't married. Married people start the day later. By this time in my life, it has a pattern which I did not organize. I am usually awoken by thoughts of what I am going to be writing.

Do you have difficulty in disciplining yourself to write?

Someone once called me a bureaucrat (among writers) because my self-discipline seemed excessive. It seemed excessive to me, too.

It looked as if I had caught the Protestant disease of worldly asceticism—actually it was only an effort toward orderliness.

Do you have any little rituals you go through to get you started writing—such as sharpen 20 pencils the way Hemingway is reported to have done?

No rituals, but I drink a lot of coffee, more than is good for me.

Do you begin at the beginning and write from an outline?

I always begin at the beginning. My ambition is to start with an outline but my feelings are generally too chaotic and formless. I get full of excitement which prevents foresight and planning. I regret it when I get into trouble: a book two-thirds done and I don't know how it is going to come out.

My faults of character emerge in my writing. I like to think things will work themselves out. But as I get older and meet more desperate people who are motivated by cravings for power and influence, I find myself more "done in the eye." When writing, I envy these paranoics and their plans.

Did you have any difficulties in switching from the novel to the theater?

No, but then I don't know whether I have done anything good for the stage.

I hesitate to say it's easy to write a play. That draws the anger of

the professionals down on you. They want you to say it required
toil. I think you should toil at learning the art, then do it as easily
as possible.

Do you notice any difference in your methods when writing the
play, *Bummidge,* and writing a novel?
As I work on it now and prepare it for the stage, I find great value
in the awareness that every word has to advance the development
of the plot. And it intrigues me.

What makes a novel worth reading long after the era in which it
was written?
Novels are about others. They lack everything if they lack this
sympathetic devotion to the life of someone else.
Sometimes when I hear that novels are done for, I believe this
kind of concern for any other human being is considered impossible. And I don't say that it doesn't have roots in selfishness.
The conviction that this sympathy is no longer available has been
the inspiration of classics like James Joyce's *Ulysses*. This is why
Ulysses consists of monologues. Dialogue is impoverished in Joyce,
all of the wealth of sensibility is internal. All connection is impoverished and brutal.
Of course, he may be right. No amount of arguing will prove that
he is wrong. But perhaps other facts may be demonstrated.

What do you demonstrate?
It's not for me to say what I've demonstrated, just why.
Romantic thought in the 20th Century has been apocalyptic
nihilism—a conviction that the world is evil, that it must be
destroyed and rise again. This one finds in D. H. Lawrence and one
sees it also in writers like Ezra Pound and the German, Ludwig
Benn.
This apocalyptic romanticism is also a political fact but, without
being in the least conservative, I deny this. I don't see that we need
to call for the destruction of the world in hope of a phoenix. If I am
not a romantic, it's for this reason.
I've a nagging sense that the human situation is not as described
in these late romantic writers. I may be disappointed in existence—but I feel I have a right to demand something other than

romantic disappointment. I think the Jewish feeling resists romanticism and insists on an older set of facts.

How does this attitude affect art?
Apocalyptic romanticism rejects art too and calls for a sterner reality. Underlying all this is a sense or perhaps a wish that the human being is through.

I am not interested in denying it as a matter of argument because there is no arguing this. Only demonstrations can be accepted; affirmations are pointless.

"Art is for Jews," I recently overheard someone say—wanting to contemptuously imply a self-indulgence which must be despised by realists.

Why do you think he felt art was just for Jews?
I suppose he thinks the Jews have been trying to put something over on civilization for 2,000 years.

You sometimes seem preoccupied with being a Jew.
I have no fight about being a Jew. I simply must deal with the facts of my life—a basic set of primitive facts. They're my given.

You once said you thought your best book would be *Herzog*. Why?
Its scale is larger. The mind of the hero is more complete. He is a man of some intelligence and, I hope, learning. In American novels in the 20th Century, there have not been many heroes who have much mental capacity.

But now I understand we're entering an era of reconciliation between the intellectuals and society. I don't think we're nearly so well reconciled as certain professors claim, nor do I agree with fashionable opinion concerning our alienation.

It is absurd to affect the low-brow style. Many novelists and poets have done that.

What is Herzog, the character, like?
Herzog is still a comic figure to me. But this time the comedy results from the difficulty of his ambition to reach a higher synthesis. He believes in certain virtues which have nearly disappeared. Goodness, duty, courage—I think they're just in hiding everywhere.

Which are the hardest characters for you to create—men or
women?

I am beginning to overcome my timidity over women. I always
had the feeling that women were doing men's things for me. I,
therefore, venerated and also feared them. But my newest insight
into life is that we belong to the same species. I think I have
created some real women in *Herzog*.

Do you ever become like the characters you are writing about?

I never realize it, it always has to be pointed out to me that I am
limping or something. When I was working on *Henderson, the
Rain King,* I imitated Henderson around the farm. I went roaring at
people, making scenes. It was one of the more trying periods.

Which of your characters is most like you?

Henderson—the absurd seeker of high qualities.

But what Henderson is really seeking is a remedy to the anxiety
over death. What he can't endure is this continuing anxiety: the
indeterminate and indefinite anxiety, which most of us accept as the
condition of life which he is foolhardy enough to resist.

He tells the King that he is a "Becomer" and that the King is a
"Be-er." I believe I meant him to say that human life is intolerable
if we must endure endless doubt. That is really what I feel is
motivating Henderson. All his efforts are a satire on the attempts
people make to answer the enigma by movement and random action
or even by conscious effort. This is why I feel Henderson and I
are spiritually close—although there are no superficial likenesses.

I don't feel close to Augie March because he is so ingenuous—
the ingenue.

Many people describe *Augie March* as your greatest work. What
do you think about it?

I am grateful to the book because it was so liberating to write it.
But I do not consider it a success because I only just discovered
a new possibility. I was incapable at the time of controlling it and it
ran away with me. I feel that Augie was too effusive and uncritical.
But it does reflect one side of my character.

In an article, Norman Mailer wonders if you are not "too timid
to become a great writer."

I'm sure I'm not a great writer in Norman Mailer's light, but then I don't want to be a great writer in Norman Mailer's light.

I neither satisfy his idea of greatness nor mine. All I can see are my problems. I'd like to stop thinking about them.

I'd like to be a person who has some other connection to life—something other than a writer who has only a narrow and professional tie.

You mean you think the life of a writer is an irrelevant one?

There's no place in this society for an artist's life. What does it relate him to: publishers, gossip columnists, displays, men of his own guild? What lies behind Mailer's dissatisfaction with other writers and me as a writer is that we are deprived of the possibility of action or social effectiveness. But then you don't become socially effective by shouting or flamboyant publicity.

Mailer seems to zero in on the end of *Henderson* as the book's failure.

I wrote it in a sort of frenzy. I was very moved in writing the last 50 or 60 pages; perhaps that doesn't reflect in the results. I'm not prepared to argue about it. It's not for me to judge.

Communication has broken down in the 20th Century. The 1920s took the novel into an impossible blind alley: the disintegration of language in Joyce; the extreme situation in Kafka; and the observance of non-art by Gertrude Stein. I find in Mailer a certain pathos; he senses a rudderless feeling in himself and all the rest. He sees me with a bit of a rudder but sailing in the wrong direction.

Do you ever call a book a failure?

Failure? It's a question of vitality. Great vitality depends on the amount of energy released. Some people think the Book of Job is a failure. I don't offer my own in comparison. But many are dissatisfied with the resolution of Job. There have been complaints that Othello should not have killed Desdemona on grounds of sexual jealousy—not noble enough reason. For Lionel Abel of Metatheatre, *Macbeth* is the only real tragedy. All else must be a failure in his eyes. The total success of one man would be a terrible affront to all the others—I'd be all alone.

Any problem in completing the play?

I wrote myself into the grave. I had thought that I could rewrite it in two weeks. It's the first time I ever had to work with people; but it's nice to work with company.

I had had in mind an old-time farce—just a series of vaudeville scenes with an excuse for a play in between them. Now I can look at the play and think someone else wrote it. I never felt that about any of my work before. I recognize only certain passages as mine—the blood ranting!

Do you have any other thoughts on yourself and the subject of writing and writers?

No, I am just a man in the position of waiting to see what the imagination is going to do next.

Saul Bellow Tells (Among Other Things) the Thinking behind *Herzog*

Robert Cromie / 1965

From *Chicago Tribune Books Today*, 24 January 1965, 8–9.

At 9:30 p.m. Wednesday a remarkable literary event will occur. Saul Bellow, author of *Herzog,* the runaway best seller from coast to coast, will make his first television appearance in five years. He will be interviewed on *Book Beat* on Channel 11 by Robert Cromie, *The Tribune*'s book editor.

Because *Herzog* is a book everyone is talking about, *Books Today* made its own tape of the show the other day when Cromie interviewed Bellow, who is on the faculty at the University of Chicago. On these two pages a highly condensed version is presented as a permanent record of the occasion.

Cromie: How long did it take you to write a book of this size?

Bellow: About three years.

Cromie: And you finished it fairly recently because I know that you mentioned the assassination of President Kennedy in it, fairly far front, unless you went back and put it in.

Bellow: Well, I was working at it, practically following it to the bindery. I don't know how many drafts I wrote. I've lost track. Anywhere between 15 and 25, I'd say. I have a trunk of manuscripts.

Cromie: It seems presumptuous to attempt to give the plot even in outline, because I would assume most of our viewers have read it, but for those who haven't it concerns a professor who has had two bad marriages and is trying to recover from the wreckage of his second one. He goes from New York to Chicago and has a little place in the Berkshires where, as the thing opens, he is holed up trying to recover, almost, his sanity.

37

You had flashbacks—it was almost like a Chinese puzzle. You've got flashback within flashback. Did you have much trouble with them?

Bellow: No, I don't think so, not with the technique of the book. Well, I simply remembered what E.M. Forster had said on aspects of the novel: that the reader will take everything that you bounce him into, provided that you bounce him hard enough. I think that if a writer is continually interesting there is no limit to the amount of innovation he can allow himself and there's no limit to the flexibility of the reader's attention, provided always, of course, that you hold his attention. So that, if you don't forget the presence of the reader, you can allow yourself all kinds of liberties.

Cromie: I think you managed it most successfully because the flashbacks are not difficult to follow. Once or twice I leafed back to be sure I was in the proper time zone.

Bellow: Well, it is a good deal like telling a long story in the parlor. You can lose everyone if you are boring, of course. But not if you know the habits of mind of your listeners—and I feel almost as if I were whispering in the people's ears, telling the story in the most intimate way. Of course, much of it depends upon the tone—the personality of the narrator. If you get the reader to accept that you can get him to accept almost anything.

Cromie: It does come thru that way. There's one part that I loved and this does, I think, show what you were trying to say, that you were sort of whispering. Herzog, of course, is talking. He says of Madeleine, his second wife, who had ditched him: "Madeleine, by the way, lured me out of the learned world, got in herself, slammed the door and is still in there gossiping about me." I think those are my favorite two lines in the whole book. Because they do so give the idea of Madeleine, who's desperate to become something herself.

Bellow: Yes, I don't want to discuss any of the characters in the book, but I am rather pleased at having created a blue-stocking like Madeleine. There are very few successful intellectual ladies in American novels. I don't know why that is. By the way, I've had a great deal of correspondence about Madeleine and other ladies in the book. Fascinating letters from women all over the country, who have taken an unusual interest in these characters.

Cromie: From what aspect?

Bellow: Well, I get letters asking me for recipes for Shrimp Arnaud, which is one of the dishes they were fixing in the book, as if I knew how to cook. What I gather from most of these letters is that ladies reading books want to find models for new behavior.

Cromie: That's an odd complaint.

Bellow: I get letters from ladies who say that the characters are too daring; that they are setting a bad example [that the ladies are setting a bad example]; some say they're not setting an example bad enough. Some say why couldn't your heroine be more like Brett in *The Sun Also Rises?*

Cromie: They want to identify.

Bellow: Not just identify, they want to go forward. They want to be able to buy the new outfits and speak the new lines and develop new forms of behavior.

Cromie: And cook the new recipes.

Bellow: And cook the new recipes. They make me feel like an editor of *Vogue*.

Cromie: Well, it's really complimentary in a sense.

Bellow: Well, it is, because they take them so seriously.

Cromie: This raises an interesting point. What does the author of a best seller do to protect himself? You, of course, have an unlisted phone number. This is one obvious thing.

Bellow: I think a writer has to decide what to do with his private life because it's so easy for him to get sucked into public life and into the mass media. There are so many writers who do enjoy going around making public appearances that I feel that most directors of the radio and television shows take it for granted that a writer is only too willing and eager to appear. And I don't like to be stingy with myself, but I do find that it puts me off balance to . . . well, a writer spends three years in a room by himself, conceiving, writing, finishing a book, and at the end of those three years of rather abnormal solitude and privacy he finds himself suddenly in the public—in the glare of all these lights.

Cromie: Blinking a bit.

Bellow: Blinking a bit and then he's supposed to embark on a new role. The role of public speaker.

Cromie: Promoter, too.

Bellow: Promoter, and sermonizer, and preacher, and moralist, and fashion plate, and even gladiator. People invite you to programs with other writers, hoping that the beasts will chew one another up, and that a certain amount of discomfiture will be shown and blood will be shed. Meanwhile, the passive spectator in his living room opens another can of beer. I feel it is bad for writers to give these gladiatorial shows to the public.

Cromie: You're quite right. Some of the television shows do try to get people with opposing viewpoints and sort of prod them into arguments.

Bellow: Well, they want drama and conflict and bloodshed. And tho I'm willing to shed my blood in the right cause, I don't want to do it in order to make the beer flow faster.

Cromie: Now that you teach literature, how do you feel about today's literature as against say the literature of 20, 40, or 60 years ago? Do you feel we have improved much in our novel writing, for instance? The reason I asked this was that *Herzog* to me is a marvelous novel, and I think dated in the sense that it is a throwback to the great novels of years ago, and a delightful throwback. It's fun to read, beautifully written, and it is a fine novel. I don't find many of these any more, at least to suit me.

Bellow: Well, about two years ago, I had occasion to read the entire output of all the novelists of 1962. I was bored silly. I found that there were some marvelous performances and no lack of talent, but what astonished me was that it was so hard to find an interesting book. That is, a passionately absorbing book, which is the only kind of book worth reading or, for that matter, worth writing.

Cromie: You mean the mechanics were there but not the heart.

Bellow: You had a lot of very good professionals performing and many virtuosos. Anyone who has written for a long time recognizes all the signs of excellent performance. Many American writers are marvelous performers, some of them close to genius on the technical level. But for some reason or other they don't move awe in the soul, don't even try any more. Some try by their extremism, but even extremism runs out of sensations too after a bit, you know. The punches don't hit quite so hard after you've gotten used to the idea, and sometimes you feel that the Puritan tradition of Americans is being exploited by shock and sensationalism. While

I believe that we all ought to be emancipated from the tyranny of Puritanism, I'm not really interested beyond a certain point in the process of emancipation itself. Sure, we ought to overcome certain sexual superstitions, for instance, if only in the interest of hygiene. Everybody knows that by now. Even the ladies' magazines show this in the psychiatric advice given in their columns. You often find very sensible ideas about the relations between the sexes, but the amount of grinding that's done on this theme in many modern novels seems to me to be past the point of utility.

Cromie: Your novel, of course, is liberated in the sense of using Anglo-Saxon words, and in some of your descriptions of bedroom scenes, but you certainly don't go to an extent which—I won't say shocks but which bores the reader.

Bellow: I think Americans tend to break issues up into literal or diametric opposites—the good guys; the bad guys. The conservatives; the radicals. Or, as in the case of many writers, the Cleans and the Dirties. The Dirties stamping their feet at the Cleans. The Cleans washing their hands at the Dirties, and so on, ad infinitum.

Cromie: Interesting thought. Who are your favorite novelists, not necessarily modern? Whom do you read when you're at home and have a free moment or a free hour?

Bellow: Well, I read the Russians a lot. The old Russians. The French, especially 18th–19th century French.

Cromie: You read them *in* French, I assume.

Bellow: Yes.

Cromie: And the Russians in translation?

Bellow: And the Russians in translation. I read a lot of Dickens and Thomas Hardy, and D.H. Lawrence, and Joyce.

Cromie: Do you also read modern novels when you have a free moment? I'm trying to figure out if you read modern things at all, except in the case of 1962, when you had to for something.

Bellow: Yes, I do read—I don't want you to get the impression that I don't admire modern writers. I do. I think we have many marvelous modern American novelists—Hemingway, Faulkner, Fitzgerald, or among living writers, Ralph Ellison, John Cheever, Wright Morris, Jim Powers. All of them are considered to be excellent writers.

Cromie: Do you start working on another novel immediately after

you finish one, as some people do, or do you have a period of
lying fallow?

Bellow: Well, I'd like to call it lying fallow. Actually, you get into
a tizzy when all this supportive work is removed. You hang on to
it until the last possible moment. When the last has been put into
the mail box, you get [a] strangely uneasy feeling. What are you
going to do now?

Bellow: One of the sources of comedy in my book is the endless
struggle of people to make sense of life and to sort out all of the
issues, and to get the proper historical perspective on oneself.
Herzog, himself, makes fun of this. He says, "Well, here I am a
man in an age, in a time, in a mass society, in a technological
transformation after a revolutionary period, in a colonial epoch or
post-colonial epoch," and all the rest of that as if he were trying to
find the co-ordinates which would describe him. It's damn hard
to describe oneself that way. The whole world runs thru your head
like an oceanic tide, and you have to, for the sake of your balance
and even your sanity, sort everything out.

My hero makes use of a phrase coined by President Wilson's
Vice President, who was a man named Marshall, a Hoosier cracker
barrel philosopher, and a great wit, who said, "What this country
needs is a good 5 cent cigar." Herzog translates this for himself
as "What this country needs is a good 5 cent synthesis." We live in
these tides of information and fact which sway us back and forth.
We're supposed to discriminate, and prepare ourselves to make
judgments. Our freedom depends on these judgments. Even our
personal life depends upon the strength of our ability to discriminate
between real and unreal things.

The human mind seems to be not prepared for this kind of
unprecedented modern crisis, and it is the humor of that kind of
floundering that I try to get into Herzog. Even the qualified intellectual doesn't know what he's doing. People keep telling him, "You
don't know what you're doing. You eggheads don't know reality.
Even a little kid in the street knows more about the actual
conditions of life than you do." This is characteristic of our period,
too, from this point of view, that people are continually saying to
one another "You don't know. I have the key. I understand reality.

You don't understand reality. I'm willing to lead you, show you, teach you." And the more susceptible people are to this kind of propaganda or bunk, the more they allow themselves to be led by the nose.

Saul Bellow: An Interview
John J. Enck / 1965

From *Contemporary Literature*, 6.2 (1965), 156–60. © 1965 by
The University of Wisconsin Press. Reprinted by permission.

*Is the period of internationalism in the novel over or could writers
in the United States learn anything from Europeans, particularly
from the recent French and German writers?*

Literature, like painting, is international today. It has in fact
always been international—European. Now it is about to become
universal. Every year we are offered more Japanese, Indian and
African books, and those Japanese, Indian and African writers read
us of course. It seems to me that recent French and German writers
have taken more from the Americans than the Americans have
been able to take from them.

*Could writers in the United States learn anything from Europe-
ans, particularly from the recent French and German?*

I take a dim view of recent French novels. Though some of them
do show a large American influence. The French have always
been drawn to our literature. At one time they were in love with
Fenimore Cooper and Buffalo Bill; the Surrealists were in ecsta-
sies over Nick Carter and Gide loved Dashiell Hammett. Sartre
swallowed a large dose of John Dos Passos. To my mind, the
main fault of current French novels is that they are so cognitive.
They lean so heavily on the history of philosopohy or on ideologies of one sort or another. The mark of the école normale is
stamped on many a brow. Often French novels take the form of
logical demonstrations or work out postulates systematically. I
prefer to get my philosophy from philosophers. This is not to say that
I am opposed to ideas in fiction. It is a great defect of American
novelists that they shun thinking. Sometimes they appear to take
anti-intellectual attitudes in order to identify themselves with the
mass of Americans and behave like untutored populists. Which
they are not. Most of them are highly sophisticated.

Do you outline your novels before writing?
I wish I were able to.

To what extent do you worry about the structure of your novels?
They give me insomnia, but I seem helpless to do anything about it.

Do you usually begin with a concept or a fable in your own work?
Fable is an Aristotelian word and I don't really feel strong enough to cope with it. I do, of course, have something that might be described as a concept—a working idea, a feeling, a sort of excitement.

To what extent do you consider your fiction a method of problem solving?
There is a general feeling abroad that we cannot justify our existence. If I shared that feeling I shouldn't be writing novels.

Do you ever, in the heat of writing, find yourself adopting a position you wouldn't consciously agree with?
Yes, very often, and I think this is the truest sign that I am doing well. If everything is going your way and you feel no challenge or strain, it is very likely that you are in the nutshell, king of infinite space.

To what extent do your characters take charge?
If I burden them with flat or dead attitudes, they seem to resent it. The main reason for rewriting is not to achieve a smooth surface, but to discover the inner truth of your characters.

In what way does teaching, especially the teaching of creative writing, influence your own work?
I don't teach creative writing. Not because I think it useless, but because it is very tedious and difficult. A man writes because he is a writer and not because he has taken courses. A writer is interesting because of his peculiar perspective. Can this perspective be taught? I think not. I know that the student longs for help, but what he develops in writing courses is generally a psychological dependency. He asks the teacher—perhaps even more important, the institution—to support him against an incredulous world which will not allow him to take things into his own hands and

declare himself a writer. This is partly a problem of egalitarianism or levelling. A beginning writer hesitates to anoint himself, to make a declaration of his very special character. And so he seeks institutional support. He goes to the universities and gets a Ph.D. in creative writing and feels himself armed for the struggle. Like any other licensed professional. But this is social assistance rather than creativity.

Could one argue that anyone who is going to teach literature ought to write a novel or at least try to write a novel?
I am often astonished at the ignorance of learned people. Even the best of teachers will sometimes fail to understand how a book is put together. I suppose that the maker of a thing, however clumsy he may be, acquires a sort of knowledge for which there is no substitute.

Have you any opinions to express about contemporary writers?
I don't really like to discuss contemporary writers. Discussion of that sort generally turns into gossip, and while I am not absolutely opposed to gossip, what I like to avoid is the sort of gladiatorial combat with other writers which the public finds so marvelously entertaining. Let me say that I admire J. F. Powers greatly. I liked *Morte d'Urban* a lot, though I thought it had some faults. I rather enjoyed Mr. Donleavy's *The Ginger Man*. I thought it was very funny and free. I admire John Cheever and Wright Morris and Ralph Ellison and William Gaddis, and many more. I liked *The Ginger Man* more than I admired it. Here and there, its victories appeared a little easy. There is a tendency in modern literature to obtain a certain relief from throwing over the accumulated restraints of earlier generations. Samuel Butler, for instance, enjoys his liberation from Victorian attitudes and rhetoric. Anderson and Hemingway do it, too. Donleavy kicks free from the prevailing rules of good fiction as well as from responsibility, marriage, etc. Of course, he does murder some sitting ducks. Marriage, which everyone murders. Family, everyone's down on the family. It isn't too hard to be radical that way—when middle-class opinion is more than half on your side. Writers are not as radical as they would like to be. That is to say, they feel an active demand for extreme positions but the imagination fails to meet the demands. The world is

far more sensational than their ideas. They cannot keep up with it, and this exasperates them.

Do you think part of the role of the writer as a public figure is to enter into a comment on contemporary events, such as politics or civil rights or world affairs?

I have no objection to writers doing that, if they feel they should; but they must genuinely feel the obligation, or the need, not fake it. You are asking me about James Baldwin, I imagine. Is that the question?

He was in the back of my mind.
Let's skip that.

Very well. What are your views on modern criticism?

My feeling about most critical writing is that it is a rival form of imaginative literature. Formerly my attitude toward criticism was entirely hostile. Now it is beginning to change. From certain critics I have learned a great deal and I admire a rather odd assortment—Erich Auerbach, David Jones, Wyndham Lewis, Harold Rosenberg. I have never liked Leavis. He is too ideological. He makes literature too political, and I dislike his views.

The best of modern writers have a formidable theoretical apparatus—Joyce, Mann, Eliot, Yeats, Pound. Unfortunately, the modern writer is obliged to think about his situation, to make an effort to understand his historical condition. For it is a modern article of faith that one must not repeat what has already been done, and every vanguard artist dreads the superfluous and has a horror of vain gestures. It should be the function of criticism to free the imagination of writers from the burden of historical evaluation. If the critic met this obligation the imagination of the novelist might be liberated. Is this what we see when we look at critical journals?

Present company always, I hope, excepted. Does this attitude of yours toward critics carry over to scholarship?

No, I don't have a similar prejudice against scholars, although I avoid mere antiquarianism.

Would you elaborate on the way you write?

Every writer learns to do a number of things expertly, and he is frequently tempted to give an expert performance whenever he is in trouble. That is to say, when in doubt, he does what he knows best how to do. He trusts his skill as other professionals do. When this happens, he is no longer the free artist—he has failed. I don't say that there is a perfect freedom for every writer, but insofar as his vocation is real, he does yearn for freedom and struggle for it.

His life, like any other life, is so hedged about by duties, obligations, contractual relationships, that if, in his chosen sphere, he loses his freedom, his defeat as a human being is total. In literature, professionalism is slavery and our literature is drearily professional and narrow. It is not smoothness of performance or virtuosity that I object to, but you have only to listen to Paganini and then to Mozart to realize the difference between the virtuoso and the artist. Paganini is all very well, but except to professional fiddlers, he is very boring.

What is your opinion on criticism of John Cheever?

I like him; he's a fine writer and his short stories are excellent. I admire the Wapshot Chronicles. He is, of course, a pro. Sometimes I wonder whether his connection with the *New Yorker* has been an unmixed blessing. It's a bad thing for any writer to wear the livery of a magazine and to become thoroughly identified with it.

Have you comments on the relationship of writers and editors and about publishing in general?

Some writers like a good deal of help from their editors, others, like myself, reject it. Editors inhabit the publishing world, have lunch and cocktails together, and represent the opinions and attitudes of their class. Or its prejudices. Some writers want to imbibe these prejudices and feel them to be beneficial. The young writer is apt to feel helpless and dependent and opens his mouth like a young bird. The publishing industry feeds him a certain number of worms.

Gloria Steinem Spends a Day in Chicago with Saul Bellow

Gloria Steinem / 1965

From *Glamour,* July 1965, 98, 122, 125, 128. Reprinted by permission of Gloria Steinem.

After many months on the best seller list, Saul Bellow's Moses Herzog has become a comfortably familiar figure to most. Not so his creator, who has granted no exclusive interviews since winning the National Book Award. Except this one. *Glamour's* Gloria Steinem persuaded the publicity-shy novelist to spend a day taking her on a tour of his native Chicago. Here is her report:

Chicago belongs to Saul Bellow. Carl Sandburg, Theodore Dreiser, Nelson Algren, and even Philip Roth have staked out some literary claim to the stockyards or the business district or skid row or the campus, but no one else has encompassed the crazy, top-to-bottom social mobility, the long progress from slum to affluence and the fast slips back again, that are peculiar to Chicago and peculiarly American. "Ever since *Adventures of Augie March*," explained one Chicagoan, "I haven't been able to stop thinking, 'This is the section Augie grew up in,' or 'That's the hotel where he tried to unionize the help.' Now, I can't even go down Lake Shore Drive without driving more carefully when I pass the spot where Moses Herzog had his accident. The lives of Bellow's characters here are as real as my own."

And, of course, it works the other way, too: Saul Bellow belongs to Chicago.

"Listen," explained Mr. Bellow, strolling in the sunshine along Lake Michigan's Chicago shore, "provincialism can be a blessing. I've lived quite a few places in New York—the Village, uptown, the West Side: all of that—I've spent seven or eight years there at least, but the literary world is ingrown and hard to avoid. Much of New York's industry is devoted to exploiting talent, so the talent gathers

49

there and talks to each other. Writers tend to lose their personal
base; they get afraid because of all the competition; they start
writing for each other."

Looking natty and not at all provincial in a dark brown suit,
sunglasses and a narrow-brimmed hat, he paused to gesture with
his walking stick at some odd-shaped structures on a grassy prom-
ontory. "That's the center of a local controversy. It's one of the
military installations McNamara wants to close, though I don't
know why; it's true that all the equipment is about twenty years
old, but it would protect us against any Russian attack from Lake
Michigan." His smile broadened as we walked past a scatterring
of early sunbathers (". . . sun *worshippers* really—they started
soon as the snow melts . . .") and back toward the parking lot. "I
can't think of a writer who had a real New York base," he said,
"since Washington Irving."

Slender, of medium height, with dark hair, eyes that seem too big
for his face and a mouth that a nineteenth century novelist would
call sensuous. Mr. Bellow makes it clear by his careful dress that
he is vain of his looks. But by exaggerating that care just a little
(he must surely be one of the few native-born Americans who can
affect a walking stick—not a cane, but an elegant stick too thin
for anything but gesturing), he seems to be making his vanity a
small joke and inviting onlookers to share it.

Now, he pointed with the stick once more before stowing it in the
back seat of his car next to a baby auto seat. "We've bought a
new cooperative apartment," he said, indicating an impressive
building facing the lake. "We haven't moved in yet, but a local
columnist ran an item about it yesterday; said the place had five
bathrooms and was the perfect home for a writer. What kind of
remark is that? Anyway, that's one difference money has made."

What about others? (Because, well received as all his books have
been, none was a best seller or made much money until *Herzog*.)
"Well, I bought this car," he said, tapping the wheel of his modest
American-made sedan. "And there's a rumor that every time I
come into class I'm wearing a brand new suit and I say to the
students, 'How do you like this cloth, eh? Just feel this cloth!'
Actually, I have bought a few new suits, but that's about all. After
a lifetime of wanting things in store windows, I'm suddenly finding

there's not very much I really want to buy. The most important thing about having some money is that it frees me from worrying about it."

He pulled off his sunglasses, blinked experimentally as he drove through the sunlight, and put them back on. "I don't usually wear these things," he said, "but the light kills me. A friend of mine died this week, an old friend, and I haven't been sleeping too much. He was a businessman—at least, he was a man who found refuge in business—and we were the same age. Forty-nine."

Silence. Longer silence. Was he sure this was the day for our Chicago tour? Maybe some other time? "Oh, come on," he said, and smiled. "It'll cheer me up."

We stopped at the University of Chicago campus to pick up Richard Stern, a fellow faculty member and novelist (*Golk,* and most recently, *Teeth, Dying and Other Sorrows*) who is joining us for lunch at a favorite restaurant of Bellow's. The restaurant turned out to be a small Chinese one underneath the Elevated on 63rd Street. Mr. Stern—a dark, solid, good-humored man in his thirties—assured me that this was one of the toughest streets in Chicago. "Southern Negroes and a few poor whites come in looking for work and they get off the train right here. Then they run into all the local mobs, the numbers guys—it's sort of calm now, but at night it goes crazy."

Inside the restaurant—which was barren and cheerful and bore the motto "Food Is Everything" on the door—Bellow ordered for all of us, and asked Stern if he had heard that Nelson Algren was to make a speech on the abolition of capital punishment. They both shook their heads in a "what next?" kind of way. Bellow, looking kindly, said that he felt Nelson Algren was the biggest argument *for* capital punishment he knew, and added firmly, "You can print that." "I used to see him a lot." said Bellow. "We went to the same Turkish bath. I always knew he was there because his cowboy boots would be standing on top of a locker. I can't imagine him talking with government officials about capital punishment.

"It's difficult." Bellow went on, "for writers to escape the temptation to be exemplary. The public wants them to be heroes, philosophers, to point the way. Walt Whitman escaped. Hemingway *wanted* to be exemplary, to be a Real Male saying 'This is the

life.' Mailer chose to offer himself as charismatic. It's so easy to
play a role before the public: women write you letters asking how
they should entertain a Jewish intellectual, or what kind of man
should they marry—everything. The hard thing to do—the thing
few Americans think is necessary—is to make the choice, close the
door, and say 'this is it, this is all I can do.' Everybody wants to be
two things at once—wild lover and faithful husband, profligate and
ascetic, a writer and a gladiator—but who succeeds? How much
time have you got?''

Back at the University again, Mr. Stern and I wandered through
the bookshop while waiting for Mr. Bellow—who had admitted
he was fresh out of money as easily as a man might admit he was
out of matches—to cash a check. In a well-known literary magazine, we discovered a review of *Herzog* that ridiculed every virtue
earlier reviewers had found in the book, and attacked the author
personally as well. Stern bought it after some debate (it also contained a favorable review—by another critic—of *his* latest book),
but we agreed not to mention it. "I know Saul has been warned
about this review," Stern explained, "but I'm not going to bring
it up unless he does. It's vicious. It's unforgivable."

But in the car, Bellow saw the magazine and, on the long drive to
the next spot on our tour, seemed quite willing to discuss it.
"There were always those who didn't like *Herzog,* but since the big
critics treated it so well—and especially since it became a best
seller—there have been many attacks. I'm fair game now. It's the
Golden Bough: I'm on top and must be cut down. I understand
that, or try to."

Stern, who had read enough of the review to be very angry for
his friend, said that this particular critic was unqualified and had an
obvious personal bias. They went into the literary politicking in
more detail, and added that other editors on the same magazine were
greatly upset by the review. I asked about the critic's background:
where had he come from? "Harvard, of course," said Bellow grimly.

We parked the car in a district full of low buildings, Negro
children playing stick ball, and store windows full of cheap merchandise. On the two-block walk to Maxwell Street, gypsy women
stationed along the sidewalk in folding chairs called out to us, but
Bellow said "no" cheerfully and made them laugh. ("Sure, they

tell your fortune," he explained, "but this is also one of the few
areas where prostitution is still open.") No sooner had we arrived
at the Flea Market-like stalls and push carts and sidewalk stores
of Maxwell Street than Bellow remembered that he hadn't put a
coin in the parking meter. He went conscientiously back, and
returned a few minutes later smiling. "I told them that if they were
such good fortune tellers, they would have told me I'd forgotten
to put a nickel in. They said, 'What does a detective worry about a
ticket?' They wouldn't believe I wasn't a detective until they'd
frisked me to see that I didn't have a gun." He laughed. "You see,
that's the good thing about Chicago. You get fed up with the university, but there are places to go."

We walked between the stores with merchandise spilling out on
the sidewalk and the peddlers' carts parked in the gutter. There
seemed to be a choice of Army surplus shirts, cardboard-soled
shoes, dime-store jewelry, satin cushions with hand-painted mottoes
like "To My Navy Sweetheart," hotdogs with sauerkraut, and a
bright purple syrup poured over cracked ice.

"Some of the most important fortunes in Chicago were started
right here," Bellow explained. "The market is half the size it
used to be—a lot of it was razed for a new highway and overpass—
but in the basement of any of these stores, you can still get the
best quality mink coat—anything you want. It's all legitimate. None
of the merchandise is hot. It's just an old-style European market."

He stopped to talk to a push cart peddler, one side of whose face
had been completely disfigured by a purple birthmark or burn.
"Hello, friend," said Bellow in Yiddish. And then in English.
"Remember me, I'm the Quotation Man." The peddler nodded
and immediately began to quote the Scriptures in Hebrew. Bellow
responded in kind. The peddler said in English, "Death awaits us
all," and went back to arranging his display of plastic jewelry.

A shop-owner stepped out of his doorway to say hello. They
talked in Yiddish, shook hands, and we walked on. "I asked him if he
was praying," Bellow said. "He said, 'God is an old man who
sleeps all day; why should I disturb him?' "

We walked past three ancient and sagging brick houses built close
behind each other so that only the first one had access to the
street. This was the old Chicago style of building, Bellow explained,

a remnant of the time when thousands of immigrants arrived every day. The houses stood alone, about to be torn down like their neighbors, but still giving off vibrations of misery. "They look older than the houses of Venice," said Stern, and asked Bellow how long since he'd been here.

"A year or so, I guess," Bellow said. "I come once in awhile. I used to work around here when I was a kid. I must have known that guy back there for thirty years, but he just knows me as the Quotation Man."

We drove around Chicago looking at landmarks—Chinatown, an Irish immigrant section now totally razed for a University of Illinois campus, a clutch of restored brownstones full of coffee houses and paperback book stores, a once respectable street now given over to hillbillies come North for jobs—and almost everywhere there was something of Bellow's life, something he has written about. The house he (and Augie March) grew up in still stands. So does the coal yard where he weighed in trucks. The hotel once owned by his older brother (Simon, to give him his fictional name) is still very big and grand. ("Did Saul ever tell you how his brother went to Europe?" asked Stern. "Well, he had some trouble with union bosses, so he sold the hotel, put his suitcase and his mistress in his big Cadillac, and drove right on the plane. He got to Europe without ever getting out from behind that wheel.")

Not all the streetcars the teen-age Bellow rode as a florist's delivery boy are now in use, but he still knows the geography of the city that the job taught him. ("I spent hours every day on those streetcars," he recalled, "sitting there clutching some big funeral wreath.") Around the university are several apartments and board-inghouses—now mostly absorbed by the Negro ghetto—where Bellow lived at various stages of academic life. But Chicago seems bent on becoming another city of concrete and glass, and the familiar landmarks are fast disappearing.

It was still only a little past three in the afternoon when we stopped at a skid row bar (a very dirty and ragged drunk was staggering out as we were walking in) that Bellow had suggested as "likely to shake you up a little, even in the daytime." All along the bar and at several tables in the cavernous room were figures who looked as if they had been sent over from a kind of sick

Central Casting. Two battered American Indian women were dancing drunkenly with each other, and vainly beckoning to men at
the bar. (The Indians, Bellow explained, came to Chicago for the
same reasons as the hillbillies and the Southern Negroes—to find
work—but many ended up on relief.) Several people—it was difficult
to tell whether they were men or women—were asleep with heads
lolling on the bar. Several more were standing upright, drinking or
swaying to the juke box, and one woman in a clean housedress
was giggling with a girl friend as if she were at a ladies' lunch
at Schrafft's.

We ordered three draft beers at the bar and tried hard to be
inconspicuous, but it was impossible. "I usually dress in something a
little more appropriate," Bellow said, looking down at his neat suit,
"and I don't usually bring a girl like you." A pockmarked Indian
was edging towards us, staggering. He put his hand out to Bellow
and said something unintelligible that sounded like a name. Bellow shook hands calmly and said, "The name is Bellow." The
Indian then shook hands all around and asked us what we were
doing there. Bellow told the Indian that we were "inspecting for the
Poverty Program and it seems like we should spread a little money
around down here." The Indian seemed to understand not only
what the Poverty Program was, but that Bellow had intended it as
a joke. They laughed together and the Indian wandered off.

A gentle-looking, middle-aged bum introduced himself to us next.
He was standing near us at the bar, and explained that he had got
drunk in Miami three weeks ago, got on a bus, found himself in
Chicago, and had been there ever since. "I come across the
bridge this morning, and I made every bar on the way, but this is
my last one. I never seen a town like this one. Man, people beat
you on the head here for a nickel."

A second man—much drunker and more surly than our neigh-
bor—began to dance in front of us with a broken glass balanced
on his head. Bellow applauded and the man looked mollified, but
then began to dance closer. Our Indian friend lurched over and pushed
the dancer away; then turned to us to suggest haltingly that maybe
we should leave now. We said goodbye and left, the stench of
stale beer and urine following us out into the street.

"Well," said Stern, "that's some bar you've got there." Bellow

unlocked car doors all around, and smiled. "Now we'll go to the
financial district," he said, "just for contrast. Besides, I have to
drop off some paper at my lawyer's office. I was supposed to do it
yesterday, but to tell the truth, I forgot." Keeping up with the
check-cashing and parking meters and paper-delivering of life
seems to be his constant, good-humored struggle.

We sat in the car, watching Bellow's slight figure weave its way
through traffic and disappear into a huge office building. "He's a
kind man, an incredible guy," said Stern. "I hope all this spotlight
and criticism isn't too hard on him."

Driving back to the university, Mr. Stern talked a little about an
espionage novel he had written some years before, and about a
book-in-progress that has to do with Ezra Pound and Venice. After
he had said goodbye, clapping Bellow on the shoulder in thanks for
the day, I asked about the contrast (even more startling if *Golk,* a
novel about television, is included) among his various writings.
Bellow looked impatient. "No one with any talent likes to do what
he's already proved he can do. Look at Augie March. I'd found a
kind of success there, a character people wanted to read about, but
I couldn't go on with him forever."

We stopped on a quiet university street to buy the *New York
Hearld Tribune*'s book review section ("I rarely read reviews at
all, but this Sunday, there's something I want to see"), and have a
final cup of tea.

"I've moved around a lot," he said, "but I'm glad to be back
here. The university gives me intellectual companionship—and that's
important after all: friends to talk to—and I can teach, but I'm not
trapped in it. I have time to write: not enough, but time." Just
now, he explained, he was finishing the last of three one-act plays
and looking forward to seeing them produced Off-Broadway.

"My first experience on Broadway," he said, referring to his
short-lived play, *The Last Analysis,* "was not exactly pleasant.
But this time, the pressure is off. And Nancy Walker, who's never
directed a play before in her life, is doing a great job with them.
She's wonderful. Brains in the theater are very rare. They all seem
to get siphoned off into physics."

"There aren't a lot of contemporary writers I enjoy either. Ralph
Ellison's *Invisible Man* is very good. So is *Works of Love* by

Wright Morris. I've always thought Morris was a greatly underrated
writer. Philip Roth can't be considered any more after *Letting Go:* his
first book was better, but he didn't follow it. I liked Donleavy's
Ginger Man, too, though nothing he did after that. Writers seem
occupied with saying that America is a fraud, that all is blackness,
bitterness, and hopelessness. That's part of the truth, but I don't
think it's all of it."

If *The Last Analysis* is produced in London as planned, Bellow
will go there. Otherwise, his future travels aren't set beyond
taking his new wife, Susan, and infant son (he has two other sons
by two previous marriages) to Cape Cod for the summer. "But
that's where I usually go. *Herzog* hasn't changed my life so much."

I said goodbye, and tried without much success to say thank you
in some way big enough to encompass the day.

"That's all right," he said, looking neat and finely drawn beneath
his thin-brimmed hat. "I hadn't been to those places in awhile.
And when I don't go, I miss them."

The Art of Fiction: Saul Bellow
Gordon Lloyd Harper / 1966

From *The Paris Review*, 9.36 (1966), 48–73. Reprinted in *Writers at Work: The Paris Review Interviews*. Third Series, ed. Alfred Kazin (London: Viking Press, 1967), 175–96. © 1966 by The Paris Review, Inc. Reprinted by permission of Viking Penguin Inc.

The interview "took place" over a period of several weeks. Beginning with some exploratory discussions during May of 1965, it was shelved during the summer, and actually accomplished during September and October. Two recording sessions were held, totaling about an hour and a half, but this was only a small part of the effort Mr. Bellow gave to this interview. A series of meetings, for over five weeks, was devoted to the most careful revision of the original material. Recognizing at the outset the effort he would make for such an interview, he had real reluctance about beginning it at all. Once his decision had been reached, however, he gave a remarkable amount of his time freely to the task—up to two hours a day, at least twice and often three times a week throughout the entire five-week period. It had become an opportunity, as he put it, to say some things which were important but which weren't being said.

Certain types of questions were ruled out in early discussions. Mr. Bellow was not interested in responding to criticisms of his work which he found trivial or stupid. He quoted the Jewish proverb that a fool can throw a stone into the water which ten wise men cannot recover. Nor did he wish to discuss what he considered his personal writing habits, whether he used a pen or typewriter, how hard he pressed on the page. For the artist to give such loving attention to his own shoelaces was dangerous, even immoral. Finally, there were certain questions that led into too "wide spaces" for this interview, subjects for fuller treatment on other occasions.

The two tapes were made in Bellow's University of Chicago office on the fifth floor of the Social Sciences Building. The office, though large, is fairly typical of those on the main quadrangles; much of it rather dark with one brightly lighted area, occupied by his desk, immediately before a set of three dormer windows; dark-green metal bookcases line the walls, casually used as storage for a miscellany of books, magazines, and correspondence. A set of *The Complete Works of Rudyard Kipling* ("it was given to me") shares space with examination copies of new novels and with a few of Bellow's own books, including recent French and Italian translations of Herzog. A table, a couple of typing stands, and various decrepit and mismatched chairs are scattered in apparently haphazard fashion throughout the room. A wall rack just inside the door holds his jaunty black felt hat and his walking cane. There is a general sense of disarray, with stacks of papers, books, and letters lying everywhere. When one comes to the door, Bellow is frequently at his typing stand, rapidly pounding out on a portable machine responses to some of the many letters he gets daily. Occasionally a secretary enters and proceeds to type away on some project at the far end of the room.

During the two sessions with the tape recorder, Bellow sat at his desk, between the eaves which project prominently into the room, backlighted by the dormer windows which let in the bright afternoon sun from the south. Four stories below lie Fifty-ninth Street and Chicago's Midway, their automobile and human noises continually penetrating the office. As the questions were asked, Bellow listened carefully and often developed an answer slowly, pausing frequently to think out the exact phrasing he sought. His answers were serious, but full of his special quality of humor. He took obvious pleasure in the amusing turns of thought with which he often concluded an answer. Throughout, he was at great pains to make his ideas transparent to the interviewer, asking repeatedly if this was clear or if he should say more on the subject. His concentration during these sessions was intense enough to be tiring, and both tapes were brought to a close with his confessing to some exhaustion.

Following each taping session, a typescript of his remarks was prepared. Bellow worked over these typed sheets extensively with pen and ink, taking as many as three separate meetings to do a complete revision. Then another typescript was made, and the process started over. This work was done when the interviewer could be present, and again the changes were frequently tested on him. Generally these sessions occurred at Bellow's office or at his apartment, overlooking the Outer Drive and Lake Michigan. Once,

however, revisions were made while he and the interviewer
sat on a Jackson park bench on a fine October afternoon,
and one typescript was worked on along with beer and
hamburgers at a local bar.

Revisions were of various sorts. Frequently there were
slight changes in meaning: "That's what I really meant to
say." Other alterations tightened up his language or were in
the nature of stylistic improvements. Any sections which he
judged to be excursions from the main topic were deleted.
Most regretted by the interviewer were prunings that elimi-
nated certain samples of the characteristic Bellow wit: in a
few places he came to feel he was simply "exhibiting"
himself, and these were scratched out. On the other hand,
whenever he could substitute for conventional literary dic-
tion an unexpected colloquial turn of phrase—which often
proved humorous in context—he did so.

Interviewer: Some critics have felt that your work falls within the
tradition of American naturalism, possibly because of some things
you've said about Dreiser. I was wondering if you saw your self in
a particular literary tradition?

Bellow: Well, I think that the development of realism in the
nineteenth century is still the major event of modern literature.
Dreiser, a realist of course, had elements of genius. He was clumsy,
cumbersome, and in some respects a poor thinker. But he was
rich in a kind of feeling which has been ruled off the grounds by
many contemporary writers—the kind of feeling that every human
being intuitively recognizes as primary. Dreiser has more open
access to primary feelings than any American writer of the
twentieth century. It makes a good many people uncomfortable that
his emotion has not found a more developed literary form. It's
true his art may be too "natural." He sometimes conveys his
understanding by masses of words, verbal approximations. He
blunders, but generally in the direction of truth. The result is that
we are moved in an unmediated way by his characters, as by life, and
then we say that his novels are simply torn from the side of life, and
therefore not novels. But we can't escape reading them. He
somehow conveys, without much refinement, depths of feeling that
we usually associate with Balzac or Shakespeare.

Interviewer: This realism, then, is a particular kind of sensibility, rather than a technique?

Bellow: Realism specializes in *apparently* unmediated experiences. What stirred Dreiser was simply the idea that you could bring unmediated feeling to the novel. He took it up naïvely without going to the trouble of mastering an art. We don't see this because he makes so many familiar "art" gestures, borrowed from the art-fashions of his day, and even from the slick magazines, but he is really a natural, a primitive. I have great respect for his simplicities and I think they are worth more than much that has been praised as high art in the American novel.

Interviewer: Could you give me an example of what you mean?

Bellow: In a book like *Jennie Gerhardt* the delicacy with which Jennie allows Lester Kane to pursue his conventional life while she herself lives unrecognized with her illegitimate daughter, the depth of her understanding, and the depth of her sympathy and of her truthfulness impress me. She is not a sentimental figure. She has a natural sort of honor.

Interviewer: Has recent American fiction pretty much followed this direction?

Bellow: Well, among his heirs there are those who believe that clumsiness and truthfulness go together. But cumbersomeness does not necessarily imply a sincere heart. Most of the "Dreiserians" lack talent. On the other hand, people who put Dreiser down, adhering to a "high art" standard for the novel, miss the point.

Interviewer: Aside from Dresier, what other American writers do you find particularly of interest?

Bellow: I like Hemingway, Faulkner, and Fitzgerald. I think of Hemingway as a man who developed a significant manner as an artist, a life-style which is important. For his generation, his language created a life-style, one which pathetic old gentlemen are still found clinging to. I don't think of Hemingway as a great novelist. I like Fitzgerald's novels better, but I often feel about Fitzgerald that he couldn't distinguish between innocence and social climbing. I am thinking of *The Great Gatsby*.

Interviewer: If we go outside American literature, you've mentioned that you read the nineteenth-century Russian writers with a good deal of interest. Is there anything particular about them that attracts you?

Bellow: Well, the Russians have an immediate charismatic appeal—excuse the Max Weberism. Their conventions allow them to express freely their feelings about nature and human beings. We have inherited a more restricted and imprisoning attitude toward the emotions. We have to work around puritanical and stoical restraints. We lack the Russian openness. Our path is narrower.

Interviewer: In what other writers do you take special interest?

Bellow: I have a special interest in Joyce; I have a special interest in Lawrence. I read certain poets over and over again. I can't say where they belong in my theoretical scheme; I only know that I have an attachment to them. Yeats is one such poet. Hart Crane is another. Hardy and Walter de la Mare. I don't know what these have in common—probably nothing. I know that I am drawn repeatedly to these men.

Interviewer: It's been said that one can't like *both* Lawrence and Joyce, that one has to choose between them. You don't feel this way?

Bellow: No. Because I really don't take Lawrence's sexual theories very seriously. I take his art seriously, not his doctrine. But he himself warned us repeatedly not to trust the artist. He said trust the work itself. So I have little use for the Lawrence who wrote *The Plumed Serpent* and great admiration for the Lawrence who wrote *The Lost Girl*.

Interviewer: Does Lawrence at all share the special feeling you find attractive in Dreiser?

Bellow: A certain openness to experience, yes. And a willingness to trust one's instinct, to follow it freely—that Lawrence has.

Interviewer: You mentioned before the interview that you would prefer not to talk about your early novels, that you feel you are a different person now from what you were then. I wonder if this is all you want to say, or if you can say something about how you have changed.

Bellow: I think that when I wrote those early books I was timid. I still felt the incredible effrontery of announcing myself to the world (in part I mean the WASP world) as a writer and an artist. I had to touch a great many bases, demonstrate my abilities, pay my respects to formal requirements. In short, I was afraid to let myself go.

Interviewer: When do you find a significant change occurring?

Bellow: When I began to write *Augie March,* I took off many of these restraints. I think I took off too many, and went too far, but I was feeling the excitement of discovery. I had just increased my freedom, and like any emancipated plebeian I abused it at once.

Interviewer: What were these restraints that you took off in *Augie March?*

Bellow: My first two books are well made. I wrote the first quickly but took great pains with it. I labored with the second and tried to make it letter-perfect. In writing *The Victim* I accepted a Flaubertian standard. Not a bad standard, to be sure, but one which, in the end, I found repressive—repressive because of the circumstances of my life and because of my upbringing in Chicago as the son of immigrants, I could not, with such an instrument as I developed in the first two books, express a variety of things I knew intimately. Those books, though useful, did not give me a form in which I felt comfortable. A writer should be able to express himself easily, naturally, copiously in a form which frees his mind, his energies. Why should he hobble himself with formalities? With a borrowed sensibility? With the desire to be "correct"? Why should I force myself to write like an Englishman or a contributor to *The New Yorker?* I soon saw that it was simply not in me to be a mandarin. I should add that for a young man in my position there were social inhibitions, too. I had good reason to fear that I would be put down as a foreigner, an interloper. It was made clear to me when I studied literature in the university that as a Jew and the son of Russian Jews I would probably never have the right *feeling* for Anglo-Saxon traditions, for English words. I realized even in college that the people who told me this were not necessarily disinterested friends. But they had an effect on me, nevertheless. This was something from which I had to free myself. I fought free because I had to.

Interviewer: Are these social inhibitors as powerful today as they were when you wrote *Dangling Man?*

Bellow: I think I was lucky to have grown up the Middle West, where such influences are less strong. If I'd grown up in the East and

attended an Ivy League university, I might have been damaged
more badly. Puritan and Protestant America carries less weight in
Illinois than in Massachusetts. But I don't bother much with such
things now.

Interviewer: Did another change in your writing occur between
Augie March and *Herzog?* You've mentioned writing *Augie March*
with a great sense of freedom, but I take it that *Herzog* was a very
difficult book to write.

Bellow: It was. I had to tame and restrain the style I developed
in *Augie March* in order to write *Henderson* and *Herzog*. I think
both those books reflect that change in style. I wouldn't really know
how to describe it. I don't care to trouble my mind to find an exact
description for it, but it has something to do with a kind of readiness
to record impressions arising from a source of which we know
little. I suppose that all of us have a primitive prompter or commentator within, who from earliest years has been advising us, telling
us what the real world is. There is such a commentator in me. I
have to prepare the ground for him. From this source come words,
phrases, syllables; sometimes only sounds, which I try to interpret,
sometimes whole paragraphs, fully punctuated. When E. M.
Forster said, "How do I know what I think until I see what I say?"
he was perhaps referring to his own prompter. There is that
observing instrument in us—in childhood at any rate. At the sight
of a man's face, his shoes, the color of light, a woman's mouth or
perhaps her ear, one receives a word, a phrase, at times nothing but
a nonsense syllable from the primitive commentator.

Interviewer: So this change in your writing—

Bellow: —was an attempt to get nearer to that primitive commentator.

Interviewer: How do you go about getting nearer to him, preparing the way for him?

Bellow: When I say the commentator is primitive, I don't mean
that he's crude; God knows he's often fastidious. But he won't
talk until the situation's right. And if you prepare the ground for
him with too many difficulties underfoot, he won't say anything. I
must be terribly given to fraud and deceit because I sometimes have
great difficulty preparing a suitable ground. This is why I've had
so much trouble with my last two novels. I appealed directly to my

prompter. The prompter, however, has to find the occasion perfect—that is to say, truthful, and necessary. If there is any superflu-
ity or inner falsehood in the preparations, he is aware of it. I have to
stop. Often I have to begin again, with the first word. I can't
remember how many times I wrote *Herzog*. But at last I did find
the acceptable ground for it.

Interviewer: Do these preparations include your coming to some
general conception of the work?

Bellow: Well, I don't know exactly how it's done. I let it alone a
good deal. I try to avoid common forms of strain and distortion.
For a long time, perhaps from the middle of the nineteenth century,
writers have not been satisfied to regard themselves simply as
writers. They have required also a theoretical framework. Most
often they have been their own theoreticians, have created their
own ground as artists, and have provided an exegesis for their own
works. They have found it necessary to take a position, not
merely to write novels. In bed last night I was reading a collection
of articles by Stendhal. One of them amused me very much,
touched me. Stendhal was saying how lucky writers were in the age
of Louis XIV not to have anyone take them very seriously. Their
obscurity was very valuable. Corneille had been dead for several
days before anyone at court considered the fact important enough
to mention. In the nineteenth century, says Stendhal, there would
have been several public orations, Corneille's funeral covered by
all the papers. There are great advantages in not being taken *too*
seriously. Some writers are excessively serious about themselves.
They accept the ideas of the "cultivated public." There is such a
thing as overcapitalizing the A in artist. Certain writers and
musicians understand this. Stravinsky says the composer should
practice his trade exactly as a shoemaker does. Mozart and
Haydn accepted commissions—wrote to order. In the nineteenth
century, the artist loftily waited for Inspiration. Once you elevate
yourself to the rank of a cultural institution, you're in for a lot
of trouble.

Then there is a minor modern disorder—the disease of people
who live by an image of themselves created by papers, television,
Broadway, Sardi's, gossip, or the public need for celebrities. Even
buffoons, prize fighters, and movie stars have caught the bug. I

avoid these "images." I have a longing, not for downright obscurity—I'm too egotistical for that—but for peace, and freedom from meddling.

Interviewer: In line with this, the enthusiastic response to *Herzog* must have affected your life considerably. Do you have any thoughts as to why this book became and remained the bestseller it did?

Bellow: I don't like to agree with the going view that if you write a bestseller it's because you betrayed an important principle or sold your soul. I know that sophisticated opinion believes this. And although I don't take much stock in sophisticated opinion, I have examined my conscience. I've tried to find out whether I had unwittingly done wrong. But I haven't yet discovered the sin. I do think that a book like *Herzog,* which ought to have been an obscure book with a total sale of eight thousand, has such a reception because it appeals to the unconscious sympathies of many people. I know from the mail I've received that the book described a common predicament. *Herzog* appealed to Jewish readers, to those who have been divorced, to those who talk to themselves, to college graduates, readers of paperbacks, autodidacts, to those who yet hope to live awhile, etc.

Interviewer: Do you feel that there were deliberate attempts at lionizing by the literary tastemakers? I was thinking that the recent deaths of Faulkner and Hemingway have been seen as creating a vacuum in American letters, which we all know is abhorrent.

Bellow: Well, I don't know whether I would say a vacuum. Perhaps a pigeonhole. I agree that there is a need to keep the pigeonholes filled and that people are uneasy when there are vacancies. Also the mass media demand material—grist—and literary journalists have to create a major-league atmosphere in literature. The writers don't offer to fill the pigeonholes. It's the critics who want figures in the Pantheon. But there are many people who assume that every writer must be bucking for the niche. Why should writers wish to be rated—seeded—like tennis players? Handicapped like racehorses? What an epitaph for a novelist: "He won all the polls"!

Interviewer: How much are you conscious of the reader when you write? Is there an ideal audience that you write for?

Bellow: I have in mind another human being who will understand me. I count on this. Not on perfect understanding, which is Cartesian, but on approximate understanding, which is Jewish. And on a meeting of sympathies, which is human. But I have no ideal reader in my head, no. Let me just say this, too. I seem to have the blind self-acceptance of the eccentric who can't conceive that his eccentricities are not clearly understood.

Interviewer: So there isn't a great deal of calculation about rhetoric?

Bellow: These are things that can't really be contrived. People who talk about contrivance must think that a novelist is a man capable of building a skyscraper to conceal a dead mouse. Skyscrapers are not raised simply to conceal mice.

Interviewer: It's been said that contemporary fiction sees man as a victim. You gave this title to one of your early novels, yet there seems to be very strong opposition in your fiction to seeing man as simply determined or futile. Do you see any truth to this claim about contemporary fiction?

Bellow: Oh, I think that realistic literature from the first has been a victim literature. Pit any ordinary individual—and realistic literature concerns itself with ordinary individuals—against the external world, and the external world will conquer him, of course. Everything that people believed in the nineteenth century about determinism, about man's place in nature, about the power of productive forces in society made it inevitable that the hero of the realistic novel should not be a hero but a sufferer who is eventually overcome. So I was doing nothing very original by writing another realistic novel about a common man and calling it *The Victim.* I suppose I was discovering independently the essence of much of modern realism. In my innocence, I put my finger on it. Serious realism also contrasts the common man with aristocratic greatness. He is overborne by fate, just as the great are in Shakespeare or Sophocles. But this contrast, inherent in literary tradition, always damages him. In the end the force of tradition carries realism into parody, satire, mock-epic—Leopold Bloom.

Interviewer: Haven't you yourself moved away from the sugges-

tion of plebeian tragedy toward a treatment of the sufferer that
has greater comic elements? Although the concerns and difficulties
are still fundamentally serious, the comic elements in *Henderson,*
in *Herzog,* even in *Seize the Day* seem much more prominent than
in *Dangling Man* or *The Victim.*

Bellow: Yes, because I got very tired of the solemnity of complaint, altogether impatient with complaint. Obliged to choose
between complaint and comedy, I choose comedy, as more ener-
getic, wiser, and manlier. This is really one reason why I dislike my
own early novels, I find them plaintive, sometimes querulous.
Herzog makes comic use of complaint.

Interviewer: When you say that you are obliged to choose between complaint and comedy, does it mean this is the only choice—
that you are limited to choosing between just these two alternatives?

Bellow: I'm not inclined to predict what will happen. I may feel
drawn to comedy again, I may not. But modern literature was
dominated by a tone of elegy from the twenties to the fifties, the
atmosphere of Eliot in "The Waste Land" and that of Joyce in *A
Portrait of the Artist as a Young Man.* Sensibility absorbed this
sadness, this view of the artist as the only contemporary link with
an age of gold, forced to watch the sewage flowing in the Thames,
every aspect of modern civilization doing violence to his (artist-
patrician) feelings. This went much further than it should have been
allowed to go. It descended to absurdities, of which I think we
have had enough.

Interviewer: I wonder if you could say something about how
important the environments are in your works. I take it that for
the realist tradition the context in which the action occurs is of vital
importance. You set your novels in Chicago, New York, as far
away as Africa. How important are these settings for the fiction?

Bellow: Well, you present me with a problem to which I think no
one has the answer. People write realistically but at the same time
they want to create environments which are somehow desirable,
which are surrounded by atmospheres in which behavior becomes
significant, which display the charm of life. What is literature
without these things? Dickens's London is gloomy, but also cozy.
And yet realism has always offered to annihilate precisely such
qualities. That is to say, if you want to be ultimately realistic you

bring artistic space itself in danger. In Dickens, there is no void beyond the fog. The environment is human, at all times. Do you follow me?

Interviewer: I'm not sure I do.

Bellow: The realistic tendency is to challenge the human significance of things. The more realistic you are the more you threaten the grounds of your own art. Realism has always both accepted and rejected the circumstances of ordinary life. It accepted the task of writing about ordinary life and tried to meet it in some extraordinary fashion. As Flaubert did. The subject might be common, low, degrading; all this was to be redeemed by art. I really do see those Chicago environments as I represent them. They suggest their own style of presentation. I elaborate it.

Interviewer: Then you aren't especially disturbed by readers of *Henderson*, for example, who say that Africa really isn't like that? One sort of realist would require a writer to spend several years on location before daring to place his characters there. You're not troubled by him, I take it?

Bellow: Perhaps you should say "factualist" rather than "realist." Years ago, I studied African ethnography with the late Professor Herskovits. Later he scolded me for writing a book like *Henderson*. He said the subject was much too serious for such fooling. I felt that my fooling was fairly serious. Literalism, factualism, will smother the imagination altogether.

Interviewer: You have on occasion divided recent American fiction into what you call the "cleans" and the "dirties." The former, I gather, tend to be conservative and easily optimistic, the latter the eternal nay-sayers, rebels, iconoclasts. Do you feel this is still pretty much the picture of American fiction today?

Bellow: I feel that both choices are rudimentary and pitiful, and though I know the uselessness of advocating any given path to other novelists, I am still inclined to say, Leave both these extremes. They are useless, childish. No wonder the really powerful men in our society, whether politicians or scientists, hold writers and poets in contempt. They do it because they get no evidence from modern literature that anybody is thinking about any significant question. What does the radicalism of radical writers nowadays amount to? Most of it is hand-me-down bohemianism, sentimental

populism, D.H. Lawrence-and-water, or imitation Sartre. For
American writers radicalism is a question of honor. They must be
radicals for the sake of their dignity. They see it as their function,
and a noble function, to say Nay, and to bite not only the hand that
feeds them (and feeds them with comic abundance, I might add)
but almost any other hand held out to them. Their radicalism,
however, is contentless. A genuine radicalism, which truly challenges
authority, we need desperately. But a radicalism of posture is easy
and banal. Radical criticism requires knowledge, not posture, not
slogans, not rant. People who maintain their dignity as artists, in a
small way, by being mischievous on television, simply delight the
networks and the public. True radicalism requires homework—
thought. Of the cleans, on the other hand, there isn't much to
say. They seem faded.

Interviewer: Your context is essentially that of the modern city,
isn't it? Is there a reason for this beyond the fact that you come
out of an urban experience?

Bellow: Well, I don't know how I could possibly separate my
knowledge of life, such as it is, from the city. I could no more tell
you how deeply it's gotten into my bones than the lady who paints
radium dials in the clock factory can tell you.

Interviewer: You've mentioned the distractive character of modern life. Would this be most intense in the city?

Bellow: The volume of judgments one is called upon to make
depends upon the receptivity of the observer, and if one is very
receptive, one has a terrifying number of opinions to render—
"What do you think about this, about that, about Viet Nam,
about city planning, about expressways, or garbage disposal, or
democracy, or Plato, or pop art, or welfare states, or literacy in a
'mass society'?" I wonder whether there will ever be enough
tranquillity under modern circumstances to allow our contemporary Wordsworth to recollect anything. I feel that art has something
to do with the achievement of stillness in the midst of chaos. A
stillness which characterizes prayer, too, and the eye of the storm.
I think that art has something to do with an arrest of attention in the
midst of distraction.

Interviewer: I believe you once said that it is the novel which
must deal particularly with this kind of chaos, and that as a

consequence certain forms appropriate to poetry or to music are
not available to the novelist.

Bellow: I'm no longer so sure of that. I think the novelist can
avail himself of similar privileges. It's just that he can't act with
the same purity or economy of means as the poet. He has to
traverse a very muddy and noisy territory before he can arrive at
a pure conclusion. He's more exposed to the details of life.

Interviewer: Is there anything peculiar about the *kind* of distractions you see the novelist having to confront today? Is it just that
there are more details, or is their quality different today from what
it used to be?

Bellow: The modern masterpiece of confusion is Joyce's *Ulysses*.
There the mind is unable to resist experience. Experience in all
its diversity, its pleasure and horror, passes through Bloom's head
like an ocean through a sponge. The sponge can't resist; it has to
accept whatever the waters bring. It also notes every microorganism
that passes through it. This is what I mean. How much of this
must the spirit suffer, in what detail is it obliged to receive this
ocean with its human plankton? Sometimes it looks as if the
power of the mind has been nullified by the volume of experiences.
But of course this is assuming the degree of passivity that Joyce
assumes in *Ulysses*. Stronger, more purposeful minds can demand
order, impose order, select, disregard, but there is still the threat
of disintegration under the particulars. A Faustian artist is unwilling
to surrender to the mass of particulars.

Interviewer: Some people have felt your protagonists are seeking
the answer to a question that might be phrased, How is it possible
today for a good man to live? I wonder if you feel there is any single
recurring question like this in the novels?

Bellow: I don't think that I've represented any really good men;
no one is thoroughly admirable in any of my novels. Realism has
restrained me too much for that. I should *like* to represent good
men. I long to know who and what they are and what their
condition might be. I often represent men who desire such qualities
but seem unable to achieve them on any significant scale. I
criticize this in myself. I find it a limitation.

Interviewer: I'm sorry; what exactly is this limitation?

Bellow: The fact that I have not discerned those qualities or that

I have not shown them in action. Herzog wants very much to
have effective virtues. But that's a source of comedy in the book. I
think I am far more concerned with another matter, and I don't
approach this as a problem with a ready answer. I see it rather as a
piece of research, having to do with human characteristics or
qualities which have no need of justification. It's an odd thing to do,
it shouldn't be necessary to "justify" certain things. But there
are many skeptical, rebellious, or simply nervous writers all around
us, who, having existed a full twenty or thirty years in this
universe denounce or reject life because it fails to meet their
standards as philosophical intellectuals. It seems to me that they
can't know enough about it for confident denial. The mystery is too
great. So when they knock at the door of mystery with the
knuckles of cognition it is quite right that the door should open and
some mysterious power should squirt them in the eye. I think a good
deal of *Herzog* can be explained simply by the implicit assumption
that existence, quite apart from any of our judgments, has value,
that existence is worth-ful. Here it is possible, however, that the
desire to go on with his creaturely career vulgarly betrays Herzog.
He wants to live? What of it! The clay that frames him contains this
common want. Simple *aviditas vitae*. Does a man deserve any
credit for this?

Interviewer: Would this help to explain, then, why many of the
difficulties which Herzog's mind throws up for him throughout
the novel don't ever seem to be *intellectually* resolved?

Bellow: The book is not anti-intellectual, as some have said. It
simply points to the comic impossibility of arriving at a synthesis
that can satisfy modern demands. That is to say, full awareness of
all major problems, together with the necessary knowledge of
history, of science and philosophy. That's why Herzog paraphrases
Thomas Marshall, Woodrow Wilson's Vice-President, who said
what this country needs is a good five-cent cigar. (I think it was
Bugs Baer who said it first.) Herzog's version: what this country
needs is a good five-cent synthesis.

Interviewer: Do you find many contemporary writers attempting
to develop such syntheses or insisting that significant fiction provide
them?

Bellow: Well, I don't know that too many American novelists,

young or old, are tormenting their minds with these problems.
Europeans do. I don't know that they can ever reach satisfactory
results on the grounds they have chosen. At any rate, they write
few good novels. But that leads us into some very wide spaces.

Interviewer: Do the ideas in *Herzog* have any other major roles
to play? The "anti-intellectual" charge seems to come from people
who don't feel the ideas are essential either in motivating the action,
the decisions Herzog makes, or in helping him to come through
at the end.

Bellow: To begin with, I suppose I should say something about
the difference in the role ideas play in American literature. European literature—I speak now of the Continent—is intellectual in a
different sense from ours. The intellectual hero of a French or a
German novel is likely to be a philosophical intellectual, an ideological intellectual. We here, intellectuals—or the educated public—
know that in our liberal democracy ideas become effective within
an entirely different tradition. The lines are less clearly drawn.
We do not expect thought to have results, say, in the moral sphere,
or in the political, in quite the way a Frenchman would. To be an
intellectual in the United States sometimes means to be immured in
a private life in which one thinks, but thinks with some humiliating
sense of how little thought can accomplish. To call therefore for a
dramatic resolution in terms of ideas in an American novel is to
demand something for which there is scarcely any precedent. My
novel deals with the humiliating sense that results from the
American mixture of private concerns and intellectual interests.
This is something which most readers of the book seem utterly to
have missed. Some, fortunately, have caught it. But in part *Herzog*
is intended to bring to an end, under blinding light, a certain
course of development. Many people feel a "private life" to be an
affliction. In some sense it is a genuine affliction; it cuts one off
from a common life. To me, a significant theme of *Herzog* is the
imprisonment of the individual in a shameful and impotent privacy. He feels humiliated by it; he struggles comically with it; and
he comes to realize at last that what he considered his intellectual
"privilege" has proved to be another form of bondage. Anyone
who misses this misses the point of the book. So that to say that
Herzog is not motivated in his acts by ideas is entirely false. Any

Bildungsroman—and *Herzog* is, to use that heavy German term,
a *Bildungsroman*—concludes with the first step. The first *real* step.
Any man who has rid himself of superfluous ideas in order to take
that first step has done something significant. When people complain
of a lack of ideas in novels, they may mean that they do not find
familiar ideas, fashionable ideas. Ideas outside the "canon" they
don't recognize. So, if what they mean is ideas à la Sartre or
ideas à la Camus, they are quite right: there are few such in *Herzog*.
Perhaps they mean that the thoughts of a man fighting for sanity and
life are not suitable for framing.

Interviewer: Herzog rejects certain of these fashionable ideas,
doesn't he—the ideas à la Sartre or à la Camus?

Bellow: I think he tests them first upon his own sense of life and
against his own desperate need for clarity. With him these
thoughts are not a game. Though he may laugh as he thinks them,
his survival depends upon them. I didn't have him engage in full
combat with figures like Sartre. If he had chosen to debate with
Sartre in typical Herzogian fashion he would perhaps have begun
with Sartre's proposition that Jews exist only because of anti-
Semitism, that the Jew has to choose between authentic and
inauthentic existence, that authentic existence can never be de-
tached from this anti-Semitism which determines it. Herzog might
have remembered that for Sartre, the Jew exists because he is
hated, not because he has a history, not because he has origins of
his own—but simply because he is designated, created, in his
Jewishness by an outrageous evil. Sartre offers a remedy for
those Jews who are prepared to make the authentic choice: he
extends to them the invitation to become Frenchmen. If this great
prince of contemporary European philosophy offers Herzog ideas
such as this to embrace (or dispute), who can blame him for his
skepticism toward what is called, so respectfully, Thought, toward
contemporary intellectual fare? Often Herzog deals with ideas in
negative fashion. He needs to dismiss a great mass of irrelevancy
and nonsense in order to survive. Perhaps this was what I meant
earlier when I said that we were called upon to make innumerable
judgments. We can be consumed simply by the necessity to
discriminate between multitudes of propositions. We have to dismiss
a great number of thoughts if we are to have any creaturely or

human life at all. It seems at times that we are on trial seven days a
week answering the questions, giving a clear account of ourselves.
But when does one live? How does one live if it is necessary to
render ceaseless judgments?

Interviewer: Herzog's rejection of certain ideas has been widely
recognized, but—

Bellow: —why he rejects them is not at all clear. Herzog's skepticism toward ideas is very deep. Though Jews are often accused of
being "rootless" rationalists, a man like Herzog knows very well
that habit, custom, tendency, temperament, inheritance, and the
power to recognize real and human facts have equal weight with
ideas.

Interviewer: You've spoken also of the disabling effects of basing
a novel on ideas. Does this mean structuring a novel according to
a philosophical conception?

Bellow: No, I have no objection to that, nor do I have any
objection to basing novels on philosophical conceptions or anything else that works. But let us look at one of the dominant ideas
of the century, accepted by many modern artists—the idea that
humankind has reached a terminal point. We find this terminal
assumption in writers like Joyce, Céline, Thomas Mann. In *Dok-
tor Faustus* politics and art are joined in the destruction of civilization. Now here is an idea, found in some of the greatest novelists
of the twentieth century. How good is this idea? Frightful things
have happened, but is the apocalyptic interpretation true? The
terminations did not fully terminate. Civilization is still here. The
prophecies have not been borne out. Novelists are wrong to put an
interpretation of history at the base of artistic creation—to speak
"the last word." It is better that the novelist should trust his own
sense of life. Less ambitious. More likely to tell the truth.

Interviewer: Frequently in your fiction the hero strives to avoid
being swallowed up by other people's ideas or versions of reality.
On occasion you seem to present him with something like the whole
range of contemporary alternatives—say, in *Augie March* or *Herzog.*
Was this one of your intentions?

Bellow: All these matters are really so complicated. Of course
these books are somewhat concerned with free choice. I don't
think that they pose the question successfully—the terms are not

broad enough. I think I have let myself off easily. I seem to have asked in my books, How can one resist the controls of this vast society *without* turning into a nihilist, avoiding the absurdity of empty rebellion? I have asked, Are there other, more good-natured forms of resistance and free choice? And I suppose that, like most Americans, I have involuntarily favored the more comforting or melioristic side of the question. I don't mean that I ought to have been more "pessimistic," because I have found "pessimism" to be in most of its forms nearly as empty as "optimism." But I am obliged to admit that I have not followed these questions to the necessary depth. I can't blame myself for not having been a stern moralist; I can always use the excuse that I'm after all nothing but a writer of fiction. But I don't feel satisfied with what I have done to date, except in the comic form. There is, however, this to be added—that our French friends invariably see the answers to such questions, and all questions of truth, to be overwhelmingly formidable, uncongenial, hostile to us. It may be, however, that truth is not always so punitive. I've tried to suggest this in my books. There may be truths on the side of life. I am quite prepared to admit that being habitual liars and self-deluders, we have good cause to fear the truth, but I'm not at all ready to stop hoping. There may be some truths which are, after all, our friends in the universe.

Mr. Bellow Considers His Planet

Jane Howard / 1970

From *Life Magazine*, 3 April 1970, 57-60. © 1970 by Time Warner. Reprinted by permission.

Maybe the evening wouldn't exactly explode with excitement, but sparks, at least, were meant to fly. In one corner, so to speak, was the cerebrally mighty author Saul Bellow—formidably learned, notoriously quick-witted, newly delivered of his seventh and most ambitious novel, *Mr. Sammler's Planet*. Facing him was a roomful of the keenest minds among Yale University's English majors. They had been hand-picked by their creative writing professor, Robert Penn Warren, to meet his old friend Bellow. Drinks and spaghetti had been served; now wits were to be matched.

For Bellow, who ordinarily likes public appearances about as much as Jacqueline Susann likes madrigal sings around Girl Scout campfires, the evening was an abrupt departure from habit. Much more than most writers of stature, he cherishes his privacy. He has no taste for television interviews, and feels no kinship at all with "those long-isolated writers who yearn to become part of the cultural furniture of the scene, emerging all too ready into the arms of the jet set like King Kong meeting the Monster from 20 fathoms." Nor does he frequent Little Literary Evenings anywhere—not even in New York or Chicago (where he lives), let alone New Haven. Yet there he was, lured to edify the promising young. There he sat captive, donnishly tweedy, physically slight and boyish despite his white hair and 54 years. And there they sat, long-haired, languid and oddly unresponsive.

Not that Bellow was dull. "Asking me what I might have been besides a writer," he told one student, "is like asking an earthworm what else he considered becoming." To another boy who sought Bellow's opinion of campus revolutionaries, he said, "The trouble with the destroyers is that they're just as phony as what they've come to destroy. Maybe civilization *is* dying, but it still exists, and meanwhile we have our choice: we can either rain more blows on it, or try to redeem it." Silence. His audience seemed unmoved by Bellow's implied attacks on the fashionable tenets that Black—and Youth and Social Consciousness and Relevance and Where It's At and Spontaneity—is necessarily Beautiful.

"Well," he said, "I see I've reduced you all to silence." More silence. "Well," he said, "it's late and I have an early train to catch."

It wasn't late at all; it was only 9 o'clock, but the group dispersed. "Ah well," said Bellow as he shrugged on his imposing sheepskin-lined coat, "they and I don't talk the same language."

The present, as readers of *Mr. Sammler's Planet* are finding at best-seller speed, by no means enchants the author. Bellow's new novel reflects his wonderment that lunar voyages should be easier to chart than unsmashed public phone booths are to find; that chaos is everywhere so commonplace; that social and sexual lunacy prevail; that so urgent a question should be the very future (if any) of this whole earth—which may, as the book ominously suggests, become "a memorial park, a merry-go-round cemetery."

That's the way Bellow thinks and talks and writes, and if his uncompromising ideas don't sit right with 20-year-old English majors, or critics twice or thrice their age, then tough luck. Bellow is not to be seduced by passing literary fashions. "I don't see any real avant-garde in sight," he says, "maybe because there isn't sufficient stability. Then years ago all the intellectuals expressed nothing but horror of mass media, but now, just as violently, that's what they're embracing. This reflects their faddishness, not to say their sneakiness and cowardice." Especially he distrusts those of his colleagues who assume "defiant, radical, independent points of view" for what he thinks are the wrong reasons. "A radical stance," he says, "is the ultimate luxury for those who already have everything else."

Bellow the public figure can be acerb, aloof and elusive. But in private he is different. At home, in his five-room South Side Chicago apartment, he is as eager a host as a lonely child at his own birthday party. Here's his soprano recorder; would you like him to play some Bach? Here's the medal he got from the French government; would you like to see it? Here's his family album; perhaps

you would like to look at his immigrant mother's passport? A
tintype of his Russian grandfather? (It is clearly to that grandfather that Bellow owes his extraordinary deep chocolate eyes—
eyes that miss nothing; eyes that can make men fidget and women
blush. Those same eyes recur in snapshots of Bellow's three sons,
now aged 25, 12, and nearly 6, each by a different ex-wife.)

Three divorces notwithstanding, Bellow genuinely cares about
his family and tries to keep in touch with all its generations and
branches. The rye bread he serves comes from his father's cousin's
bakery and is spread with chicken liver chopped by a niece. His sons
all live in different cities, but "I see them as often as I can," he
says, "and sometimes bring them all together. When that happens
we all get along fine. They're like each other's uncles."

He shows you around his apartment: dark wood, green sofa,
books, lake views. Then he offers to guide you around what he
once called "that somber city," only his tour, commencing with the
obligatory view of the skyline panorama from the Outer Drive,
isn't somber at all. It proceeds to the open markets of Maxwell
Street, whose proprietors Bellow addresses in fluent Yiddish. Next
his 10-year-old Mercedes, which he bought last year for $1,000,
heads south back to his own part of town, into neighborhoods he
says are being "cauterized" by the University of Chicago (where
he teaches English to graduate students and belongs to the august
Committee on Social Thought).

He suggests lunch at a good, unsung Chinese place under the
elevated tracks, then a beer at a student hangout named Jimmie's,
where to his pleasure nobody recognizes him. Then back northwest
to the part of town where Bellow grew up—as did the hero of *The
Adventures of Augie March,* which won him the 1954 National Book
Award for fiction. It also won him so much acclaim that "I could have
exploited it, become a household name or standard brand, and
ruined myself by never working any other vein."

Instead Bellow has burrowed in many literary veins. He has
written plays, for instance, none of which have fared well in their
brief Broadway runs. He has also written stories, criticism and
essays, and plans later this spring to help bring out a new literary
magazine, *Locations.*

His favorite work of all, at this point anyway, is *Mr. Sammler,*

whose aged and half-blind hero is a Polish refugee from the Nazis
now ensconced on the Upper West Side of New York City. "I had
a high degree of excitement writing it," Bellow says, "and
finished it in record time. It's my first thoroughly nonapologetic
venture into ideas. In *Herzog* [for which he got a 1964 National
Book Award for fiction] and *Henderson the Rain King* I was kidding
my way to Jesus, but here I'm baring myself nakedly."

Ideas always outweigh plots in Bellow's novels. His people tend
to be brooders, musers, and writers of letters more than they are
doers. Of such action as there is they are witnesses and victims,
who always resemble, in some way or another, their creator. Bellow
is himself Herzogian in that he is a Canadian-born intellectual,
alluring to women and given to endless philosophizing. He is also
Hendersonian, in that he is something of an anthropologist (Northwestern University granted him his bachelor's degree in that
subject in 1937) and very much of a compulsive traveler. When
Sammler was done, he considered celebrating with trips to Mo-
rocco, England, Mexico or all of the above (and ended up sending
postcards from Kenya).

"I think I must have lived in upwards of 200 places in my life,"
he says. "I guess I could list them all for you, if I felt like it, but
I don't." He will allow that "there are places, people, houses and
women with whom I have a feeling of renewing very old anteced-
ent relations. It's a sort of *dèjà vu* when something about the light,
the moisture, the plants or the color of stones gives me the sense
of renewing an old and valuable connection—the Yiddish word is
angenehm. The new not only recollects but *becomes* the old."

Would he prefer to have lived earlier? "I have, in a way. My life
in Canada was partly frontier, partly the Polish ghetto, partly the
Middle ages. My second wife used to say I was medieval pure and
simple. I've always been among foreigners, and never considered
myself a native of anything. My father was the same way. In Russia,
he imported Egyptian onions, in Quebec he bootlegged for American rumrunners, in Chicago he sold coal. I was brought up in a
polyglot community by parents who spoke many languages."

Yiddish was the first of those languages, but Bellow is not
preoccupied with his Hebraic origins, or with such questions as
"Whither the Jewish Novel?" He would rather talk of subtleties.

"One of the pleasures of writing," he volunteers, "is being able
to deal in certain primitive kinds of knowledge banished from
ordinary discourse, like the knowledge brought by smells. I must be
a great smell-classifier." He writes evocatively of the damp stench
of the subway, the odor of tomatoes as they burst on a vine, and the
multitude of scents generated by women who, he says "smell more
strongly and variously than men, and to me more pleasurably."

The other sex, however, preplexes both Bellow and his heroes.
"What do women want?" he has Herzog wonder. "They eat
green salad and drink human blood." One lady in *Sammler* is
credited with a "high annual tearfall." Of today's brassiere-
burning militants Bellow says, "I'm afraid they'll have dragging
breasts. I'm all for freedom, short of degeneracy. As John Stuart
Mill foresaw, women today show all the characteristics of slaves in
revolt. They're prone to the excesses of the lately servile, the
newly freed. I'd like to see their increased freedom accompanied
by human development. Gentleness and generosity, which *used*
to be considered feminine qualities, are certainly not contemptible—are they?"

Even so banal a topic as the weather can inspire Bellow. "I thrive
on a certain amount of smoke, gloom and cold stone," he says.
"Sometimes it's not good to see things too clearly." He seldom
stays for very long in hot, bright places and has no yen to
"transport my neuroses to a more fertile climate; they're doing fine
right here. A wave of gloom comes over me whenever I step out
of a plane into California. I know it's just like the Midwest, only
sunnier and gloomier. Here things are more strident and gristly."

His next book probably will concern either Washington, D.C. or,
of all the gristly places, Gary, Ind. "On and off I've been writing a
little something about Gary," he says, "having to do with the way
white workers are getting prosperous and going off into the dunes
and farmlands, leaving the city a vast black slum. Will it explode? I
don't know. That's prophecy, which isn't my business."

What he does regard as his business is to take sharp cognizance
of what goes on around him, "achieving stillness," if he can
manage to, "in the midst of chaos." That is an ambition he shares
with Mr. Sammler, an unwitting "registrar of madness," distracted
from peaceful contemplation by the people whose lives intersect his.

The book's other characters are as vivid a lot as Bellow has ever
conceived. There is a Hindu scientist, from precisely the other
side of the globe, who shares Mr. Sammler's concern for earth and
earthlings. There are also: an elegantly sinister black pickpocket,
an effusive young radical, a well-meaning widow who doesn't know
when to shut up, a dying surgeon, and the surgeon's grown
children—a ne'er-do-well son and a voluptuous psychoanalysand
daughter. Best of all, there is Mr. Sammler's own memorably
loony daughter Shula, who schlepps shopping bags to free lectures
and sermons, wearing a yak's hair wig.

It is like Bellow to have made his new hero a septuagenarian. His
talk suggests he's heard quite enough glorification of the new,
Now Generation. "In the way the young declare the obsolescence
of the old," he says, "there's a kind of totalitarian cruelty, like
Hitler's attitude toward Jews, or Stalin's toward kulaks. These kids,
I predict, will face a lot more trouble than their elders. If I were
an enterprising real estate man in California I'd build a colony not
for the old but for the soon-to-be-senile young."

Saying this, Bellow sits at a rolltop desk in his dormer-windowed
office at the university; wearing horn-rim glasses. He talks nonstop, not only of the overrated young but of his own generation—
"the first to see the clouds from above"—which, let's not forget, has
problems, too. Especially, he implies, those of his literary and
academic colleagues who suffer from the persistent American
feeling that "the intellectual life is somehow not virile. Artists and
professors, like clergymen and librarians, are thought to be female. Our populist tradition requires the artist to represent himself
as a man of the people, and to conceal his real concern with thought.
Maybe that's why we don't have more novels of ideas." Maybe
that's also why "the really powerful men in our society hold
writers and poets in contempt, because they get no evidence from
modern literature that anybody is thinking about any significant
questions."

"The real problem," he says, "is the problem of death. If people
don't know how to come to terms with it, and souls have no
preparation, then the only thing is to be externally young and in
pursuit of pleasure, and further sexual and hedonistic horizons." A
nobler course is the obligation Bellow and Mr. Sammler feel they

have: to reflect and consider and clarify—not so much to explain
as to distinguish.

Some fellow writers have always been among Bellow's friends,
but others interest him less. Norman Mailer, for example, "has
learned all one can from the modern masters, but he uses his skill
and talent to present himself far too prominently for my taste.
He's a public actor, swinger, a gladiator and punch-trader, who
brings a message of emancipation to his middle-class brothers."

(When another eminent writer's name came up, a visitor to
Bellow's apartment said, "Oh, I met him once, he seemed nice
enough."

"We all do," said Bellow, "until you get to know us.")

Bellow often seeks out the company of men like Dave Peltz, an
ascot-wearing contractor from Gary, with whom he plays squash.

"You know what my buddy is?" asks Peltz, who has known
Bellow since they both were 14. "My buddy is one of the few
unpolluted people left in the world." His buddy has, indeed, a
Sense of Wonder worthy of the late Rachel Carson. With awe exceed-
ing that of a child, he gazes at baby chicks pecking their exhausted
way out of eggshells at the Museum of Science and Industry, or
at exhibits extolling mankind's giant leaps in space, or at an exceptionally vivid color television set, showing a basketball game.
Bellow doesn't care a thing about sports, but his brown eyes stay
transfixed to that screen. He notices things. His characters may
seem passive, but their creator is not. "I'm a very determined
struggler," he says. "I've always sought exposure, and never
really been any good at taking cover." And he waits warily, to see
what will happen. "Civilization," he says, "is standing on a tight
long rope over an abyss. There are too many crushing and possibly
insoluble problems. Now seems a particularly chancy time to rock the
boat merely for the sake of *joie de vivre*."

A Conversation
with Saul Bellow

Chirantan Kulshrestha / 1972

From *Chicago Review*, 23.4–24.1 (1972), 7–15. Reprinted by permission.

I interviewed Saul Bellow on January 12, 1971, in his office in the Committee on Social Thought, University of Chicago. The conversation was recorded on tape and the resulting transcript passed on to him for revision. Bellow went through the transcript carefully: while he did not depart from the views expressed in the conversation, he altered sentences, phrases, and punctuation at many places to achieve greater clarity and precision. My thanks are due to Ellen Wetherell for transcribing the conversation from the tape.

Interviewer: Most reviewers of *Mr. Sammler's Planet* have complained that the novel is so "weighty with wisdom" that the ideas in it tend to cloud the tale. Now, if this is true one is faced with a contradiction in your development as a novelist because in an article in *The New York Times Book Review* at the time of the publication of *Henderson the Rain King* you had attacked novels that lacked concreteness and particularity and turned more or less into abstractions. I'd like to know how you reconcile the abundance of ideas in *Mr. Sammler's Planet* with what you said in the article I have referred to.

    Bellow: Well, the article that I wrote in *The New York Times* was against the American vice of over-interpreting the text and finding symbols where none existed, of trying to justify the reading of fiction by its symbolic value and projecting symbols into works or imposing symbolic interpretations on works that I very much objected to and still object to. Now it may be that the critics of *Mr. Sammler's Planet* are right. I have no way of knowing whether the book succeeds or not, but in my own defense I think it is possible

to say that people do not read attentively and are not very willing
to undertake hard work. It is hard work, a book like that. Each
word is very carefully weighed and connected, closely connected,
to the man. The internal processes of Mr. Sammler require the
very narrowest attention. You have to see that he is never speaking
out of character and that he never says anything simply for the
sake of saying the thing, but what I wanted to create—I don't know
how successful I was in this—was the thinking of such a person
never disconnecting the thought from the person, so that these
things are not presented in the book as sermons, but rather as a
monologue. Perhaps the monologue is too long and perhaps it is
tedious, possibly it breaks down—I don't know. It seems to
me—and it seemed to me when I wrote it—that it was sustaining
itself through the passion of the thinker or the passion of the speaker
and that it was justified, that there was no superfluous word or
movement in the book. The idea, therefore, is that these thoughts
are so intimately embedded in the mind of Mr. Sammler and are so
much a part of his subjective state that I myself do not think of
them as mere exercises in thought. And the two matters, that is my
essay in *The New York Times* and my writing of this book, have
very little to do with each other.

Interviewer: Let me ask here a somewhat irrelevant question out
of sheer curiosity. I have in mind the discussion that takes place
between Mr. Sammler and Dr. Govinda Lal, an Indian scientist, on
the future of the moon. Why did you choose an Indian to talk at
such length with Mr. Sammler?

Bellow: I think that Mr. Sammler is a man whose ordinary
relations to life have been disturbed, to say the least. He began as
a Polish intellecutal; an Anglophile Polish intellectual; he was
trapped in a war and that war wiped out all the familiar landmarks.
Now he is in New York which to him is a very exotic place still. He
feels that his condition is exotic. Not abnormal or even aberrant,
but the vividly unaccustomed. So his feelings have a planetary
character. What better then than to have somebody of whom you
would expect to be exotic but who on the contrary is closer than
anybody else? It is simply that the accidents don't matter. It
would happen like that. It would be someone from far away with
whom he could have immediate intimacy, and, of course, these

things are not always matters of deliberate choice. It occurred to me that way—I mean, it was *given* when I first started to write the book, so my explanation of it is hindsight, purely, because I started with the fact. I am just trying to explain the fact to you, to interpret it. My interpretation may be incorrect.

Interviewer: After the publication of *Herzog* you said in your *Paris Review* interview that you would like to represent "good men" in your novels and that if till then you had not represented any it was because you were still trying to know who and what they were and what their condition was. Since Mr. Sammler, to me, is very much a "good man," do I take it that you have at last realized your own conception of goodness?

Bellow: Well, you see I myself have been the victim of a prejudice against good men. I don't mean personal prejudice, I mean a literary prejudice. Literature in the last hundred years has specialized in being "realistic" about virtue and it has been very hard for writers to combine intelligence with kindliness. I don't think you find many intelligent persons in the literature of the last hundred years who are also kindly. I don't know why that is. It's as though it became an important duty to disabuse oneself of false virtue and to discover the hypocrisy of the good and expose it as a bourgeois pretense and a humbug and so on. Literature has not stopped doing that.

I am afraid that I was weak in this regard, didn't know how to justify the virtue of the virtuous. See how it is even for a writer like Dostoyevsky who has such an extraordinarily powerful vision of goodness. How hard it is for him to introduce good characters! Prince Mishkin who is his best, his saint, is also an idiot, and Alyosha Karamazov is really rather pale in contrast with Dmitri and Ivan in *The Brothers Karamazov*. It has for some reason been very difficult for intellectuals to show goodness as fully developed. Nine-tenths (to guess at a fraction) of what a man writes is determined for him unconsciously by social circumstances and by historical forces of which he is unaware. He is immersed in these things and his truth may not be discerned in his own generation. One must wait and see whether one's work has any value or not. That is hidden from the writer.

Interviewer: *Mr. Sammler's Planet* seems to me to suggest an affirmation of the terms of life all men hold sacred in their hearts; in the long conversation Mr. Sammler has with Dr. Lal you relate these terms to "the sense of God." This, I suppose, would immensely satisfy researchers who look exclusively for religious meanings in your novel. But then doesn't it somehow contradict your earlier warning against overt "Affirmation and Life Affirmers the princes of big time . . . who whoop it up for life"? Of course I concede that the affirmation in *Mr. Sammler's Planet* is very cautious and does not grant complete trust in things like the transforming magic of personality and final solutions.

Bellow: Well, let me try to answer that question. I am interested neither in affirming nor denying anything. A "character" has his own logic. He goes his way, one goes with him; he has some perceptions, one perceives them with him. You do him justice, you don't grind your own axe. I have no axe to grind, one way or the other. This man seemed to me to be the sort of man to whom this would be happening: he happens to have religious feelings. I did not choose such a person for the purpose of expressing my own religious convictions. I was simply following the thread of his being. I found a clue and I was winding it up going inwards. It brought me to religion. If it had brought me elsewhere, I'd have written something else. One doesn't arbitrarily invent these things in order to put anything across. That's what I am trying to say to you.

Interviewer: In your meeting with writers in Israel you are reported to have spoken in some detail of the competition between the writer and the media in the United States. What, according to you, are the possible ways in which a novelist can meet the challenge of the media?

Bellow: Fifty or sixty years ago, let's say seventy years ago, at the turn of the century, writers became aware of the pollution of their language by journalism and cheap printing, by sensational writers, by education, by popular culture, which contaminated poetry and which made it necessary for writers to find some way to purify themselves and to purify the language—a general attempt at purgation in a writer like Mallarmé who said very explicitly that he was trying to give a finer sense to the words of the tribe: *"les mots de la tribu."* Well, now we are up against another—we are up against a sequel to that. The mass-media today, a magazine like *Time*, employs techniques developed by an earlier generation of avant-garde writers. These young journalists in *Time, Newsweek,* or *Life* or *Esquire* or *Playboy,* in television or on Broadway or in criticism are employing the very techniques that Joyce or Gertrude Stein and Hemingway and others employed and they are using all the known devices of art. In which Harvard has educated them. One must, naturally, do something that they cannot do. Well, how does one do it? Well, that's really a spiritual, aesthetic question which I can't briefly answer. But it has something to do with the feeling of what your art is, what it's for, what it has to do with the consciousness of mankind, what it has to do with the deepest states of being of mankind and what it has to do with tradition. Art must be understood as a purgation of consciousness. Among the things to be purged are these latest infections, the poisons of the sophisticated media. Can this be done? Well, I don't know. By ordinary means? I don't know that either. But one must have some very powerful command of one's art in order to cope with this invasion of foreign bodies. I feel that I have such a command of my art and I am waiting to see where that will lead me, what measures I will take. Whether they will succeed or not, I can't say. I see most of my efforts as being something in the nature of an experiment, an experiment and a battle. One doesn't necessarily win one's battles. I may be defeated, I may not make it. I don't know that.

Interviewer: I could infer that when I read *Mr. Sammler's Planet.* With its strong sense of contemporaneity and with that long discussion on the future of the moon at its center, the novel seemed to be placed directly on the cross-wires of history. You *were* at something different, attempting something close to what Lionel Trilling has been saying about the novel of ideas and the form it is going to take in the future.

Bellow: Well, people are quite afraid of this kind of writing. Americans, of course, are democratic with a small "d." Populistic. They have pursued avant-garde ideas, but they have always brought them back again to the small "d" democratic public: people like Hemingway, or even people like e. e. cummings, who, with their great interest in the most advanced art of the twentieth century, still wanted to come back to the ordinary man with their

new devices. This is a healthy impulse. I think that Hemingway
was probably right except that he succumbed to prejudice himself.
He succumbed to some of the small "d" democratic prejudices of the
society. He was anti-intellectual and populistic at the same time
that he was an avant-garde writer of a really daring and original
kind. But that is one of the peculiarities of American literature. I
strike most Americans of that sort as being a foreigner; something
between a European and an American. Closer to the European than
the American. Whatever the case may be—most people are interested
in the case. That is to say, they are not willing to pay particular
attention to the subtleties of the particular case. I can't say that I
wholly blame them. It is a terrible demand to make on people, to
say, "I am going to write a book in which you must peel away all
preconceptions and you must read and hear and think in an entirely
new way." People want to know what your warrant for this is, on
what authority you require it. I don't really blame them for that.
One of the things that has happened is that authority in all forms
in this revolutionary period is under fire and this affects art a great
deal because art lives through the authority of the writer. He is
the author, and authorizes certain things to be. If you deny his
authority then you deny his art, and in this age which feels itself
to be so revolutionary and which is more dishevelled than revolutionary, the hatred of authority is very deep. It runs over into art.

Interviewer: Now a question relating to a personal problem. I
have always had trouble "placing" *Seize the Day*. Although
chronologically it appears in 1956, between *The Adventures of
Augie March* (1953) and *Henderson the Rain King* (1959), I have
been more inclined to group it with *Dangling Man* (1944) and *The
Victim* (1947). The justification is both formal and thematic; it is
as tightly organised as the first two novels, and, in spite of its makeup of a victim novel, it moves to a very unexpected transcen-
dence, suggesting thus a relationship with and an advance on the
victim-group. Could I have your clarification?

Bellow: That's right. That's very shrewd, an excellent observation. That's the way I think of it myself. You are very right. It
really is true that Wilhelm belongs to the victim-group.

Interviewer: My own feeling was that the novel was written
earlier and held over, but I had no way of proving that . . .

Bellow: Well, it was written over a period of years and I don't remember now when it was begun. You may be right even about it. However, I have long since done with that. It wasn't written in the same mood, but the state of mind is similar. *Seize the Day* is victim literature, very much like *The Victim* itself. I was a little shocked at this myself—after having written *Augie March*—at the slovenliness of it. I felt that there was something delirious about the writing of *Augie March*. It over-ran its borders.

Interviewer: I am told that in recent years there has been a great change in the attitude of the Jewish Community towards your work. To what do you attribute this change? Would you describe yourself specifically as a Jewish writer?

Bellow: I don't really know the answer to that. I don't think that any literature should be so special that it can't be understood by non-communicants—put it that way. Its human quality should appeal to anyone. If it doesn't, it's a mistake. Something wrong. It's too parochial. No good literature is parochial. All good literature has some color of this sort because there is no such thing as a generalized human being. He's an Irishman, or an Italian, or an Indian, or a Japanese, whatever it is that he is, he is. We in America have a feeling that perhaps it would be a nice thing, if we had a generalized human being who didn't have these characteristics, but only, let's say, desirable American characteristics, shared by all. There is really no such thing. It's a total impossibility and it would be an undersirable thing, if anyone could achieve it.

Interviewer: Does it mean then that the reason why your heroes—except Henderson—are Jewish is that they are the kind of people you have known and found worth writing about?

Bellow: Yes, I like to know what I'm talking about. Henderson is not a Jew, but he has been accused by some of being a sort of a convert. But that's false, that's simply not the case. One has one's character—a given—and that's it. He had better be faithful to the given and if other people don't like it that's unfortunate. I have never consciously written as a Jew. I have just written as Saul Bellow. I have never attempted to make myself Jewish, I've never tried to appeal to a community, I never thought of writing for Jews exclusively. I never wanted to. I think of myself as a person of Jewish origin—American and Jewish —who has had a certain experience of life, which is in part Jewish. Proportions are not for me to decide. I don't know what they are: how much is Jewish, how much is Russian, how much is male, how much is twentieth century, how much is midwestern. That's for others to determine with their measuring sticks. I have no sticks myself.

Interviewer: This is of some satisfaction to me because I have often been told that unless I acquaint myself fully with Judaism I cannot understand the special Jewish slant of your fiction.

Bellow: I think that's nonsense. It really is. One of the charms of life in the twentieth century is that a variety of human beings pass before you, people who were formerly unknown or could only be dealt with mythologically. You know we don't do it mythologically nowadays, not that way. We don't create Jews as Marlowe created them in *The Jew of Malta* or as Shakespeare did when he created Othello. There is something mythic about these characters. But we are somewhere in between: instead of myth we have some kind of knowledge, some kind of anthropology, some kind of recognition of the humanity of exotic peoples. We do not romance these exotics as Gauguin did in *Noa Noa,* or Melville did in the South Seas, or D. H. Lawrence did in Mexico. More actual now, and more intellectual. This is not necessarily a gain. But I still object to this Jewish label. I think it false and wrong. I don't blame the Jews for applying it, for they have to strengthen their public position as well as they can. Since the holocaust they have become exceptionally sensitive to the image the world has of them and I think that they expect Jewish writers to do good work for them and propagandize for them. In that respect I was a great disappointment to them. Since then, Philip Roth has made me more acceptable by writing *Portnoy's Complaint.* Naturally, they prefer Malamud and me to the sexual Jewish wildmen who have recently appeared in fiction.

Interviewer: As one with some pretensions to creative writing I want advice from you. I am a Hindu, a secularised Hindu. I don't go to temples or sit in worships, but there is a way of life that comes to me naturally, which I cannot avoid, which is very much a part of my being, and which I cannot but call Hindu. There is much in the Hindu way of life that fascinates me with its creative possibilities, but much that would appear irrational to the scientific mind. Writing about that seems such a risk, such a step in darkness . . .

Bellow: You should take a risk. You should take a chance. What I would say to this is simply that your imagination in its most open days was formed by the Hindu religion. How could you possibly repudiate or renounce that? Your mind takes its color from this and it is one of the great gifts of your life. For whom should you repudiate this? You should not repudiate it for anybody. It's part of the power of your imagination by now and so you should cherish it as such. Not as belief, not to defend against rational argument or by rational argument, but simply as a fact of your life. For it is a fact of your life. That's how I view my own Jewishness. That's where the great power of it comes from. It doesn't come from the fact that I studied the *Talmud,* or anything of that sort. I never belonged to an orthodox congregation. It simply comes from the fact that at a most susceptible time of my life I was wholly Jewish. That's a gift, a piece of good fortune with which one doesn't quarrel. It is what exists in feeling that matters. But what people ascribe to you—well, they ascribe all kinds of strange things to you. One might just as well forget about that.

Saul Bellow in the Classroom
Sanford Pinsker / 1973

From *College English*, 34 (1973), 975–82. © 1973 by the National Council of Teachers of English. Reprinted by permission.

Writers are one thing between hard covers and often quite another when you must meet them at train stations, behind lecture podiums, and in the give-and-take of classrooms. Saul Bellow's advance press was hardly good. He could be, I was told, cranky or shy or downright bored. How would he react to the undergraduates of my Contemporary American Novel class and, more importantly, how would they react to him? Suddenly, the whole idea looked foolish, rather like asking Einstein to teach introductory physics. Not that my students would turn the visit into a shouting match a la *Mr. Sammler's Planet*. At its most radicalized, Franklin & Marshall was no Columbia. But there are times when silence can be worse than boorish manners. In short, Saul Bellow in the classroom was a risk.

What follows is less a formal interview than a scorecard which each reader can fill in for himself. My students had read a handful of authors—Ralph Ellison, John Barth, Bernard Malamud, Joyce Carol Oates, Kurt Vonnegut, Jr., etc.—along with *Herzog* and *Mr. Sammler's Planet*. And, yet, there are limits to even the best mix of willing readers and good discussion. When one is eighteen, it is easier to imagine Tralfamadore than a divorce. As Bellow had remarked in his address to the college: "Poetry and painting make one peculiarly observant, and the artist is often like one condemned to observe. The facts, presenting themselves, cannot be rejected. One is obliged to note them and to note them in a certain style." At the time, he was referring to Joyce's Leopold Bloom (in a heavyweight talk entitled "Who's Got the Story: Writing After Joyce"), but the sentiments were pure Bellow. That—as much as anything else—was the reason I wanted him to talk with my students. He could articulate what I vaguely felt or had hunches about—or, sometimes, missed entirely. He met with us on the following morning (22 May 1972). And here is what happened:

93

Class: Critics often talk about the "ideas" in your work, especially when referring to *Herzog* or *Mr. Sammler's Planet.* What *is* the relationship between a contemporary writer and the world of ideas?

  Bellow: Well, American writers always imagined that they were populists—that is, writing about the people, for the people, etc. I would say that from at least the time of Whitman on this was so. Of course, the "people" did not know Walt Whitman was writing for them. Nevertheless, his democratic loyalties were very strong. His language, however, was anything but the language of the people. It's when you get to a writer like Carl Sandburg that you see the meeting of the two. I don't think Whitman even had the notion of using a popular language. When he *did,* it was a rarity and it came as an interesting interruption in what he was saying: "Now, son, pack up your duds!" in *The Open Road* or "The Yankee is mighty cute." But if you read the bulk of Whitman's poetry, you discover that the language he uses is rather special. Very sophisticated language is combined with a populist attitude. Hemingway, for instance, is an extremely sophisticated writer and, yet, his attitudes were intensely populistic. All his ideas—his Modernism, if you will—went into style. The result is that the ideas are implicit; he seldom discusses them *explicitly.* Now most American populist writers of the James T. Farrell or John Steinbeck sort don't bother with ideas very much. Their characters don't have them. If there are ideas, they belong to the whole class of people they are writing about. The individuals themselves can be rather unremarkable, if not downright dumb. Now it seemed to me that at a certain point we had gone as far in America as stupidity would get us. We were living in a very sophisticated society—on the technological side, extremely sophisticated—surrounded by all sorts of curious inventions and writers still insisted on sitting on the curb playing poker and talking about whores. It seemed to me to be a little artificial. You know, out of loyalty to the people, to cling to your original dumbness. Since it *was* extremely artificial, it was time, I thought, to give it up. I'm not trying to develop a literature for intellectuals. It's just that I'm not afraid of ideas and when I have to deal with them, I do.

  Class: Herzog is out to achieve a synthesis both for himself and, presumably, the entire society. If his first book—*Romanticism and Christianity*—dealt with the history of those ideas, would it be fair to say that Herzog is testing out the implications of Romantic thought on the contemporary world?

Bellow: I think the people in Western countries live Romanticism all the time. They don't even know it, but they do. They think of the proper mode of being as highly stimulated, ecstatic, a life of infinite possibilities, the individual utterly free, his main responsibility to fulfill himself and to realize his own desires as richly as he can.

Class: But at one time those were good dreams, weren't they? When did it all become the nightmare you suggest?

Bellow: It becomes a nightmare when you have as many people on junk—of one sort or another—as you do in this country. It's purely a Romantic thing. The great junk-users of the nineteenth century were also the great painters and writers of the nineteenth century. It's sort of a secession on individualistic terms from the collective life. And it's very peculiar. People don't realize how much they are in the grip of ideas. We live among ideas much more than we live in nature. There are more artifacts than natural objects about us. So that when people talk about intellectualism in modern literature, I'm always surprised at the inconsistency of it. People's lives are already filled with mental design of one sort or another. If you don't have it yourself, your environment has it. If your environment hasn't got it, your government has it.

Class: You mean, I take it, what Herzog calls Reality Instructors. Aren't Herzog's mental letters a rage against all that, a way of having it out in a more private way?

Bellow: Well, he's a person in a very agitated and almost mad state who is resisting everything, including his own intellectual life. That he fights almost as much as anything else. As I was writing the book, I began to understand what I was doing. It was something like this: the man was trying on the roles which had supported him before and he was doing them one after the other—the father, the lover, the husband, the scholar, the avenger. He puts them on and takes them off like clothes. None of them really fit. They had all been misleading. And this is really the source of his irony toward them. As if to say "Look at what I have been doing and imagining that I could remain a sane and intelligent person. Of course I was not sane. Of course I was not intelligent." This is his goodbye to

all of these roles. That's why, at the end of the book, he has nothing
more to say. He's at a point of personal balance.

Class: The moment comes in prayer, an acceptance that the
synthesis cannot—at least for the moment—be made.

Bellow: Yes, I think a person finally emerges from all this nonsense when he becomes aware that his life has a much larger
meaning he has been ignoring—a transcendent meaning. And that
his life is, at its most serious, some kind of religious enterprise,
not one that has to do with the hurly-burly of existence.

Class: In the final lines of *Mr. Sammler's Planet,* something of
the same sort appears. I'm thinking of the speech about the human
contract and the terms "we know we know we know. . . ."

Bellow: Well, I think it's *always* the basic note of a religious
outlook. You read the New Testament and the assumption Jesus
makes continually is that people know the difference immediately
between good and evil—as soon as you present it to them. And
that is, in part, what faith means. It doesn't even require discussion.
It means that there is an implict knowledge—very ancient, if not
eternal—which human beings really share and that if they based
their relationships on that knowledge, existence could be transformed. So it's by no means a new idea. It's older than the hills.
It's only startling in this different context. I don't know that I
have any program of this sort. I don't think that I *do,* consciously.
I never know what I'm going to do until I've done it.

Class: How do you see the difference between what Herzog calls
"potato lovers" and that other camp of people known as the
Reality Instructors.

Bellow: Potato love is a weak emotion that people often have of
friendliness and a melting heart toward other people, the real
source of which is terror. It's a low-grade emotion, like potato sap.
Reality Instructors are people who think they know the score. You
don't. They're going to teach you.

Class: What are the connections between the Romanticism we
have been talking about and the brutal realism which occurs so
often in *Herzog* and *Mr. Sammler's Planet?* Do you mean to suggest
that one is a logical outgrowth of the other?

Bellow: Well, the reason Sammler would be particularly vulnera-

ble to Romanticism is that Nazism was an extremely Romantic
movement.

Class: Romanticism ends, then, in the concentration camps?

Bellow: It gets into that. It gets into all kinds of things. It also
gets into art and at certain moments there is a fusion between art
and authoritarianism. You read any good book on the concentration
camps and you'll find immediately how much Romantic art there was.
What *scenes* there were which might have come from fiction or
drama—of people being hung to the strains of Viennese band music.
A book called *The Concentration Camp Universe* (by David Rous-
set) points out that there was a strong element of play or playful-
ness in the very idea of a concentration camp. And that there were
a good many art ideas at work there. It was a sort of terrible
surrealistic game. But to get back to your question about the idea
of reality being so punitive, I suppose nineteenth-century leaders
of thought inherited from Christianity the idea that people might be
engaged in some worldly play and illusion, but the real things
would catch up with them and give them a punch in the nose. Then
they would find out how foolish their lives were. The warning
implied was: "Get hold of yourself before it's too late. Don't spend
your life among shadows. Come to terms with reality." Well, the
idea of reality often had a sort of Calvinistic tinge. Reality may be
very terrible—"Sinners in the Hand of an Angry God." "You
watch out! You may be among the damned!"—all of these things
transferred from the religious sphere to the sphere of philosophy
and especially *political* philosophy. We have that now too. This
toughness is the toughness of the ant toward the grasshopper. It's
all right for you to fiddle in the fields, but you wait—one of these
days it's going to be cold and you'll be unprepared and then you'll
find out what reality is. Now, I think in a world where people had
better have an "earnest" grip on reality in order to survive, it
becomes a mental-moral project to understand your surroundings,
yourself, and the society you live in, etc. This is supposed to be
achieved on a sort of personal basis. You and I and all of us are
supposed to bring off this enormous and difficult piece of analysis.
We're never going to do it. But there are always people who feel
peculiarly competent to tell you how it is. Take something like
Seize the Day. There's this charming lunatic named Dr. Tamkin.

He thinks he has the answers. He has them all. Now, Wilhelm is in
pain and confused and the good doctor gets hold of him and says:
"Don't worry. I'm going to set you straight." And then I remember something from my own childhood. A lady from next door of
whom I was very fond gave me a mirror to repair which had become
loose in the frame. I was certain it could be fixed. At that time my
idea of fixing things was to hit them with a hammer. So I did. It
shattered the mirror. Since then I have been very careful about such
things. It is very tempting to imagine you are going to fix things,
but mirrors are awfully easy to break with hammers. And these
Reality Instructors are out among the mirrors with their little
hammers.

Class: We have been told that Moses Herzog is a minor character
in *Ulysses* and some critics have gone on at length about the
parallels between the two books. Is that the sort of thing you had
in mind?

Bellow: One had absolutely nothing to do with the other. It had
to do with the fact that my father had given me a book when I was an
adolescent written by a certain Moses Herzog. And this stayed with
me. The Joyce thing is purely a coincidence.

Class: Do you happen to remember what the book was?

Bellow: Well, I *thought* it was Moses Herzog. I looked again and
it was an edition of the Old Testament in Hebrew and English,
but the name was really Moses Hertz. I suppose I didn't want it to
be Hertz subconsciously, because that's a car rental agency and
I didn't want to get involved with that. However, I had no idea that
I would be mixed up with Joyce. And, actually, when I later
found out about it, I discovered that Herzog is a real Dublin name
and that they were a prominent Dublin family. In fact, Moses
Herzog had been the Chief Rabbi of Dublin. If the name has any
significance in *Ulysses,* it is that Bloom (who has fallen away from
the faith) might remember the name Moses Herzog as one which
reminded him of organized religion. But *I* had no such idea.
However, I'm used to people taking off in the wrong direction full-
speed. In my boyhood I knew so many people trying to scrape
together a living by selling neckties, razorblades, and shoelaces that
I never have any objection to people using *me* in that way.

Class: Would you say *Herzog* is an autobiographical novel or, to

put it another way, what is the differnce between fiction and
autobiography where a book like *Herzog* is concerned?

Bellow: Well, autobiography is probably the hardest of all things
to write. When people say "Is this fiction or autobiography?"—as
though it were easier to write autobiography than fiction, that's a
mistake. It's very hard for any person to give a real account of his or
her life. You try it sometime. You'll find out how hard it is. If you're
asking me if I owned a house in the country and whether my wife
kicked me out, etc., I don't know that that sort of personal thing is
really relevant. I mean, it's a curiosity about reality which is *impure,*
let's put it that way. Let's both be bigger than that.

Class: In *Mr. Sammler's Planet,* you talk about imitation, suggesting that one must learn to be satisfied with it, rather than the
reality itself. I wondered what you meant by that.

Bellow: I mean, first of all, in that particular passage to construct
an argument against the absurd ideas of originality which belong
to the Romantic tradition. As if every individual had to re-invent
himself and everything that surrounded him in an original way. As if
to *live* were an act of genius, as though we had no resemblance
whatever to people who preceded us. All this sort of stuff is obviously
wrong. I went to a natural history museum once. I had a friend who
worked in the shops of the Field Museum in Chicago. He took me
on a tour. I saw how a dinosaur and fish skeletons were assembled.
Then he took me to an enormous room, filled from top to bottom
with small drawers. And he began to pull out these drawers. They
were filled with specimens of hummingbirds. Thousands of sub-
species of hummingbirds from all over the world. They were all
heaped up in these drawers with little bands on their tiny legs,
identifying them. And I thought, how powerful the stamp of the
species is on all these individuals. How overwhelming in any life
the presence of the species has got to be. And, yet, in our new-
found liberty—and it *is* relatively new in human history—we have the
idea of breaking away from the type, which has been the author of
our existence from the beginning. It's true that individuality is
also marked and that probably each one of those birds was unique
in its own way, but you pretty soon get the idea of how potent the
power of this common stamp is to all beings. It's something that in
our day and age we really don't know much about. We really do have

the idea of being self-created individuals of genius, etc., as if we don't derive *from* anything. That's really a very false idea, carried to such lengths. It's an immoderate idea. All through ancient times and clear through the Renaissance into modern times—the Renaissance hasn't really been over for very long; I suppose the eighteenth century is *still* the Renaissance—people had the idea that if they wanted something they could not do better than to study the great models and imitate them. After all, that's what *Don Quixote* is about, isn't it? He did it madly, but he did it in line—or in the light of a great tradition. And he says, in so many words, that the individual has to learn greatness from others, to which he will add a quality of his own. But what he adds is only an increment to the rest. But we, in the tradition of the nineteenth century, think we are our own authors, from the ground up.

Class: Are you suggesting, then, that the twentieth century itself cannot provide such models?

Bellow: I think we have plenty of examples of people who might with benefit influence us. By "imitation" I don't mean a silly copying or slavishness. I simply mean a strong conscious realization of the superiority of a certain class of human beings or of a certain kind of conduct. Because there's plenty of *imitation* now. There's almost nothing but. To anybody who knows a little history and who walks around the streets of a big city, the amount of imitation is absolutely alarming. But people are unaware—as they go around in their costumes—that they're involved in an imitation. They do it anyhow, because human beings are not very fertile in ideas. There are only a few *big* ideas and very few new ideas are added to the stock in *any* generation. I can think of only a very small handful of people in the twentieth century who were truly original. You have to wrack your brains.

Class: Do you think that writers like Vonnegut or Barth or Hawkes represent anything significant on the contemporary scene or are they merely a phase? To put it another way, are more traditional novels—like yours perhaps—dying out?

Bellow: Well, everything is dying. We're all sitting here—or, in my case, *standing* here—dying. Are "traditional" novels (whatever that means) dying out? You mean, you'd rather back a winner. But we don't know who the winner is going to be. I don't think anybody knows. We're all engaged in historical analysis, trying to guess what is going to endure and what is going to fall to the ground. But I don't think that because people are filled with this frantic question that they're any better off and that they are really on the track of the modern. After all, it isn't so much a matter of gestures as it is of substance. Anybody can make the modern gestures. Anybody can think up *new* gestures to make, if he has any theatrical talent. I'm not one to knock theatrical talent—I like it very much—but is it *all* really a matter of theatrical talent? I don't know. What I'm really getting at is this: that for about a hundred and fifty or two hundred years we have been obsessed with the notion that unless you stand at the crossroads of history, you're going to become obsolete and your work forgotten. And since nobody wants to be obsolete, everybody is in a sweat to stand at the vital corner. But how do you know you're at the vital corner? Just because you *think* you are there is no proof that you are. And just because you make passes or gestures which are supposed to tell the world that you are standing at that vital corner doesn't mean that you're with it, *really*. I don't think that many of those writers you named are really with it. They are writers who have managed to create a very successful fashion and with the aid of the publishing world and the editing world and the scholarly world, they've gotten a very considerable boost. As to whether or not they're the real thing, nobody will know until we've all kicked the bucket.

Class: To what extent have the mass media replaced the popularity and even *need* for the novelist? I'm not sure that this makes any sense, but I wondered how a novelist justifies—to himself if nobody else—what he does in an age where television, records, movies, etc. compete for the audience and seem to be winning?

Bellow: It's a tougher question than you think. At one time novels made life understandable to a great many people who wanted to know what daily reality was about. And you're quite right that novels now have to hold their own against competitors who are also doing that. It always seemed to me, though, that the mass media are also dealing in fictions. They're not giving you a true account of what's happening either. They're just giving you a simplified, acceptable, digestible picture which is colored convincingly by reality. They put it over on you that they know what

Nixon is up to behind the scenes. There is a fairish amount of information in these accounts, but, in a way, they are fictional too and are even presented in, say, *Time* magazine in a language borrowed from the twentieth-century novel. Since the people who write for magazines are ex-college students like yourselves—people who have studied modern literature and have some talent for writing—they learned how to do what Joyce was doing or Hemingway or Faulkner or Proust. What you read in these magazines, then, is a kind of literature, derived from literature, and purporting to be news. It gives people the feeling that they are in contact with reality at last. Well, we're not getting true information; we're getting a lot more illusion which *looks* like information. The advantage of literature in all of this is that it may be able to pierce through the illusions and reach some truth. The problem is that people are in love with expertise now and they don't like amateur opinion. I think this is one of the difficulties of the present-day writer. A French reader in the nineteenth century will accept from Balzac what Balzac told him about the goldsmith's trade or about the way a country doctor lived or about a courtesan's life in Paris. They were satisfied with a pretty good approximation. But we want more of Kinsey or Masters and Johnson. In other words, people have a craving for what seems to them to be more exact information and, therefore, they are not willing to take on faith the simulacra they used to get from novelists before. On the other hand, the experts— the ones who *really* know a subject—know very little besides that subject, perhaps because space is limited in the human mind. If they are highly specialized, they know one thing extremely well, but they don't know much else. So how do you put together the big picture? You put together the big picture—if you're a journalist—by visiting a lot of experts and getting their testimony and trying to knit it all together. But you're not going to understand the expert testimony if you're only a poor reporter because it takes a lifetime really to understand expert testimony. This is the fix that we're in. This is why I am telling you that the journalists are still writing a kind of fiction, only it's a very inferior kind of fiction. So that when you wonder if the communications industry is going to drive the novel out, what you're really asking is based on Gresham's Law—namely, will bad money drive the good money out. Well, I

don't know, but it will probably make some changes. First of all,
I don't think that novelists can continue to hope to reach as great a
public as they used to reach and to be heroes of their times—as, say,
Dickens was or Ibsen or Victor Hugo or any of those great national
heroes who were thought to be the voices of their age, prophets
in their own countries. I don't think that any novelists or poets will
stand in this position again because that day is gone. And anybody
who has such an idea of recovering vanished glory is being very
Quixotic about it. But one doesn't *need* that. In a society like
this, if a writer can be sure that 10 or 20,000 people will be interested
in his art, he is doing pretty well. He's doing at least as well as a fancy
glass blower or a good dog breeder. It's a limited public, but how
many people do you need?

Class: You are often compared and contrasted to other American-
Jewish writers we have studied in this course—people like Bernard Malamud, Philip Roth, Bruce Jay Friedman, and others. What
is your own reaction to labels like this?

Bellow: I didn't invent that, you know. I got stuck with it.
Suppose you had an uncle in the wooden handle business and the
wooden handle business went out of date and was broke. And you
got stuck with a big inventory of wooden handles. Well, you
would want to go around and attach wooden handles to as many
things as possible. I'm just an unfortunate creature who gets a lot
of these handles attached to him. This whole Jewish writer business
is sheer invention—by the media, by critics and by "scholars." It
never even passes through my mind. I'm well aware of being Jewish
and also of being an American and of being a writer. But I'm also
a hockey fan, a fact which nobody ever mentions. For every fish in
the ocean, there seem to be a thousand ichthyologists. And you
really shouldn't ask the fish ichthyological questions, because he
doesn't know anything about science. I know *I* don't. I sometimes
look up through the water and see those guys leaning over, but,
thank goodness, I have no desire to study them.

An Interview with Saul Bellow

Joyce Illig / 1973

From *Publishers Weekly*, 22 October 1973, 74–77. © 1973 by
Publishers Weekly. Reprinted by permission.

Saul Bellow doesn't like to be interviewed. Even if you hadn't been
told this by several people at his publishing house (Viking), you
could figure it out from the company he keeps. Moses Herzog
wouldn't like it. Neither would Arthur Sammler. Bummidge might
consent but then hide behind the curtains with his shoes showing,
or lie down on a couch with his glasses on so he wouldn't have to face
the questions but could see his answers better. It's painful enough
to try to be private when you've gone public with seven novels, short
stories and a play—all of which make you an important American
writer and a spokesman for the Midwest. Augie March exhaled
Chicago and Saul Bellow has lived there for most of his life.

Bellow agreed to talk and to meet me in New York on a visit to
his publisher. (He's rewriting his next novel, "Humboldt's Gift.")
When he appeared in the doorway of Viking's conference room, he
was already in a rush to leave.

His clothes were dandy—all in one brown or another. He wore a
hat pulled down like a guy standing under a street lamp in the
opening of an Alan Ladd movie. He could have been on his way to
Belmont. Instead, he sat down and looked worried.

PW: Does a school of writers still exist in Chicago?
SB: There used to be, in the old days, something called a "Chicago school." It had a certain reality in the days of Dreiser or
Anderson, Carl Sandburg, Floyd Dell and Ben Hecht. There really
was such a group in Chicago. There is no such group today. The
earlier group reflected the fact that Chicago had become a regional
capital. Gifted people were coming from the surrounding region
and states—Iowa, Indiana, Wisconsin, Michigan—and Chicago was
then *the* big city, they say, which brought them together. It had the
excitement of a city. It had art. It had new architecture, Sullivan

architecture. Above all, it had newspaper jobs for them. For the most part they were employed by the newspapers. Newspapers in those days were something more than advertising throwaways with a margin of copy on each page followed by the business department of the paper. Several things happened all at once to put that to an end. One was the mechanization of news gathering. The other was the professionalization of journalism. You no longer had literate people doing a job. You had old "leg men" or city room guys or people of that sort or graduates of journalism schools. It no longer attracted people of talent nor did it want to. Journalism didn't give them jobs and so Chicago began to lose its hold on these people. They were drawn away by two rival centers, California and New York. They headed either for Broadway or for Hollywood and so Chicago as a regional literary center was drained.

PW: When did the exodus take place?

SB: That began to take place in the late twenties. By the time the depression hit Chicago, there was nothing to make Chicago a literary center except the WPA [Works Progress Administration], which was Roosevelt's gift to the arts in America. I suppose the intention really was to keep the bums out of trouble and to prevent them from joining subversive organizations. When we got out of school and had no jobs and no income, we were all tickled to have a WPA Writers Project job.

PW: What was your Writers Project job?

SB: It was to sit in the Newberry Library mainly and to organize the statistics about newspaper publishing. For a time, it was that. Then, John D. Frederick, who was the head of the project in Chicago, a very decent and imaginative man, gave me a job of writing biographies of Middle Western authors. None of them, I'm sure, were ever meant to be used. I'm glad to say that they've all disappeared. I kept no copies and I'm certain that there are none in the files.

PW: Wouldn't you like to see them now?

SB: No, I'd hate to see them.

PW: Why?

SB: I'd be distressed. I was only 22 years old and I knew nothing.

PW: Aren't you curious about the comparisons you could make?

SB: No, thanks. I know all about that. [*There is a long pause.*]

No, I don't think that Chicago is a regional literary center. I don't
think there is any such thing as a Chicago school of writers any
more. There are writers who have lived in Chicago, who live in
Chicago, who've been struck, if not stung, by Chicago, who've
been knocked down and run over by Chicago. Or who have, as Nelsen
Algren once said, "an unrequited love affair with Chicago." But
Chicago is an American city. That is to say vigorous, charming in
its own brutal way, philistine, lacking in culture fundamentally,
except for a few islands like the universities and the art establish-
ments of the city. But it is for the most part a philistine city.

   PW: Yet, you have spent most of your life writing there, haven't
you?

   SB: Yes, it's true that I have been there most of my life.

   PW: Then, how does someone like yourself survive?

   SB: That is a curious question. Well, where is an American writer
to go? I had the good luck to miss New York in the sixties.
Perhaps it was foresight to leave New York in the sixties, as if I
knew intuitively that it was going to go mad. It did go mad. This was
no place for a writer. This was a place for performers, virtuosi
exhibitionists, self-advertisers and promoters, people in the publicity game who describe themselves also as writers. It was no place
for a writer. In fact, it was quite depressing for a writer. The
country had no center for literature and the arts. New York is not a
center for literature and the arts. New York is a place where all the
stuff gets packaged, and where auxiliary or associated careers are
made in publishing, in editing, among agents, among literary
journalists, and for hustlers. But as for literature, it doesn't thrive
in promotional centers like New York. I don't see that there are
any interesting writers in New York itself, apart from these salaman-
ders of the Mailer type who know how to live in the fire, and I'm
not that sort. So I'd gone away. Was I to go back to Paris? Paris is
deader than a doornail for an American writer. London is not a
center, either, it looks toward New York. Then what one has is a
group of imaginary centers each reflected elsewhere. So there is
no locus for it anywhere. And one has to live with the brute facts of
one's society. Though America is a fascinating country, to which
I am devoted—I'd better be devoted to it because it possesses me
heart and soul—I don't imagine for a moment that it's what one

might call a cultivated society. There's a lot of public excitement about culture. But there is no such thing in actuality as American culture.

PW: Did you want to return to your roots?

SB: Well, I don't know whether they're actually roots. Sometimes I think they are a lot of tangled old wires. [*He laughs.*]

PW: Fine ones, though. But it seems that no matter where you were, you would come back to Chicago. Did it lure you back? Or was it a safe feeling?

SB: No, I wouldn't say that Chicago is safe. I think I live in one of the most dangerous neighborhoods to be found in North America. [*Laughs again, pleased.*]

PW: You know I mean creatively—was it a safe feeling?

SB: Well, I don't know about that. I had a hunch that it might be feasible there since it was hopeless elsewhere, and hopeless in a way which filled me with rage and despair. I don't thrive on rage and despair. I'm not by nature a desperate person. I am, however, an irritable and aggressive one, and get my dander up.

PW: I bet you do.

SB: So I knew that in the early sixties on the Eastern seaboard I was living in a state of high irritation which was incapacitating. I read the papers and the new books. I met the writers, the painters, the critics, the art establishment, the jet set, the flossy women and I responded with very little other than rage to all this. I thought I'd better remove myself from the scene.

PW: What's the longest you were here in New York in one chunk of time?

SB: Well, like every ambitious provincial, I came to take the big town. I showed up at the end of World War II. The job was done by about 1963 or 1964. So I would say that I was in the East for about 18 years. Two of these years I spent in Paris. Some of the time I was in Nevada, and also in Minnesota, but I lived in the East for about 14 or 15 years straight through. Everything in my life is a matter of decades. After the war I came back to Chicago and packed up my wife, my one-year-old child, my worldly goods and we took the train to New York. We had no place to stay. We barged in on some friends in Brooklyn Heights, on Pineapple Street. Then we heard of a place near Quarry, New York, so we went up there. I

supported myself then by writing brief notes. I got $5 for novels
and $10 for nonfiction books. I could turn out five or six a week if I
stayed up nights reading. So I was able to make 40 and 50 bucks
a week.

PW: How did you get the jobs and where did your work appear?

SB: The man who founded Penguin Books in this town and is
now a publisher, Victor Weybright, was very kind to me. He was
then preparing his first Penguin list. He was considering a great,
great number of books. He used me to screen books for him. I
wrote these reports for Weybright. I also did this for the *New
Republic* and for the *New York Times Book Review*. There was a
very generous man at the *Times* who knew what my situation was
and who, if he didn't have any work for me, used to take an
armload of review copies off the shelf and give them to me. I would
take them to 59th Street and sell them to a secondhand dealer. So
that was the way I supported myself for some time.

PW: Are you teaching now?

SB: Yes. I teach at the University of Chicago. I teach literature
there. I don't teach writing courses.

PW: I see it's important to you to make the distinction.

SB: Yes, because I don't like teaching writing.

PW: Is there a profound reason for that?

SB: It makes me too unhappy to read some of the inept things.

PW: You're sensitive about your talent. Do you have a great deal
of respect for yourself as a writer?

SB: I think that people who write well are people who take a
certain attitude toward themselves. Considerably more is involved
than technique. One sees oneself as a certain kind of human being.
I don't think that that peculiar act of initiation can be transmitted
in a classroom. How am I going to describe to a young man or
young woman the operation on one's soul which is necessary?
You can't do that. So it's really misleading to say, well, I'll teach
you to put together words on a page, or how to hook your reader
or how to find a symbol or how to balance your narrative or
anything of that sort.

PW: Who are you? What are you? [*After a long pause he doesn't
answer.*] With the wealth of literature you've created, by now

you could say, "I'm an amalgam of all the characters I've created."
I don't want to put words in your mouth.

SB: No, don't. I'll take them right out. I don't know that that's
really so, and I wouldn't like to describe myself because I would
rather remain mysterious even for myself. We've all adopted from
science the practice of telling ourselves what the critter is, in so
many words, and I don't think that any act of positive cognition will
really surface. We don't know who this is or what this is. [*pause*]
But writing courses are very helpful to young people who leave
home to go to the university, secretly craving to write and who
are then able to tell their parents, the folks back home, that it's OK,
I'm taking a course in it at the U. . . . This gives them a cover
which they don't otherwise know how to create for themselves.

PW: The New York *Times* had an article about the physical and
attitudinal changes in Chicago. Does this affect you?

SB: What abides in Chicago is the people of the city, many of
whom I've known from childhood. These are intrinsically interesting to me. I don't care what happens to the Loop. It's of interest to
me, but I don't live by that. I've seen too many neighborhoods in
Chicago—familiar to me from childhood—destroyed, razed to the
ground, rebuilt or left empty, to attach myself to the city in that way.
That can only breed sadness in your heart. No, what I'm attached
to in Chicago is a certain kind of person or to put it differently, a
form of personality with which one becomes familiar in Chicago
after many years.

PW: Is there a way of making me feel what that form of personality is?

SB: Only through what one writes.

PW: But don't you think that even in a small way, the environment makes a difference to you as a writer?

SB: I would adore a thriving and nourishing environment in
which people of all sorts met in a common language, extraordinary interests, wonderfully developed personalities and all the rest
of that rich, nutritious bed which we associate with culture of the
great ages: Elizabethan England. Renaissance Italy, 19th century
Paris, but that has never existed in the United States for anyone.
It didn't exist for Poe or for Melville. Whitman insisted that it
existed here. That he could discover it and prove that it was here.

Mark Twain attached himself to a frontier society. Henry James and
T. S. Eliot ran away from it altogether because they felt the
poverty of it. But we who have grown up in this have no choice
except to struggle with it. We know in the depths of our being how
humanly significant it is, so we listen to what the schools have
always described as culture. It's something else. It's a strange
new condition that's shared by the rest of mankind which is rapidly
approaching it too. The British, the French and the Italians are
speeding towards it in their own fashion. They, too, lack the vital
food of culture which was so easily available in the past. They
haven't got it anymore. All of civilized mankind is entering this
peculiar condition in which we were pioneers. That's why Chicago is
significant. We experienced it before the others did. We experienced
the contemporary condition before the others were aware of it.

   PW: In what way is that development unique to Chicago?

   SB: Well, Chicago, I believe, is a symbol of it. In Chicago, things
were done for the first time, which the rest of the world later
learned and imitated. Capitalist production was pioneered in the
stockyards, in refrigerator cars, in the creation of the Pullman, in
the creation of farm machinery, and with it also certain urban and
political phenomena which are associated with the new condition of
modern democracy. All that happened there. It happened early.

   PW: I hear a lot of so-called image makers in New York trying to
adopt Chicago. They talk about new buildings and fancy shops
along Michigan Avenue, museums and theater. Isn't most of that
just creating a new face, not a new pulse?

   SB: That's right, but this country is great for that kind of thing. I
go to the Art Institute and look at pictures. I also talk to intelligent
people in Chicago. There are many there. They live in a sort of Fort
Dearborn condition, behind palisades, so to speak, because the
streets are not safe. The city empties at night, just as much as
Dubuque, Iowa. You don't go down to the Loop any more
because at night it's dangerous. Anyhow there's nothing to see in
the Loop at night except a blue movie where some super 007 with
fancy pistols is shooting down whitey. I don't exaggerate when I
say Fort Dearborn situation because one feels that one is surrounded by hostile savages. There's quite a lot of that in every city;
it's all the more naked in Chicago because the city at night is so

uninviting that one doesn't venture out except to go and see intelligent friends. I don't know what medieval Spain was like, but imagine that there are certain similarities. You ride from one castle keep to another and you gallop over the drawbridge and the portcullis rises for you, and you spend an agreeable evening with your friends eating good food. What else is there to do? As you get older and flirtations dwindle or become less interesting, you spend . . . [*His laughter finishes the sentence.*] You can go out and admire the city as a tableau. You can admire it scenically. You can go downtown and visit the marvelous structures, look at the skyline, admire the color of the lake, show your visiting friends the wonders of the Miracle Mile and all the rest of that. But what is it really? It is really a sort of stirring and dramatic showpiece which at certain hours you can enjoy.

PW: Bill Styron gathers a literary and political crowd at his house in Martha's Vineyard. Are your intelligent friends a more diversified group?

SB: Styron is, if I may say this without offending him, on a Scott Fitzgerald system. Beautiful people and so on. I adore them when I meet them but I don't go out of my way to encounter them. I'm aware that I'm living through some sort of crisis in the history of civilization and I like to talk to people who know a great deal about various aspects of it. This entertains me much more than drinking with the boys and girls. Now I do divert myself in Chicago. I leave the university fortress to go to play squash twice a week downtown with businessmen, stockbrokers, lawyers, psychologists, builders, real estate people, and a sprinkling of underworld characters and old school friends who are not particularly aware that I am a writer. I make liberal use of the professional camouflage so they are a bit undecided in their mind as to which I am. Consequently, I am not continually identified by people as a writer. This I find a great blessing. I don't like to appear always under the single aspect: the writer. I like to be anonymous, diffuse, unnoticed. But of course, many Americans when they become writers, having performed enough and performed well the killing job of writing a book or two, want to unbend and enjoy the fruits of being a writer. Being a writer is extremely agreeable socially. Writing is damned hard.

PW: Will you appear on television to promote your books?

SB: I don't think I should appear on television to huckster my books because that's no part of my deal.

PW: With whom?

SB: With myself. With the gods, or with the public. I'm delighted when my books reach a large public. I want as many people as possible to read and understand my books. But I see no point whatever in hustling them on television because I am not a soup or a cleanser. And I feel polluted when I make a public pitch for it. I haven't done it since the days of Tex and Jinx and Mary Margaret McBride, when it brought my gorge up, and I quit then and there. I haven't done it since.

PW: Are you bringing your new novel out soon?

SB: In answer, may I quote E. M. Forster, in a favorite statement?

PW: You're compared to him a lot.

SB: Well, I don't like to be compared to him. We're sexually too different. But he said, and I appreciate this greatly, "How can I know what I think till I see what I say?" And I'm not done saying, so I don't know what I think.

Some Questions and Answers

Saul Bellow / 1975

From *New Review*, 2.18 (1975), 53-56. Reprinted in "Some
Questions and Answers: Self-Interview by Saul Bellow," *Ontario Review*, 3 (1975), 51–61. © 1975 by Saul Bellow. Used
by permission.

*How do you, a novelist from Chicago, fit yourself into American
Life? Is there a literary world to which you belong?*

When I entered the Restaurant Voltaire in Paris with the novelist
Louis Guilloux some years ago, the waiter addressed him as
'Maitre.' I didn't know whether to envy him or to smile. No one
had ever treated me so reverentially. And as a student I had sat in
Chicago reading of *salons* and *cénacles,* of evenings at Magny's
with Flaubert and Turgenev and Sainte-Beuve—reading and sighing. What glorious times! But Guilloux himself, a Breton and a
former leftwinger, seemed uncomfortable with his title. It may be
that even in Paris literary culture is now preserved by smarmy
headwaiters. I am not altogether sure of that. What is certain is
that we have nothing like it in America—no Maitres except in dining
rooms, no literary world, no literary public. Many of us read,
many love literature, but the traditons and institutions of literary
culture are lacking. I do not say that this is bad, I only state it as
a fact that ours is not a society which creates such things. Any
modern country that has not inherited them simply does not
have them.

American writers are not neglected, they mingle occasionally
with the great, they may even be asked to the White House but
no one there will talk literature to them. Mr Nixon disliked writers
and refused flatly to have them in, but Mr Ford has invited them
together with actors, musicians, television newscasters and politicians. On these great evenings the East Room fills with celebrities
who become ecstatic at the sight of other celebrities. Secretary
Kissinger and Danny Kaye fall into each other's arms. Cary
Grant is surrounded by Senators' wives who find him wonderfully
preserved, as handsome in the flesh as on film and they can hardly

113

bear the excitement of personal contact with greatness. People
speak of their diets, of travel and holidays, of vitamins and
problems of aging. Questions of language or style, the structure of
novels, trends in painting are not discussed. The writer finds this a
wonderful Pop occasion. Senator Fulbright seems almost to recognize his name and says, 'You write essays, don't you? I think I can
remember one of them.' But the Senator, as everyone knows, was
once a Rhodes Scholar.

It is actually pleasant on such an evening for a writer to pass half
disembodied and unmolested by small talk from room to room,
looking and listening. He knows that active public men can't combine government with literature, art and philosophy. Theirs is a
world of high-tension wires, not of primroses on the river's brim.
Ten years ago Mayor Daley in a little City Hall ceremony gave
me a five hundred dollar check on behalf of the Midland Authors'
Society. 'Mr Mayor, have you read *Herzog*?' asked one of the
reporters standing by. 'I've looked into it.' said Daley, yielding no
ground. Art is not the Mayor's dish. But then why should it be? I
much prefer his neglect to the sort of interest Stalin took in poetry,
phoning Pasternak to chat with him about Mandelstam and,
shortly afterwards, sending Mandelstam to die.

Are you saying that a modern industrial society dismisses art?
Not at all. Art is one of those good things toward which it feels
friendly. It is quite receptive. But what Ruskin said about the
English public in 1871 applies perfectly to us. 'No reading is possible
for a people with its mind in this state. No sentence of any great
writer is intelligible to them.' Ruskin blames avarice. '. . . so
incapable of thought has it (the public) become in its insanity of
avarice. Happily, our disease is, as yet, little worse than this
incapacity of thought; it is not corruption of the inner nature; we ring
true still, when anything strikes home to us . . . though the idea that
everything should 'pay' has infected our every purpose so deeply . . .'

You don't see avarice as the problem, do you?
No. 'A people with its mind in this state', is where I lay the
stress. We are in a peculiarly revolutionary state, a critical state that
never ends. Yesterday I came upon a description of a medical
technique for bringing patients to themselves. They are exposed

for some minutes to high-frequency sounds until they are calm
enough to think and to feel out their symptoms. To possess your soul
in peace for a few minutes you need the help of medical technology.
It is easy to observe in bars, at dinner tables, everywhere, that
from flop house to White House Americans are preoccupied by the
same questions. Our own American life is our passion, our social and
national life against a world background, an immense spectacle
presented daily by the papers and the television networks—our
cities, our crime, our housing, our automobiles, our sports, our
weather, our technology, our politics, our problems of sex and
race and diplomacy and international relations. These realities are
real enough. But what of the formulae, the jargon, the principles
of selection the media prefer? TV creates the exciting fictions, the
heightened and dramatized shadow events accepted by the great
public and believed by almost everyone to be real. Is reading
possible for a people with its mind in this state?

*Still a book of good quality can find a hundred thousand readers.
But you say that there is no literary public.*
An influential book appears to create its own public. When
Herzog was published I became aware that there were some fifty
thousand people in the United States who wanted to read my novel.
They had evidently been waiting for something like it. Other
writers have certainly had the same experience. But such a public
is a temporary one. There is no literary culture that permanently
contains all of these readers. Remarkably steady and intelligent
people emerge from the heaving wastes of the American educational system. They survive by strength, luck and cunning.

What do they do while waiting for the next important event?
Exactly. What can they read month in, month out? In what
journals do they keep up with what matters in contemporary literature?

*What about the universities? Haven't they done anything to train
judgment and develop taste?*
To most Professors of English a novel is an object of the highest
cultural importance. Its ideas, its symbolic structure, its position
in the history of Romanticism or Realism or Modernism, its higher

relevance require devout study. But what has this sort of cultural study to do with novelists and readers? What they want is the living moment, they want men and women alive, and a circumambient world. The teaching of literature has been a disaster. Between the student and the book he reads lies a gloomy preparatory region, a perfect swamp. He must cross this cultural swamp before he is allowed to open his *Moby Dick* and read, 'Call me Ishmael'. He is made to feel ignorant before masterpieces, unworthy, he is frightened and repelled. And if the method succeeds it produces BAs who can tell you why the *Pequod* leaves port on Christmas morning. What else can they tell you? No feeling for the book has been communicated, only a lot of pseudo-learned interpretation. What has been substituted for the novel itself is what can be said about the novel by the 'educated'. Some professors find educated discourse of this kind more interesting by far than novels. They take the attitude towards fiction that one of the Church Fathers took towards the Bible. Origen of Alexandria asked whether we were really to imagine that God walked in a Garden while Adam and Eve hid under a bush. Scripture could not be taken literally. It must yield to higher meanings.

Are you equating Church Fathers with Professors of Literature?
Not exactly. The Fathers had sublime conceptions of God and Man. If Professors of Humanities were moved by the sublimity of the poets and philosophers they teach they would be the most powerful men in the university and the most fervent. But they are at the lower end of the hierarchy, at the bottom of the pile.

Then why are there so many writers at the universities?
A good question. Writers have no independent ground to stand on. They belong to institutions. They work for newsmagazines and publishing houses, for cultural foundations, advertising agencies, television networks. And they teach. There are only a few literary journals left and those are now academic quarterlies. The big national magazines don't want to publish fiction. Their editors want to discuss only the most significant national and international questions and concentrate on 'relevant' cultural matters. By 'relevant' they mean political. The 'real' questions facing us are questions of business and politics—energy, war, sex, race, cities,

education, technology, ecology, the fate of the automobile industry,
the Middle East crisis, the dominoes of Southeast Asia, the moves
of the Russian politburo. These are, of course, matters of the
highest importance. More accurately, there are questions of life
and death at the heart of such important public matters. But these
life and death questions are not discussed. What we hear and read
is crisis-chatter. And it is the business of the cultural-intelligentsia
(professors, commentators, editors) to produce such chatter. Our
intelligentsia, completely politicized and analytical in temper, does
not take much interest in literature. The members of this elite *had*
literature in their student days and are now well beyond it. At
Harvard or Columbia they read, studied, absorbed the classics,
especially the modernist classics. These prepared them for the
important, the essential, the incomparable tasks they were des-
tined to perform as functionaries in the media, the managers of
scores of new enterprises. Sometimes I sense that they feel they have
replaced writers. The cultural business they do is tinged by literature, or rather the memory of literature. I said before that our common
life had become our most passionate concern. Can an individual,
the subject of a novel, compete in interest with corporate destin-
ies, with the rise of a new class, a cultural intelligentsia?

*Do you suggest that when we become so extremely politicized we
lose interest in the individual?*
Exactly. And that a liberal society so intensely political can't
remain liberal for very long. I take it for granted that an attack on
the novel is also an attack on liberal principles. I view 'activist' art
theories in the same way. The power of a true work of art is such
that it induces a temporary suspension of activities. It leads to
contemplative states, to wonderful and, to my mind, sacred states
of the soul.

And what you call crisis-chatter creates a contrary condition?
I should like to add that the truth is not loved because it is *better*
for us. We hunger and thirst for it. And the appetite for truthful
books is greater than ever, sharpened by privation.

To return for a moment to the subject of a literary world . . .
No tea at Gertrude Stein's, no Closerie de Lilas, no Bloomsbury

evenings, no charming and wicked encounters between George
Moore and W.B. Yeats. Reading of such things is very pleasant
indeed. I can't say that I miss them, because I never knew
anything like them. I miss certain dead friends. Writers. That
Molière put on the plays of Corneille, that Louis XIV himself
may have appeared, disguised, in one of Molière's farces—such
facts are lovely to read in books. I'd hardly expect Mayor Daley
to take part in any farce of mine. He performs in his own farces
only. I have, however, visited writers' clubs in Communist countries
and can't say that I'm sorry we have no such institutions here.
When I was in Addis Ababa I went to the Emperor's Zoo. As
Selassie was the Lion of Judah he was perhaps bound to keep a
large collection of lions. These poor animals lay in the filth of dim
green cages too small for pacing, mere coops. The leonine brown of
their eyes had turned blank and yellow. Bad as things are here
they are not so bad as in the Emperor's Zoo or in writers' centers
behind the Iron Curtain.

*Not so bad is not the same as good. What of the disadvantages
of your condition?*
    There are moments of sorrow, I admit. George Sand wrote to
Flaubert, in a collection of letters I looked into the other day, that
she hoped he would bring his copy of her latest book on his next
visit. 'Put in it all the criticisms which occur to you,' she said.
'That will be very good for me. People ought to do that for each
other as Balzac and I used to do. That doesn't make one person alter
the other; quite the contrary, for in general one gets more determined in one's *moi,* one completes it, explains it better, entirely
develops it, and that is why friendship is good, even in literature,
where the first condition of any worth is to be one's self.' How
nice it would be to hear this from a writer. But no such letters
arrive. Friendships and a common purpose belong to a nineteenth-
century French dream world. The physicist Heisenberg in a recent
article in *Encounter* speaks of the kindly and even brotherly
collaboration among scientists of the generation of Einstein and
Bohr. Their personal letters were quoted in seminars and discussed by the entire scientific community. Heisenberg believes that
in the musical world something of the same spirit appeared in the

eighteenth century. Haydn's relations with Mozart were of this
generous affectionate kind. But when large creative opportunities are
lacking there is no generosity visible. Heisenberg says nothing
about the malice and hostility of less lucky times. Writers today
seldom wish other writers well. Critics use strength gathered from
the past to pummel the present. Edmund Wilson wouldn't read
his contemporaries at all. He stopped with Eliot and Hemingway.
The rest he dismissed. This lack of goodwill, to put it at its
mildest, was much admired. That fact speaks for itself. Curious
about Canadians, Indians, Haitians, Russians, studying Marxism
and the Dead Sea scrolls, he was the Protestant majority's big
literary figure. I have sometimes thought that he was challenged
by Marxism or Modernism in the same way that I have seen the
descendants of Orthodox Jews challenged by oysters. Historical
progress demands that our revulsions be overcome. A man like
Wilson might have done much to strengthen literary culture, but
he dismissed all that, he would have nothing to do with it. For
temperamental reasons. Or Protestant majority reasons. Or perhaps the Heisenberg principle applies—men are generous when
there are creative opportunities, and when such opportunities dwindle
they are . . . something else. But it would have made little difference. At this moment in human evolution, so miraculous, atro-
cious, glorious and hellish, the firmly established literary cultures
of France and England, Italy and Germany can originate nothing.
They look to us, to the "disadvantaged" Americans, and to the
Russians. From America have come a number of great irrepressible solitaries like Poe or Melville or Whitman, alcoholics, obscure
government employees. In busy America there was no Weimar,
there were no cultivated princes. There were only these obstinate
geniuses writing—why? For whom? There is the real *acte gratuite*
for you. Unthanked, these writers augmented life marvelously.
They did not emerge from a literary culture nor did they create
any such thing. Irrepressible individuals of a similar type have lately
begun to show themselves in Russia. There Stalinism utterly
destroyed a thriving literary culture and replaced it with a horrible
bureaucracy. But in spite of this and in spite of forced labor and
murder the feeling for what is true and just has not been put out. I
don't see, in short, why we should continue to dream of what we

have never had. To have it would not help us. Perhaps if we were to
purge ourselves of nostalgia and stopped longing for a literary world
we would see a fresh opportunity to extend the imagination and
resume imaginative contact with nature and society.

*Other people, scholars and scientists, know a great deal about
nature and society. More than you know.*
True. And I suppose I sound like a fool but I nevertheless object
that their knowledge is defective—something is lacking. That
something poetry. Huizinga, the Dutch historian, in his recently
published book on America says that the learned Americans he
met in the Twenties could speak fluently and stimulatingly, but he
adds, "More than once I could not recognize in what he wrote
the living man who had held my interest. Frequently repeated
experience makes me hold the view that my personal reaction to
American scholarly prose must still rest upon the qualities of the
prose itself. I read it with the greatest difficulty; I have no sense
of contact with it and cannot keep my attention fixed on it. It is for
me as if I had to do with a deviant system of expression in which
the concepts are not equivalent to mine, or are arranged differently." The system has become more deviant during the last fifty
years. I want information and ideas, and I know that certain highly
trained and intelligent people have it—economists, sociologists,
lawyers, historians, natural scientists. But I read them with the
greatest difficulty, exasperated, tormented, despairing. And I say
to myself, "These writers are part of the educated public, your
readers. You make your best efforts for them, these unpoetic or
anti-poetic people. You've forgotten Ortega's philistine professional, the educated Mass-Man . . . etcetera." But none of this
matters. Philistine intellectuals don't make you stop writing. Writing
is your *acte gratuite*. Besides, those you address are there. If you
exist, then they exist. You can be more certain of their existence
than of your own.

But whether or not a literary culture exists . . .
Excuse me for interrupting but it occurs to me that Tolstoi would
probably have approved of this and seen new opportunities in it.
He had no use for literary culture and detested professionalism in
the arts.

*But should writers make their peace with the academic Ivory
Tower?*

In his essay "Bethink Yourselves" Tolstoi advises each man to
begin at the point at which he finds himself. Better such Towers
than the Cellar alternatives some writers choose. Besides, the
university is no more an Ivory Tower than *Time* magazine with its
strangely artificial approach to the world, its remote-making mana-
gerial arrangements. A writer is offered more money, bigger
pensions, richer security-plans by Luce enterprises than by any
university. The Ivory Tower is one of those platitudes that haunt the
uneasy minds of writers. Since we have none of the advantages of a
literary world we may as well free ourselves from its banalities.
Spiritual independence requires that we bethink ourselves. The
university is as good a place for such thinking as any other. But
while we think hard about the next step we should avoid becoming
academics. Teachers, yes. Some are even moved to become
scholars. The great danger for writers in the university is the
academic danger.

Can you conveniently give a brief definition of academic?

I limit myself arbitrarily to a professorial type to be found in the
Humanities. Owen Barfield refers in one of his books to "the
everlasting professional device for substituting a plethora of *talk*"
about what matters for—what actually matters. He is sick of it,
he says. Many of us are sick of it.

America's Master Novelist:
An Interview with Saul Bellow

Walter Clemons and Jack Kroll / 1975

From *Newsweek*, 1 September 1975, 32–4, 39–40. © 1975 by
Newsweek, Inc. All rights reserved. Reprinted by permission.

Saul Bellow watches the young man with a camera who circles him,
crouches and moves in for a close shot.

"What the hell are you and I doing?" he asks mildly. A handsome
man, 60 this year, who dislikes being photographed, Bellow is
submitting to a candid session in a London hotel room. "I'm getting
paid and you're getting famous," says the photographer, snapping
away in his cheerful, practiced way.

"I can't get any famouser. I'm already too famous," says Bellow.
Then the notion of celebrity makes the foremost American novel-
ist burst out laughing. "When I'm stopped in the street," he says,
"I'm usually asked if I'm the guy who made 'Never On Sunday'—
Jules Dassin, whom I'm said to resemble."

Bellow's career has been a striking refutation of Scott Fitzgerald's
remark that there are no second acts in American lives. He has not
succumbed to any of the classic fates America seems to reserve for
most of its major writers. He did not crack up, like Fitzgerald; he
was not consumed by his own myth, like Hemingway; he did not
suffer from long-delayed recognition, like Faulkner. Nor is Bellow
a specimen of that other American phenomenon, the writer as
show-biz personality or sudden superstar. Unlike Norman Mailer,
perhaps his chief rival in sheer significance as a contemporary
American writer, he has never dramatized his own persona as a
major component of his art. And, unlike E. L. Doctorow, whose
recent *Ragtime* has made him an instant millionaire after several
well-received but non-bonanza novels, Bellow has never felt the
pressures of outlandish success.

He is indeed an enormous success, complete with best sellers,
prizes and honorifics, but above all he is a major artist and
steadfast craftsman who has, almost miraculously, steadily matured

and deepened, in book after book. Now, with the publication this week of his eighth novel, *Humboldt's Gift* (487 pages. Viking. $10), he consolidates the place assigned to him by Philip Roth, who identi- fied "the great inventors of narrative detail and masters of narrative voice and perspective" as "James, Conrad, Dostoevski and Bellow."

Humboldt's Gift is an exuberant comedy of success and failure, in which Bellow deals directly for the first time with the writer's life in America, including, implicity, his own. It is his funniest book and his most openly affectionate, even in its satiric side glances. It speaks most movingly of aging, and the felt loss of the sorely missed dead. It even proposes—and this will make some readers restive—a supernatural dimension beyond the crowded comic stage on which its characters collide.

The story tracks the parallel careers of two American writers. Charlie Citrine is a Pulitzer Prize historian, successful Broadway playwright, "Chevrolet" (as a Chicago gangster malaprops) of the French Legion of Honor and, in his late fifties, "a goofy chaser" of a voluptuous younger woman named Renata, whom he will be unable to keep if his ex-wife succeeds in stripping him of his money in a fang-and-claw divorce action.

The book also deals with one of the keenest American anxieties— the fear of death. Charlie keeps trim playing paddle ball at his Chicago club. But he isn't entirely reassured by his doctor's com- ments about "my amazingly youthful prostate and my supernor- mal EKG. Strengthened in illusion and idiocy by these proud medical reports, I embraced a busty Renata on [a] Posturepedic mat- tress."

Above all, Charlie is haunted by the death of a friend of his youth, the brilliant poet Von Humboldt Fleisher. Charlie read Humboldt's first poems in the '30s and came out of the Midwest to look him up in Greenwich Village. In Humboldt's company Charlie met the best talkers in New York. "Under their eloquence," he remembers, "I sat like a cat in a recital hall." As Humboldt's fame began to sink in the late '40s, Charlie's began to rise. Humboldt dropped dead in a seedy Times Square hotel in the '60s. Charlie now dreams of him and wakes crying with happiness at his memory and with regret that he dodged Humboldt the last time he saw him, wasted and stumbling down a New York street.

It's no secret that Humboldt is a loving portrait of Delmore Schwartz, whose precocious early poems prefigured the flowering of the powerful generation of poets who came to the fore in the '40s—Robert Lowell, Randall Jarrell, John Berryman. A woman who remembers Schwartz's electrifying youth says that Humboldt's talk in this novel brings him back with heartbreaking clarity. As Charlie Citrine remembers him, Humboldt was "a hectic nonstop monologist and improvisator, a champion detractor. To be loused up by Humboldt was really a kind of privilege. It was like being the subject of a two-nosed portrait by Picasso or an eviscerated chicken by Soutine."

For Citrine—and Bellow—Humboldt's rise and fall personifies the fate of the American artist who hunts glory in a hard-nosed society. Charlie reflects that "Humboldt did what poets in crass America are supposed to do. He chased ruin and death even harder than he had chased women. He blew his talent and his health and reached home, the grave, in a dusty slide . . ." America, thinks Charlie, ghoulishly enjoys this spectacle. Charlies sees the poet as the great American scapegoat, who is loved precisely because he can't make it. Poets exist, he says, to "justify the cynicism of those who say, "If *I* were not such a corrupt, unfeeling bastard, creep, thief, and vulture, I couldn't get through this either. Look at the good and tender and soft men, the *best* of us. They succumbed, poor loonies'."

Bellow says that "the history of literature in America is the history of certain demonic solitaries who somehow brought it off in a society that felt no need for them. In Chicago, where I grew up, we dreamed of the literary life—we were mad for it, but never got a smell of it. I went to Greenwich Village like everybody after college. It wasn't very glamorous, but I did get a feeling in New York that you weren't a bum or an outcast if you wanted to write."

Bellow is now in a position to look back on the writer's life from the vantage point of a survivor who has never even suffered from writer's block. But he looks back without complacency. "I feel I've fallen short of my talents," he says. "Always—in this new book, too. And I've fought inertia in myself. Charlie in *Humboldt's Gift* feels he's snoozed through his life, missing the significance of the great events of his time. I've fallen short of full wakefulness too. I've struggled with torpor.''

Reading his novels, you would hardly know it. Books are of course the chief events of a book-writer's life, but with a master like Bellow the books are like battles in the life of a great general, filled with captured truths, dazzling strategies, difficulties overcome and even a few dearly fought losses. His first two novels, *Dangling Man* (1944) and *The Victim* (1947), caught the tensions of wartime and postwar America, especially *Dangling Man,* which described with rare honesty and power the anxieties of a young man waiting to be drafted. With *The Adventures of Augie March* (1953), which won Bellow the first of his three National Book Awards, he made a stylistic breakthrough into the pungent colloquial idiom of his later fiction. The very first words of *Augie* ("I am an American, Chicago born—Chicago, that somber city—and go at things as I have taught myself, free-style") signaled the most exciting thing that can happen in literature—the unmistakable sound of a major new voice.

What many regard as Bellow's masterpiece appeared three years later. *Seize the Day* is a stunning, excruciating short novel about the downfall of Tommy Wilhelm, a loser who dreams of a quick killing on the market. Like the great short novels of Herman Melville, *Seize the Day* is at once lyrical and gritty. Bellow's evocation of New York's upper Broadway, with its cavernous shabby-genteel hotels and benches filled with old pensioners, established him as the most powerful poet of urban America. He knew this subject backward, but his next novel, *Henderson the Rain King* (1959) was about Africa, which he had never visited. In a feat of vivid imagination he produced a romance about an eccentric millionaire on a spiritual safari. It remains a special favorite of his. Of all his characters, Bellow has said, Henderson, the quixotic seeker of higher truth, is most like himself.

His next novel, *Herzog* (1964), was a best seller, NBA winner and the kind of book that goes beyond literature. For critic Julian Moynihan the appearance of *Herzog* suggested that things might be looking up for American civilization in general. Moses Herzog is a big, juicy character—comic, tragic, ridiculous, profound. As cuck-

old, Jew, composer of unmailed letters to everyone from Willie
Sutton to Spinoza, Herzog is both a great outsider and a great
Everyman who touched a nerve in readers all over the world. "I
received two or three thousand letters from people pouring out their
souls to me," says Bellow, "saying 'This is my life, this is what
it's been like for me.' And then I understood that for some reason
these themes were visited upon me, that I didn't always pick
them, they picked me. I began to have a little respect then for my
own hunches, and also I felt that you could be a charlatan with
this kind of power, and you'd better be careful with it."

With *Mr. Sammler's Planet* (1970) many felt Bellow had in fact
mishandled his great power. Always a conservative in the best,
classical sense of that word, Bellow in this novel shrinks his usual
humane magnanimity to a narrow, almost paranoid view of the
social turmoil of the '60s. Critic Alfred Kazin wrote that *Mr.
Sammler* was not so much a novel as "a brilliantly austere set of
opinions . . ." and used such terms as "uncharitable" and "moral
haughtiness" to describe the disapproving attitude of Sammler-
Bellow toward women, Negroes and almost everyone "on the ugly
alarm-laden streets" of the same West Side he had treated so pierc-
ingly in *Seize the Day.*

Bellow himself is intolerant of the shortcomings he sees in his
early work. "In *The Victim* I was very much under the spell of
Dostoevski's *The Eternal Husband.* In *Augie March* I got stuck in
a Sherwood Anderson ingenue vein: here are all those people and
isn't life wonderful! By the last third of the book I wasn't feeling
that way any more. I've always thought that the germ of a novel
is found in the first few pages. You start a certain way because it's
liberating, and before you're through you find it inhibiting. I
didn't know what to do with those inhibitions in the last third of
Augie March, and I can't bear to reread it. I can reread *Henderson
the Rain King* with pleasure. I reread *Herzog* two or three times a
year—looking, mind you, for goofs I made."

With the confidence born of a mastery that few American writers
have achieved, Bellow sees very few goofs in *Humboldt's Gift.*
"The nice thing about this book," he explains, "which I was really
struggling with in *Herzog,* is that I've really come into a cold air
of objectivity about all the people in the book, including Charlie. It

really came easily for me to see him as America saw him, and thereby America itself became clearer." It seems clear that Bellow is talking about himself as well as Charlie. When he says, "Charlie is a very funny fellow, isn't he?" Bellow is ratifying the comic muse as the chief agent of his vision amd mastery.

For Saul Bellow is a very funny fellow—like such other funny fellows as Gogol, Dickens and Mark Twain. Philip Roth put it nicely when he referred to Bellow as "closing the gap, as it were, between Damon Runyon and Thomas Mann." Bellow himself refers to his method offhandedly as "kidding my way to Jesus." Precisely because he is basically pessimistic about the drift of things, Bellow knows the liberating power of comedy. "*Humboldt,*" he says, "is very much a comic book about death." Then he adds: "I'm going to have my knuckles rapped for this book. There's this lady who says to Charlie Citrine, 'You're laughing and kidding and having a wonderful time, but life will come crush you like an empty beer can.' Well, that was actually said to me by a very tough, existential lady who's a critic. She's the type who, if she got some handsome young man to sleep with her, would rake his face with her fingernails, just to prove an existential point."

Born in Lachine, Canada, in 1915, the youngest of four children of Russian immigrants, Bellow moved with his family to Chicago when he was 9. A friend of those days, Dave Peltz, remembers Solomon Bellows, known as "Solly"—he dropped the "s" from his surname and took the name Saul when he began to publish—as the outstanding member of a group of Tuley High School friends who dreamed of someday becoming famous writers.

Every Friday night, these precocious Chicago kids went to the Mission House in the tattered multi-ethnic neighborhood around Humboldt Park—a name possibly reflected in the title of Bellow's new book. Dave Peltz remembers these sessions well. "Anyone could get up and speak, and we'd sit and listen while they argued politics and religion." Solly Bellows was the most precocious of the lot—a good runner on the track team, a fair swimmer, middling tennis player, but a remarkable writer even then. Sam Freifeld, now a Chicago attorney, recalls that Solly was fond of reading his work out loud among friends. In the back leaf of a copy of Oscar Wilde's poems, Bellows and his friends scribbled the titles of books

they would someday write, copping their favorite lines from
Wilde's verse. Solly was particularly fond of the phrase, "Black
leaves whirling in the wind," which he thought would make a
terrific book title.

Peltz, who now owns a home-improvement company in Gary,
Ind., lunches with his boyhood friend once a week. "Last week
he gave me Diderot's *Rameau's Nephew* to read," says Peltz. "I
don't have time to educate myself in literary matters. So he feeds me
the proper material and when I finish it we discuss it. And I bring
him something different. My work takes me into all kinds of neighborhoods. I tell Saul stories that help keep him connected."

Bellow still draws on the raffish Chicago scene for such "connections." In a poker game with novelist Nelson Algren, columnist
Studs Terkel and two underworld characters, Peltz lost heavily, was
advised by Terkel not to pay and promptly got two cement blocks
through the windows of his home and a threat on his life. "I paid
up," says Peltz. From this incident came Charlie Citrine's encounter in *Humboldt's Gift* with the exquisite mobster Ronald
Cantabile, one of Bellow's great comic creations.

The father of three sons by his first three marriages, Bellow lives
quietly in Chicago with his fourth wife, Alexandra, a beautiful
Romanian-born mathematician who teaches at Northwestern University. He plays racquet ball at a local athletic club but shuns
the Chicago literary community. "Saul is not a pop character,"
says Peltz. "He enjoys a couple of drinks before dinner, a quiet meal
and a glass of brandy afterwards. He prefers to sit in civilized
circumstances." Some think Bellow's withdrawn life is eccentric,
and Freifeld, who had a falling-out with Bellow while representing
him in one of his three divorces, avows that "Saul Bellow is a
great artist but a lousy friend." The complex truth was probably
best summed up by Bellow himself when he told the lawyer: "I
know you think I'm a square, Freifeld, but there's no name for the
shape I'm in."

Bellow has been on the faculty of the University of Chicago since
1962, as a member of the Committee on Social Thought. This is a
flexibly organized department that accepts only 25 to 30 students a
year. "It was designed to break the academic lockstep, to free
students from required courses, to allow more independent-minded

work," explains sociologist Edward Shils. As a member of the committee, and its chairman since 1970, Bellow is not a mere ornamental writer-in-residence. Last year he taught tutorials on the novel from Defoe to Joyce and this fall he will be teaching Tolstoy's shorter works.

Bellow, who got a B.S. in anthropology and sociology from Northwestern in 1937, has had what he calls "intellectual romances" with various ideologies—Marxism in his youth, Reichian psychology later. But he has been conspicuously apolitical in a period when many of his fellow artists have taken strong activist positions. The most celebrated occasion was President Johnson's 1965 White House arts festival, which the poet Robert Lowell declined to attend, citing his disagreement with the Administration's Vietnam policy. Twenty leading artists and writers signed a telegram supporting Lowell's position; Bellow and John Hersey wouldn't sign. "The President intends, in his own way, to encourage American artists," Bellow's statement read. "I consider this event to be an official function, not a political occasion . . . I accept in order to show my respect for [the President's] intentions and to honor his high office." The statement won him few friends; some of his colleagues harshly accused him of having lost touch with history.

But Bellow's position is more complex than that. "What man with his eyes open at this hour could not be interested in politics?" he says. "I only wish people talked about it at a deeper level than Chappaquiddick or Scoop Jackson or who's-gonna-get-the-nomination. I don't think we know where we are or where we're going. I see politics—ultimately—as a buzzing preoccupation that swallows up art and the life of the spirit."

The life of the spirit is very much on his mind these days. Some early readers of *Humboldt's Gift* have been startled by Charlie Citrine's espousement of anthroposophy, the creed of the early twentieth-century occultist thinker Rudolf Steiner, who believed in the transmigration of souls and opposed the dominant scientific view of the universe. How seriously are we meant to take these passages in the novel? Answer: very seriously indeed. Bellow discovered Steiner through a book called *Saving the Appearances* by Owen Barfield, a remarkable British writer who now lives in retirement in Kent after a long career as a lawyer. One of the

main purposes of Bellow's trip to England this summer was to talk
with Barfield.

For Bellow, Barfield's work represents a vigorous claim for the
importance of poetic imagination. "Read *Saving the Appearances,*" he says, "and then Rudolf Steiner's little book on theosophy—your hair will stand on end! I was impressed by the idea
that there were forms of understanding, discredited now, which had
long been the agreed basis of human knowledge. We think we can
know the world scientifically, but actually our ignorance is terrifying."

When he discusses these matters, Bellow's face lights up with
youthful enthusiasm. Like Charlie Citrine, who receives a message left behind by his deceased friend Humboldt: "Remember: we
are not natural beings but supernatural beings," Bellow in this
most open-hearted of his novels embraces, at least as an imaginative
possibility, the notion that "*this* could not be *it* . . . We had all
been here before and would presently be here again."

A surprising turn in the thinking of a worldly Chicagoan who has
tasted his share of the satisfactions of the here-and-now. But the
forms of "successful" life in the American here-and-now prove
illusory in *Humboldt's Gift*. Charlie Citrine, on the one hand,
realizes late in the day that he has slept through most of his life: "I
have always had an exceptional gift for passing out," says Charlie.
"I look at snap-shots taken in some of the most evil hours of
mankind and I see that I have lots of hair and am appealingly
youthful. I am wearing an ill-fitting double-breasted suit of the
Thirties or Forties, smoking a pipe, standing under a tree, holding
hands with a plump and pretty bimbo—and I am asleep on my feet,
out cold. I have snoozed through many a crisis (while millions died)."

Still more insidious than Charlie's lethargy is Humboldt's reaching for the high-voltage wire of fame, of being *someone*. Bellow's
voice softens with regret when he speaks not only of destroyed
poets who were his friends, but of Marilyn Monroe, with whom
he was acquainted when she was married to Arthur Miller: "I
always felt she had picked up some high-tension cable and
couldn't release it," he says. "She couldn't rest, she found no
repose in anything. She was up in the night, taking pills and
talking about her costumes, her next picture, contracts and money,

gossip. In the case of a beautiful and sensitive creature like that, it was a guarantee of destruction.''

There's been nothing remotely comparable to that in Bellow's own life. But he wryly describes a recent White House dinner he watched from the sidelines. ''I was not there as a celebrity, only as a marginal retainer,'' he says. ''But I watched the celebrities falling into each other's arms—Kissinger and Danny Kaye in a tight embrace. The only people who behaved decently were those like Margaret Truman who had recovered their humanity or never lost it. The others, their eyes wildly rolling at other celebrities, you couldn't hold their attention when you talked to them. What was I doing there? Neither Hubert Humphrey nor Nelson Rockefeller functions as I function. The common ground I could find with them would be *their* common ground, if by some mighty, transcendent act of imagination I could project myself there, alongside them.''

As the most honored American novelist of his age, Saul Bellow now enters a dangerous period, of which he is cannily aware: ''Many American writers cross the bar in their 60s and 70s,'' he says, ''and become Grand Old Men, gurus or bonzes of the Robert Frost variety. This is how society eases us out. Sees us off on the immortal train, with waving and cheering and nobody listening. Just as well, because there's nothing but bombast coming from the rear platform. If I last long enough, I assume this will happen to me too. And then there are two possibilities. Either you've run out of imagination, in which case you're ready to be puffed up, held down like a barrage balloon by the cables before you float off into eternity. Or your imagination keeps cooking, in which case you're lucky. You're among the blessed. No man knows which way he's gonna go. He can only hope.''

At 60, Saul Bellow is not ready to be puffed up, held down, or floated off. Instead he makes us the gift of a masterly novel—wise, challenging and radiant.

A Talk with Saul Bellow

Joseph Epstein / 1976

From the *New York Times Book Review*, 5 December 1976, 3, 92–93. © 1970 by the New York Times Company, Reprinted by permission.

Joseph Epstein: Noel, Nobel. The *New York Times Book Review* has asked me to interview you for its special Christmas Books issue. The mood is supposed to be celebratory, both of the season and, more important, of your having won the Nobel Prize for Literature. But I thought the occasion might be better used to ask you to formulate answers to some questions I have about your literary career and the Nobel Prize.

Saul Bellow: Well, you are not Eckermann, I am not Goethe, and this, our City of Chicago, is most distinctly not Weimar. But let's go ahead anyway. Shoot.

JE: What is the importance of praise to a writer? What, to you, is the best kind of praise?

SB: I think the answer is perhaps best put in an American context, for the question of praise is a trickier one here than in other countries, especially in countries where there is a literary establishment that is in a position to confer praise. In the United States, though, it is either feast or famine: one is either totally ignored, which is damaging, or becomes the center of attention, which is almost always unreal. Here it is the media which confer praise; and I think it is fair to say that the media aren't interested in literature but in publicity, in celebrity, in filling the space and killing the time allotted to them.

For myself, I have no reason to complain. I have had my share—and even more than my share—of recognition; and of all kinds and coming from all quarters. I think—I hope—I have received enough praise to have weaned myself away from the need for it. By now I think I have a clear enough eye to know both how good and how bad I am as a writer.

As for the second of your questions, the best praise I have had came from the young men with whom I started out in Chicago, most of whom are now dead. In particular I was much moved by the praise of my friend Isaac Rosenfeld, who was of course not only himself an estimable writer but who went out of his way to praise *Augie March,* to tell me how significant he thought it was. His praise was, and shall always remain, very special to me.

JE: What, I wonder, would you have felt, especially after all the stories about your last year being a close runner-up to Montale, if you had been passed over for the Nobel Prize this year?

SB: Last year, after a momentary feeling of disappointment, I felt rather relieved that Montale won the prize. As I said, I have gotten a great deal of recognition, and I like to think I wouldn't have minded if I had been passed over. Perhaps this is the calm hindsight of a winner speaking, perhaps not.

One of the things one fails to realize till one has won it is that the Nobel Prize for Literature has many extraliterary aspects. Winning it makes you an eminent person; it gives you certain kinds of power. I have never had much taste for the power that goes with eminence.

As usual, there is the comic side. Journalists are fond of pointing out to me all the great writers who did not win a Nobel: Tolstoy, Proust, James, Joyce. They ask how it feels to be among the company of such distinguished literary figures as Sully-Prud-homme, Carl Spitteler, Wladyslaw S. Reymont, and Halldór K. Laxness. It causes me to scramble to remember that some pretty fair figures did win the Nobel Prize, among them Yeats, Mann, Eliot, Camus.

JE: As a writer who has shown himself fully alive to the world's status comedy, how do you think your own rise in status, as a Nobel Prize winner, will affect both your view of yourself and the day-to-day conduct of your life?

SB: One thing you may count on, and this is that I am not about to start thinking of myself as Saul Bellow who won the Nobel Prize for Literature for 1976. I am too old and canny for that. Moreover, I don't think that what recognition I have won thus far has turned my head; at least I hope it hasn't.

The worst fear I have as a writer is that of losing my feeling for the common life, which is, as every good writer knows, or should know, anything but common. To think of oneself as a Nobel Prize winner is finally to think of oneself as an enameled figurine in a China cabinet, and I don't intend to find myself in a China cabinet.

One of the things of interest about becoming a laureate is to note the attempt at exploitation of the Prize by institutions and the media. For a time the telephone here didn't stop ringing with offers: to accept honorary degrees, to go on talk shows, to make statements of one kind or another. A downtown club here in Chicago even offered me a free membership. We ought to go there one evening for dinner with our wives, order an enormous dinner, and not pay the bill.

One becomes aware of how many cultural promoters there are in this country: men and women whose job it is to drag you to the podium, to hold you tight while you are being photographed, propping you up like a corpse in a coffin. As a Nobel Prize winner one could become, if one is not careful, a cultural functionary, to be trundled out in honorific robes whenever the occasion requires. I wish I had the coldness, or strength of character, or whatever it takes, to turn my back on the publicity connected with the Nobel Prize, as Samuel Beckett has done. But I apparently do not. Instead when I am made an offer I usually just say thank you very much.

JE: Do you look forward to the award of the Nobel Prize increasing the size of the audience for your books? This might be a good place, too, to clear the air on the subject of your once supposedly calling yourself a "large-public" as opposed to a "small-public" writer.

SB: I truly do not know if the Nobel Prize brings a writer more readers. I do know that, as e. e. cummings once put it, I would rather have "better than more readers." I am grateful to learn that someone has taken the time and trouble to read my books. Yet I am sometimes also a bit depressed when someone who has read something I have written comes up to me to ask "What does it mean?" As if a novel were a puzzle, or a code, to which only the author and certain highly erudite readers had the key. Such a response shows the rather demoralizing effect of the teaching of literature in our universities. But if the Prize should bring me more readers, and among those additional readers are better read-

ers, then I should be most pleased, though, as I say, I am not at
all sure that winning the Nobel Prize has such an effect.

On the question of "large-public" and "small-public" writers,
the distinction, which is a useful one, was originally made by
Wyndham Lewis, who noted that in the middle of the 19th century
writers of great power—among them Dickens, Tolstoy, Dostoyevsky—wrote and seemed to be understood by a large public, whereas
later in the 19th century and early in the 20th century a different
kind of writer, no less of a genius but with something odd and
difficult about him—Rilke, Joyce, Proust, Mallarmé are examples—appeared, though the difficulty of such writers made them
perforce writers for a "small public." I grew up under the
influence of these small-public writers. I revered them then, and in
many respects continue to revere them now. But in an interview
in *The New York Times* of some months ago, a reporter garbled the
distinction badly, making me sound as if I thought myself a large-
public writer and as if there was, in my view, something degrading
about being a small-public writer. Of course, I neither think nor
intended anything of the kind.

Which is not to say that I, along with every writer, do not want
as large an audience as possible, but there are limits to such a
desire. I want to be read on my own terms, which are small-public
terms—to be, in my books, as odd, difficult, idiosyncratic as I
need to be in order to get said what I feel needs to be said.

JE: Some time ago you remarked that you thought yourself a
most fortunate man, because when you published a novel 50,000
people bought it in cloth covers, 5,000 people read it through, and
300 people reacted to it. Do those figures still apply? Or do they now
need to be revised upwards?

SB: Perhaps this is a question better answered by an agent, or
statistician, or literary accountant. But if pressed for an answer,
I should say that the figures probably do need to be revised upward.
I think I nowadays get more response from unknown readers than
I used to get. Many of these letters are very penetrating; not all are
completely approving, but then I am not completely approving of
myself. In recent years, I would say that I have learned more from
these letters than I have from formal criticism of my work. So many
current critics—you can fill in the names for yourself—remind me

of nothing so much as the figure of the man who steps to center
stage with his thumbs looped in his suspenders, giving off an air of
tremendous confidence, as if to say, "I've got the poop." Well,
as I see it, he doesn't have the poop, just the suspenders.

But my view is that a writer should reach as many people as
possible—not with a message but with a point of view arising
from his freedom as a writer, the nonpartisanship of his heart, and
the happy responsibilities of the imagination. When it is going
well a novel affords the highest kind of truth; a good writer can lay
claim to a disinterestedness that is as great as that of a pure
scientist—when he is going well. In its complicated, possibly even
mysterious, way, the novel is an instrument for delving into
human truths.

JE: Do you imagine a perfect reader for your novels?

SB: Well, I do not start out assuming that I am *sui generis*. What
I think I might have, apart from the techniques that I have learned
about my craft over the years, is a certain clairvoyance about
discovering issues, questions, problems before they are seen by
most others—sometimes in a general, sometimes in a quite particular way. After publishing *Herzog,* for example, I was interested
to learn that all sorts of people wrote letters to the famous that they
never sent, à la Moses Herzog. More generally, I find that the
things that agitate, confuse and sometimes indeed frighten me about
our time agitate, confuse and frighten a great many others. As a
novelist, it is a good part of my job to attempt to formulate, as
dramatically and as precisely as I can, the pain and anguish that
we all feel. Now more than ever, it seems to me, it becomes the
writer's job to remind people of their common stock of emotion,
of their common humanity—of the fact, if you will, that they
have souls.

JE: One of the comforts of winning a Nobel Prize, I should think,
is that you might now feel more free to compare your work with that
of important writers of the past without seeming altogether vain in
doing so. In this regard, will the winning of the prize in any way affect
your work?

SB: To begin with, it is a cold comfort, if I may say so. The truth
is, even though I have been at it for nearly four decades, I have
always felt myself, as a writer, to be an apprentice or journeyman.

Although I hope my books have given off greater reverberations than are perhaps to be found on their pages, I nonetheless feel that I have exercised my imagination on certain private kinds of people—with working out obsessions about people I loved who are now dead.

But now certain things have intervened to change my interests. In the book I recently did on Israel I discovered that it was as easy to write about great public matters as about private ones. All it required was more confidence and daring.

Possibly the award of the Nobel Prize has, in an indirect way, bolstered that confidence further. Whatever the reasons, I feel it is time to write about people who make a more spirited resistance to the forces of our time. (True, they sometimes go under, such people, but that is another matter.) I am not saying that, as a novelist, I have suddenly become super-ambitious. Not at all. What I am saying is that I think that it is time for me to move on now.

JE: With a small handful of exceptions, I think it fair to say that the novel today does not generate the kind of excitement that it once did among intelligent readers. Is the writing of novels nowadays more difficult, or is it that our novelists are less good?

SB: I think it is hard to judge talent in a situation that is itself so difficult. It is harder for a novelist to cast his spell over a reality that is so convulsive as ours is at present. We're going through an interregnum at present, a terrible time of impatience. People are unquestionably more troubled, agonized, less certain of themselves. They are not only often without kindness but actively wickeder to one another. The cost of real virtue has gone up. Instead we have the false virtue of phony liberalism. In the midst of this one turns to the novelist and says: "Well, Bud, what have you got to say about this?" It's not to be wondered at if the novelistic imagination isn't often up to it. Besides, most novelists are little different than most people: they refuse to think things through anew but prefer instead to do the same old things in the same old way. But to answer your question: I am not sure if novelists today are less good than they once were—there has always been a great number of bad writers in the world—but I am sure that, the situation being what it is, they have to be very good indeed to make legitimate claims upon the attention of a public so deeply stirred and agitated.

JE: On more than one occasion, I have heard you refer to yourself as not a novelist but as a "historian of society." Could you elaborate a bit upon what that term means to you?

SB: I think of myself as a historian of society in that I cannot exceed what I see. I am bound, in other words, as the historian is bound by the period he writes about, by the situation I live in. I blame myself for not often enough seeing the extraordinary in the ordinary. Somewhere in his journals Dostoyevsky remarks that a writer can begin anywhere, at the most commonplace thing, scratch around in it long enough, pry and dig away long enough, and, lo!, soon he will hit upon the marvelous. I tend to believe that, at least most of the time.

Whether he is conscious of it or not, I think that every modern novelist has a theory of history. I think that I have, till recently, held for the most part to modernist assumptions about history. It is only recently that it has begun to occur to me that in fact we did not live with these assumptions, and that we were deeply moved by others. Therefore, I have begun to think of shucking these old assumptions off. At the moment that leaves me a historian of society without a theory of history.

JE: A great many of your readers were left confused about the emergence of interest in the work of Rudolf Steiner shown in your last novel. Many people who, I suspect, have never read Steiner, as I have not read Steiner, have been able to score rather easy points by remarking on the "vapidities of Rudolf Steiner" and taking other, similar cheap shots. But I wonder if your interest in such matters does not reflect an interest in the higher and wider questions: the design of the universe, the origin of evil, the origin (as mysterious, I should think) of goodness, and so forth. Do such questions occupy your thoughts more than they once did?

SB: I think people were confused by seeing Rudolf Steiner's work pop up in a novel a good part of which was comic in intent. I do admit to being intrigued with Steiner. I do not know enough to call myself a Steinerian. The college professor in me wants to administer a quick quiz to those who knock him to see whether they have done their homework. I think it enough for now to say that Rudolf Steiner had a great vision and was a powerful poet as well as philosopher and scientist.

When I was a child I read the Bible, when older I read Plato, St. Augustine and Dante. Should I, as an adult, erase all traces of this reading? Is it kid stuff compared with, say, R. D. Laing and *The Village Voice?* I am moved to take Plato, et al. seriously. I hope I will be forgiven if I choose not to see this as a sign that I am slipping.

JE: Shall we stop here?

SB: Let's. Before we weigh down too many Christmas stockings.

JE: Merry Christmas to all.

SB: And to all a good night.

Common Needs, Common Preoccupations: An Interview with Saul Bellow

Jo Brans / 1977

From *Southwest Review*, 62 (1977), 1–19. Reprinted in "A Feeling for Where the Nerves Lie." *Listen to the Voices: Conversations with Contemporary Writers* (Dallas: Southern Methodist Press, 1988) np. © 1977 by Jo Brans. Reprinted by permission.

Saul Bellow, the author of eleven books, among them *The Adventures of Augie March, Herzog, Mr. Sammler's Planet,* and *Humboldt's Gift,* received the Nobel Prize for Literature in 1976.

Jo Brans is a member of the faculty of the Department of English at Southern Methodist University. She interviewed Bellow when he visited Dallas in November, 1976, to speak at SMU's Literary Festival.

Brans: You said recently that you began to write books because you love literature. And I thought that was the best answer to the question of "why" that anybody had given. But it seemed to be a strange answer. You didn't say anything about expressing yourself or revealing your feelings. None of that Rousseau stuff.

Bellow: If I thought the project was about myself I would value it less. It isn't really about myself. What I have discovered over the years is that although it began with me, it is an activity that affects other people, and that I have the knack of expressing some of their unexpressed thoughts and feelings. For instance, for many years I had fantasies in which I wrote letters to people. Then I thought, oh, what an odd thing. Wouldn't it be amusing if I wrote a book about a man who, going out of his mind, is writing letters to everybody. And then I discovered that hundreds of thousands of people were doing just that—always had been doing that.

Brans: Writing mental letters?

Bellow: Yes. And so this was some evidence to me that I enjoyed some "clairvoyant powers." I had had that before, from my very first book. When I published *Dangling Man,* many people wrote me and said that they found their own situation in this. And then I began to realize that I had some feeling for where the nerves lay. That the enterprise was not really about me, that I was on loan to myself, as it were, and that I was doing something that expressed common needs, common preoccupations. If it were just about myself I don't think that it would have meant so very much to me, because I haven't all that much use for myself—myself as such, my own ego, pride of accomplishment, or what you like. I think I had not an abnormal amount of such pride, but a relatively low amount. I would have been satisfied with a far more modest success. I never wanted to uncork the genie, or raise the lid of Pandora's box. I began to see some years ago that it was a Pandora's box.

Brans: You mean your success? Or the connection that you made with people?

Bellow: No, the connection was important, but the success was something else again, because the success meant that I was supplying a need, a public need—of a cultural kind. And that I was expected to act the culture figure, to be a public utility, an unpaid functionary, something between a congressman and a clergyman. And I saw that people felt they had a right to bring to me everything that troubled them in this province.

Brans: That's what Sammler says about himself—that he is a priest or a psychologist.

Bellow: Yes, you begin to feel that way pretty soon.

Brans: When you say clairvoyant, do you mean that somehow intuitively or mystically you speak for other people? That somehow you are a kind of scapegoat figure as a writer and you bear the burden of other people, and you write about that? You have sometimes quoted Whitman, that the poet in America must create archetypes of Americans. Are you creating archetypes that come from all the people?

Bellow: Well, I used the word clairvoyant. I might have chosen simpler, less mysterious language and said that because I'm concerned with what affects so many people, I have trained myself in an attitude of mind which provides just that sort of material. It may not be clairvoyance, but I have sometimes definitely sensed that it's a little more than a natural process. Something beyond positivistic, rationalistic common sense, or the clear light of day.

Brans: That seems a curious thing for you to say, when your books are so full of ideas.

Bellow: Well, not all ideas are clear and rational. And not all ideas belong to the modern idea system of scientific provability, or whatever you want to call it.

Brans: I'm sympathetic to that. I know things all the time that I don't think through rationally, that are not even available to rational thought. But it seems really remarkable to me for a writer somehow to feel that he speaks for all kinds of people with whom he's never come in contact.

Bellow: I think it's true, though. And I don't like to question the sources of my own ideas and feelings too closely. That is to say, I avoid the assumption that I know the origin of my own thoughts and feelings. I've become aware of a conflict between the modern university education I received and those things that I really felt in my soul most deeply. I've trusted those more and more.—You see, I'm not even supposed to have a soul.

Brans: Who says you can't have a soul?

Bellow: The soul is out of bounds if you have the sort of education I had. I got my bachelor's degree as an anthropologist. And I read Marx and Bertrand Russell and Morris R. Cohen; I read the logical positivists. I read Freud and Adler and the Gestalt psychologists and the rest. And I know how a modern man is supposed to think. The hero of my last book says, "If you put a test before me I can get a high mark, but it's only head culture." The fact is there are other deeper motives in a human being, which I don't like to call unconscious, because that's a term preempted by psychoanalysis, but I say to myself, "I have always behaved in such a way that I cannot escape the conclusion that I believe things I'm not consciously aware of believing. That I have hopes I can't justify. And that I have affections I can't explain by the modern system in which I was trained." Then you come to the point of choice. Do you believe the psychoanalytic explanation of your deeper motives? Or do you simply say, "These are my deeper motives, I don't care what psychoanalysis has to say about them." I've made the second

choice. I don't care any longer whether my ideas square with the
modern canon, which I have taken to calling the canon of head
culture. I know that people live by something far deeper than
head culture; they couldn't live if they didn't. They couldn't survive
if they didn't. What a woman does for her children, what a man
does for his family, what people most tenaciously cling to, these
things are not adequately explained by Oedipus complexes, libi-
dos, class struggle, or existential individualism—whatever you like.
Now, I know that psychoanalysis has found a natural preserve
for poets and artists called the unconscious. A writer is supposed
to go there and dig around like a truffle hound. He comes back
with a truffle, a delicacy for the cultural world. The poet is a
wonderful Caliban, the analyst is the Prospero who knows how
to put his discoveries to a higher purpose. Well, I don't believe that.
I don't believe that we go and dig in the unconscious and come
back with new truffles from the libidinous unknown. That's not the
way it really is.

Brans: How do you think it really is? If you act on what you get
from this part of yourself . . .

Bellow: There are persistent ideas, the truth of which we recognize when we meet them in literature. You read Tolstoy—it's not
uncommon that a character of Tolstoy will hear an inner voice. We
all know what that is. We immediately recognize it. We know how
the soul of a child speaks to the child. We've experienced it
ourselves, only there's no room for it in the new mental world that
we've constructed, which is less and less a world and more and
more a prison, it seems to me. But we know all these things when
people talk to us about them. Our immortal hopes we know. We
understand what they are. We don't dismiss them out of hand.
And it's not just because of ancient superstition, it's because there
is some unacknowledged information that we have. It's about time we
simply dealt with it directly and without being so evasive.

Brans: Now you're being Rousseau. You use this "we" so
bravely. Aren't you making the assumption that what you think
is really what everybody thinks? Isn't that a sort of Rousseau claim:
I know my heart, so I know men?

Bellow: "Je sens mon coeur, et je connais les hommes." Well,
there's a good deal to it.

Brans: How do you know that I'm not completely unlike you, and that you can talk about *we* all you want, but what you really mean is *I?*

Bellow: I sense that when I say these things you don't actively disagree with me. At least, you're agnostic enough not to dispute them immediately. You'll think matters over.

Brans: No, I'm not an agnostic at all. You know that I agree with you—I'm playing, I guess. Tell me about your teaching. What has been the importance of your teaching to your writing? You taught Tolstoy last year, didn't you?

Bellow: Yes, and Conrad.

Brans: Do you feel as frustrated about teaching as I do sometimes? What do you think about it? You teach graduate students all the time, who presumably feel lucky to be there, and who are dedicated to ideas—to what you have to say to them.

Bellow: I suppose so. In Chicago it's very hard to find people to talk literature to. You find them at the university, and that's the long and the short of the thing. There is no literary culture in the United States. There are no colleagues to discuss novels with. Most of the critical articles that you read in magazines or newspapers are scandalous. And there is no community, so you talk to young people who know something. It's a great comfort. And, after all, why should one lock these things within one's bosom? I can't even talk to my wife about them. She's a mathematician. She's wonderful—she knows all kinds of things, but she doesn't know this, just as I don't know pure mathematics.

Brans: But you both are using symbols, symbol systems.

Bellow: Yes, but I'm dealing in broad human facts to which all human beings have access. Only an elite has access to what she does. I think there are only twenty people in the world who actually understand her theorems—this eliminates most mathematicians.

Brans: So she really has to keep it locked within her bosom, whether she wants to or not.

Bellow: Yes, it's hard for her—hard for her to live with a man who doesn't understand these things. I know that. We have other kinds of understanding, but her situation with me is not very different from my situation with most people in Chicago—mechanics, secretaries, lawyers, dentists, engineers, criminals, stockbrokers, or hoodlums. I can meet with them, we can find common ground, there's a lot we *can* talk about. But we don't talk about what matters most. Neither they nor I can do that.

Brans: Can you talk to your students about that?

Bellow: Not directly. I have to talk to them about *The Red and the Black,* which is what I am doing this term, but one can put a lot of things into that, and they understand.

Brans: So in your teaching, then, you find this common ground where you can meet, and where you can really exchange experiences safely.

Bellow: I think that the university contains all that there is left in this country, or indeed in most countries, of a literary culture.

Brans: Maybe what we do in classrooms in a university is really our religion.

Bellow: No, I wouldn't go so far as that. It's not my religion. But it really is the only avenue I have for expressing certain feelings and thoughts—or for talking shop, which can be important if you're deprived of it. I never much liked talking shop, but occasionally one does like to discuss one's trade.

Brans: And this gives you a chance to do that.

Bellow: I do it indirectly. I never talk about myself, and I never talk to students about what I'm writing, or what I'm thinking about my own work. But that I can obliquely touch upon some of these questions gives me nearly the kind of gratification I'm looking for. That's what it's meant to me all these years. Perhaps students learn something from it too.

Brans: Yet you've been very critical of academics. Isn't there a contradiction here?

Bellow: I'm critical of academics who take masterpieces and turn them into discourse in the modern intellectual style. I'm against that, of course. I am not for the redescription of *Moby Dick* by Marxists and existentialists and Christian symbolists, respectively. What does that do for *Moby Dick* or for me? It doesn't do anything. It only results in the making of more books—King Solomon has already warned us against that in Ecclesiastes.

Brans: You make me very uncomfortable because I don't know exactly where you draw the line. And when I was coming to talk to you today I felt that somehow I might be doing some kind of

disservice to your books by asking you questions about them. I
thought, I'm supposed to take these books that mean a great deal
to me—I'm supposed to understand what they mean. If I ask
direct questions about them, maybe it's sacrilege.

Bellow: I'm well prepared to defend myself against these incur-
sions, if that's what they are. But there's no reason why people
shouldn't talk about books. There is a prerequisite, though, which
is that they should be deeply stirred by the books. They should
love them or hate them. But not try to convert them into . . .

Brans: Theory?

Bellow: Yes. Or chatter. There's no need to babble about these
things. They *can* be talked about. But so much of literary criticism
is babbling.

Brans: I'm not sure I understand exactly what you mean by
babbling. Do you mean using special terminology? Or talking
about little things and ignoring big ones?

Bellow: Critics often translate important books—write them
again, as it were, in the fashionable intellectual jargon. And then
the books are no longer themselves. They have been borrowed by
Culture, with a capital C. There are two things here that we must
clearly distinguish. One is the work of art with its direct effect on
people. The other is a work of art as a cultural commodity, as a
piece of society's property in Culture. In the second form, art
becomes a fertilizer for the cultivation of languages, vocabularies,
intellectual styles, ornaments, degrees, honors, prizes, and all the
rest of that. That's Culture with a capital C. That's what I'm
talking about. And this is what always happens. Our model for it is
the Christian religion, which started with faith and ended with
churches.

Brans: Are you afraid you will become a Culture object?

Bellow: I think we must all be on guard against it. I don't want to
become a support of the new clergy. Why should I? It's none of
my business!

Brans: You think sometimes that you might be drawn into writing
for these people?

Bellow: You're on the right track. The public has changed. It now
includes more people who have gone to college. Until recently
contemporary literature was not part of the curriculum. If you were

a lawyer with a good education, or an engineer, or a physician, or
a clergyman, it was assumed that you could read a novel. You didn't
need ten manuals in order to read it. There is a process of
mystification associated with this, you see.

Brans: Do you think writers are tempted to contribute deliber-
ately to this process of mystification?

Bellow: I feel no such temptation. But many modern writers do.
They reflect the rise of the intellectual level of the public. There
is a public of professional intellectuals for whom poets and novelists
perform a function. Take somebody like Joyce, especially in
Finnegans Wake. He is writing for a small public of intellectuals—of
highly skilled readers, people who know the history of modern literature and are amused by puzzles. The same thing is true of Thomas
Mann. Of Eliot. Of all the small public writers.

Brans: Is this what Stendhal called his happy few?

Bellow: The happy few in Stendhal were people of spirit and
energy and genius and passion and imagination and all the rest of
that. They weren't necessarily intellectuals.

Brans: Not the literary intelligentsia?

Bellow: In the modern sense, you see. But Joyce was trying to
please a certain kind of public, to which he himself belonged.
These were scholars, or amateur scholars—people who liked mental
games, people who would not be put off by a multitude of
references to Homer or to Vico or Thomas Aquinas, or Irish history;
and this reflects a change in the public and the writer's relation to
that public. I don't blame writers for this; I'm simply pointing to
the fact that modern art has a far larger intellectual burden than it
ever had. And at certain points it really becomes an exercise in the
history of the art itself, so that it's for people who know that
history. I'm not against an elite literature, mind you. That's not
really what I'm talking about. What I'm talking about is the
amount of modern intellectual freight in literature and painting. One
can find this agreeable, but you can't say that it is literature in the
older sense.

Brans: Which was intended for the man in the street?

Bellow: Yes, at least the novel was.

Brans: Do you see yourself, then, as writing for that man in
the street?

Bellow: I don't know him well enough to write for him in that
direct way. But I have a good deal of feeling for him. I know that
at bottom I'm just the same kind of human being. There are cultural
differences, but I know they are only that. They may not be differences of the heart. I don't like the snobbery implicit in the idea of
the "mass man" developed by Ortega, his German predecessors, and
his recent successors.

Brans: This mindless creature who goes around cultivating his
body. You don't think he exists?

Bellow: In some respects. I don't think that it fully characterizes
anyone.

Brans: I really could argue with you. What about people who go
habitually to singles bars, that sort of thing? Instant Dionysus.

Bellow: Yes, well, they are standardized in their quest for joy or
diversion. But how do we know what their souls suffer in abreac-
tion from this? We don't know. Do we really think that in their
secret human agonies over what they do, they are still standardized? We don't know that.

Brans: But surely if their sufferings are real there should be some
way of finding something—something more particular.

Bellow: It would be nice if they had a language for it. A wonderful
liberation. Unfortunately "education" and the mass media fill them
up with formulas.

Brans: You don't want to write for a literary intelligentsia. And
your books sell beautifully. Do you think of yourself as somehow
serving all of those people?

Bellow: No, I write as I do because I am what I am. I can't really
help myelf.

Brans: You're not trying to teach people how to live?

Bellow: No.

Brans: But your books seem so much as if you have the answers.
Before I met you I thought, "Here's a man who has the answers,
and if I can just ask him the right questions, then he'll give me the
right answers." And I wondered if maybe you had that sense of
yourself at all? And when you began talking about clairvoyance, I
thought that's what you meant, partly. So you don't see yourself
as a teacher of the masses.

Bellow: Not necessarily. . . . Although when I think about it, I do

believe that I have something of importance to transmit. Just how
to name it, I don't know. But I think of myself as speaking to an
inviolate part of other people, around which there is a sort of neatly
sacred perimeter, a significant space, if you like, a place where the
human being really has removed to, with all his most important
spiritual possessions. Yes, that I do think about. I'm not very clear
about it, but I don't have to be because I'm not a philosopher. All
I have to do is feel it, and that I do feel.

Brans: That you're talking to someone other than the social
being?

Bellow: Yes, I'm talking to human beings who have certain permanent attributes—that there is something in them—as in myself. I've
never doubted it. I don't think of myself as different in that way.
On the contrary, I think of myself as ordinary in many ways. But
when I say ordinary, I don't mean what people commonly mean by
ordinary. I mean something extraordinary which is in every
human being. At the moment there is no place for this extraordinary
universal possession. It's rushed out of sight by material preoccupations (which I have too), by fear, by fashion, which is the child of
fear. But I really do think that I am talking to a part of people
that I know is there and that they know is there. Though my books
may not make sense to many readers. Perhaps the sound of my
voice communicates this sense of things.

Brans: I've been curious about that. I've wondered why people
bought *Herzog* so enthusiastically, because it's hard to believe
that most people feel quite as fragmented or as confused as Herzog,
and yet the book has sold millions of copies. So evidently there is
something . . .

Bellow: I think they recognized certain things in it. The theme of
divorce, the feeling of being shut out, their humanity denied by
the arbitrary acts of those who are very close to them, evicted,
deprived of a connection that they thought they had. And in
Moses Herzog a kind of self-critical comic sense, an amused objectivity toward himself, almost amounting to courage.

Brans: The straw hat, and the striped jacket, and the whole bit?

Bellow: Yes, putting up a resistance to these crushing antagonists.
Even if it's only a comic resistance.

Brans: That's the best kind. But I don't think it is only comic.

Do you? It ends with Herzog sitting out in the sun, the flowers, the candles, the whole thing. The whole thing about grace. Do you think your life is touched with grace?

Bellow: Not exceptionally. But I think of Herzog in a different way. I think of him as a man who, in the agony of suffering, finds himself to be his own most penetrating critic. And he reexamines his life, as it were, by reenacting all the roles he took seriously. And when he has gone through all the reenactments, he's back at the original point.

Brans: That's wonderful! I never thought of that, Ok, reenactment of what?

Bellow: The professor, the son, the brother, the lover, the father, the husband, the avenger, the intellectual—all of it. It's an attempt really to divest himself of all of the personae . . .

Brans: The social selves?

Bellow: That's right. And when he has dismissed these personae, there comes a pause.

Brans: But that's grace—"Thou movest me." Or is Herzog just like a cat, accepting the life of the universe, or something?

Bellow: It's better than his trying to invent everything for himself, or accepting human inventions, the collective errors, by which he's lived. He's decided to go through a process of jettisoning or lightening. That's how I saw the book when I was writing it. And I wrote it with passion, because I believed in it with a passion. I thought, "Enough of this."

Brans: Then, is Madeleine necessary to him because she causes all these things? Is she like Proust's *madeleine,* the thing that makes you think, remember all the past—reenact the past?

Bellow: Oh, he loved her deeply. She wounded him horribly, and he is trying to live with the wound. And he's also very angry, of course, and critical.

Brans: And he's wrong about her, isn't he? I mean, she's not what he said she was, is she?

Bellow: No, she's both better and worse than he said she was. But of course he's at war and he can't be fair. But he loves her, and he loves the child, and he feels that she's replaced him with Valentine, a liar, a phony, and there's something of the phony in her, to which the phony Valentine appeals.

Brans: But he's such a loser! You know, no woman can take such a loser. At a point, you just have to get away from somebody like that.

Bellow: Well, it isn't that he's a loser. It's that he's so chaotic; no woman can stand so much disorder. It's not the losing at all, it's the chaos, and the complexity of life which would tire a woman out, just trying to follow it. This complexity is intolerable, I agree.

Brans: Right. You mean simple losing would be ok, but complicated losing not so good. But tell me about Humboldt—he's even more complex. I tried first of all to fit Humboldt into John Berryman. But of course biographically he's very close to Delmore Schwartz.

Bellow: Yes.

Brans: And I began to see that he probably wasn't either of those men exactly.

Bellow: No, he's not.

Brans: There seem to be stories about both of them in the character. The thing I remember is something about pushing the big girl downstairs that you wrote about Berryman. And that sounded like Humboldt chasing the girl through her apartment. But you're saying something about the artist and what the writer has to expect in that book.

Bellow: American society likes its artists and writers, certainly, it's proud of them, it rewards them, but it doesn't know what the hell they're all about—and there's a sort of vulgar cheerfulness in its relation to them. Some of the writers share this same vulgar cheerfulness. They make something of it, at times. Think of Allen Ginsberg's line, "America, I'm putting my queer shoulder to the wheel."

Brans: You mean writers feel responsible.

Bellow: It isn't just that they feel responsible. They feel attached. Attachment. Piety. Even when they think it awful. When Humboldt feels his talent leaving him, he begins to clown. He's putting his poet's shoulder to the wheel. We too are America's children. It's this part that Citrine finds Humboldt guilty of playing.

Brans: You mean the artist-in-residence?

Bellow: That's right, when there's a slackening of the talent, then there come all these other games that the poet invents.

Brans: Like the whole con thing about going to Princeton.

Bellow: Exactly. Or the automobile, or the farm, or the relations with women.

Brans: Which are often the things that sell books of poetry. Don't you think that's true?

Bellow: That's right. But there's something really promotional, exhibitionistic, and impure about it. And Charlie knows that, you see.

Brans: But Charlie is successful.

Bellow: Charlie is not really successful. Charlie is a man who, by having success, has excused himself from success. Charlie is like Julien Sorel in *The Red and the Black*. When he gets to the top of society, there's nothing to do but shoot Madame de Rênal and get his head cut off.

Brans: He doesn't care any more.

Bellow: Of course not.

Brans: I like that.

Bellow: That's exactly the Charlie position in the book. That's why he'd rather hang around with card players and bums and tramps.

Brans: Does he think they're more genuine?

Bellow: It isn't that he thinks they're more genuine. No, everybody's equally genuine or false. It's just he thinks they express the ludicrousness of the position.

Brans: The games are all out in the open.

Bellow: That's right.

Brans: Charlie resembles you a lot in the outward aspects. I think of a matador executing dazzling veronicas, with the cape very close to the real human body. Tell me how not to see Citrine as Bellow.

Bellow: I would have to suffer from dissociation of personality to be all these people in the books. I can't possibly be all of them. I lend a character, out of pure friendship, whatever he needs, that's all.

Brans: The amazing thing about Charlie is all the love he has, for these bums, and for the people in his past, for almost everyone.

Bellow: True. Nobody has noticed the amount of affection in that book. The critics are unaware of that sort of quality in a book.

Brans: He loves his past, in a way that seems so accurate. I can't remember anything that happened to me yesterday. Things just leave me all the time. But I can remember everything about the past. I can remember precisely a certain day in Mississippi when I was fifteen. And this is the sort of thing I think your books bring so vividly to life. I don't mean they're all recollection. I think you're creating them. But you focus on these things that seem important to me but that most people, or at least most current writers, don't care about. Do you think that somehow the ability to remember or to create memory is important for a novelist?

Bellow: In my own case these memories serve to resurrect feelings which, at the time, I didn't want to have. I had them. They were very powerful. But they were too much for me to deal with, and I covered them over with cynicism or wit or whatever. And now I realize how much emotion was invested in them, and I bring them back.

Brans: You mean in loving your family?

Bellow: Yes.

Brans: Did you feel at the same time that they were really not you, and that you were trapped in this family?

Bellow: No. I always had a great piety about my life. I always thought my life—I didn't think about it as my life when I was a kid—I thought it the most extraordinary, brilliant thing in the whole history of the universe that we should all be together. And there was so much unusable love that in the end it turned against itself and became a kind of chilliness, and for many years it stayed that way. The Marxist attitude toward the family, the modern attitude toward mothers, or fathers, or . . .

Brans: Mothers can't do any good. There's no way!

Bellow: And all the rest of it. And then I realized that I was simply fooling myself. That it had really been a feast of love for me which I couldn't persuade the others to share. They weren't aware of it in me. Mostly not. Sometimes they were.

Brans: Do you really think it would have made them uncomfortable? You say that, sometimes, in the novels. Citrine, for example, feels that Julius is uncomfortable with the love that Charlie has to give him—that it really is superfluous or shouldn't be expressed. It might be there, but it shouldn't be shown in any sort of overt way.

Bellow: Yes, because Julius has made his way in life as a tough business operator.

Brans: Why do you so often have your heroes the brothers of all those tough-minded businessmen who've made lots of money?

Bellow: Because they're all over the place. After all, I am a historian. Every novelist is a historian, a chronicler of his time. Of course I write about business types.

Brans: People making lots of money? Being successful?

Bellow: Well, it's the history of the United States, in a way. Here we sit in Dallas. Isn't it the history of Texas?

Brans: Can we talk about *Sammler*?

Bellow: Sure.

Brans: That was the first one of your books that I read. I think it came out in the *Atlantic*. As I began reading it, I was absolutely dumbfounded.

Bellow: Why?

Brans: I thought it was a real accusation. I thought I was supposed to take all this stuff about the mass man to heart.

Bellow: No, not really. I'll tell you how I saw it. There's enough European in me to be able to look at America as a foreigner.

Brans: Is that true? You really still feel close enough to Europe?

Bellow: Yes, I do, through my family. My parents were immigrants. They spoke in Russian. In 1920 their table talk was still about the Czar, the war, the Revolution.

Brans: Well, I thought *Sammler* was just a gripy old man's opinion of the world, when I first read it. Then I read it again, and I began to see that you had a distance from Sammler, and that he was not your spokesman. At least I imagined that he was far grouchier than you would have been. And I finally decided that the book was a limited affirmation of America. And that what people like Angela had was a kind of energy, a kind of creativity, that Sammler could only grudgingly recognize.

Bellow: *Sammler* would have been a better book if I had dealt openly with some of my feelings, instead of filtering them through him.

Brans: You mean everything had to come out with a kind of bias because of him?

Bellow: Not a bias in the ordinary sense. But he is a Lazarus—a man back from the dead.

Brans: You were talking earlier about these experiences, these feelings that we all have, and you think there are certain of those experiences that Sammler no longer has. Is he disenfranchised somehow?

Bellow: Well, I think he's cold, because he's known the grave.

Brans: I think *Sammler* is a wonderful book. I don't have any reservations about it. Once I discovered that Sammler wasn't the voice of God, or something, then I was comfortable enough with it. It was only when I thought that he had all the answers that I was . . .

Bellow: Oh, he doesn't have the answers. If he had had all the answers he would have been the religious man he wished to be. In reading Meister Eckhardt he was feeling his way. He was only beginning to acknowledge the first stirrings of religion.

Brans: He was terribly bound to being a human creature, in spite of all his mysticism and so forth.

Bellow: Yes, but then you see it was really a sort of an exotic report on life in the United States; it was not condemnatory.

Brans: It was misread, then.

Bellow: Of course it was misread. We started out earlier by talking about criticism. One of the troubles with criticism is that it's simply linear, if you know what I mean—sketchy. The novelist never feels he's got anything until he has it in all the density of actual experience. Then he looks at a piece of criticism, and all he sees is the single outline of thought. It's not the same thing. And you can't deal with a phenomenon that way. So he never really trusts criticism, because it lacks the essential density.

Brans: Well, the critic has to make a point. He has to take a line, and then he has to develop the line. I haven't written much, but from what I've written I know that you feel all these things rushing in upon you from the book, and yet you can't, for your own sanity's sake, try to say all there is to say about the book, and what you finally want to keep saying is, "Go read it. Go read this novel, and you'll see what I mean."

Bellow: Or, "Don't go read it."

Brans: Do you think of yourself as a survivor, like Sammler or Citrine?

Bellow: No, I think of myself as horribly deprived of people whom I loved and who are dead.

Brans: You know, I really loved John Berryman. I never even knew him, but I believed in him, in Henry. I hate to face what he became at the end. But you must have known that bad side of Berryman. I'm sure he called you late at night, and all that. . . . the terrors.

Bellow: I know, but he was full of feeling. . . . He was a real man. John and I were very close in spirit as writers, I think. He knew it, and we would sometimes talk about it. He wrote a little piece once after *The Adventures of Augie March* came out, in which he said that this book had cleared the way for him to do certain things. Maybe it was so. But he loved literature. That is rare even among writers. John gave himself to it, heart and soul.

Brans: Why was he such a disaster, though? Why did his life have to be such chaos? Your life is not like that. You've controlled your life.

Bellow: Yes, I know. Oh, I didn't have to face the kinds of things he faced—the suicide of a father—coming out on the porch and seeing his dead father in the morning.

Brans: Don't you think at a certain point you just grow out of that? Or you move away from that? You take control of yourself.

Bellow: Well, he lacked control.

Brans: But in his poetry he had fine control.

Bellow: Yes, in his poetry he had the control. In his life there was none at all. Then because he decayed physically he knew he must die soon. He was really sick. He had no liver any more, he lacked muscular coordination. He was getting dirty. And it was getting to be pretty pukey. And he knew it. His pride suffered from it. And he probably said, well, enough. He was a derelict, in hospitals. And he just stopped it.

Brans: It seemed to me a deprivation for the rest of us that he should do that. I felt really angry because he'd do it.

Bellow: Well, he thought he was on the wagon, and he thought he was straight with his wife, and he thought he was out of the woods, and all of that Boy Scout optimism of somebody who feels, "At

last, I'm on the right path." And then he went off completely, got
drunk again—horribly drunk. Disappeared for days, and found
himself in bed with some strange girl.

Brans: But you see, I don't buy this "found himself" thing: I
mean, he got there. He did it.

Bellow: Yes, but in disgust with himself. Of course he did it. He
had no further use for himself. And I believe he thought he didn't
want to write, that he had done it all.

Brans: The death of the poet. Like Humboldt. But Rinaldo
Cantabile survives. Now there's a name! I can't say it without
rejoicing that you thought of it. Why a musical name for a thug?

Bellow: Well, I know the common people in Chicago; the bums,
or whatever you like, in Chicago all have these unfathomed
cultural and intellectual ambitions, and they don't know what to do
about them really. They bring the greatest enthusiasm and devotion to these things, but at the same time they're clumsy, stupid,
arrogant, ambitious.

Brans: You mean like Rinaldo, who thinks he's going for the big
time, and then somehow it all. . . . I never have enjoyed anything
as much as when Citrine bests him. It was so marvelous. I was so
afraid that somehow he was going to be in service to Rinaldo
forever.

Bellow: Oh, no.

Brans: And Rinaldo really gets put down. But he's a splendid
character. Tell me, you're a daring writer: why haven't you ever
used a modern woman as your protagonist? I don't agree with some
of your critics who say that you don't understand women, and
that you have only a Schopenhauerean attitude toward women.

Bellow: Well, I don't. No, unfortunately I just struck the women's
movement at a bad time.

Brans: But why haven't you ever written from the point of view
of a woman? Why do you always have to have Madeleine as
interpreted by Herzog, and Renata as interpreted by Citrine?

Bellow: Well, I sometimes think of doing it; I just never got
around to it. I was working out problems that couldn't be worked
out that way. The only thing I ever wrote about a woman directly
was a story called "Leaving the Yellow House." About Hattie. I

loved her. But of course you could say she's an older woman. She's
an old lady.

Brans: But your women do seem to be around mostly just to
stick on band-aids at opportune times, or they leave when things
get rough. There's this attitude toward women. I think it's because
the women always are filtered, or falsified, through the minds of
the heroes.

Bellow: Maybe. But I thought there were some rather nice women
in this last book. I thought Demmie Vonghel was an awfully
nice woman.

Brans: Oh, she's fine. I loved Demmie.

Bellow: She's a real sort of American—you know—young lady.

Brans: But she dies. And then there's Renata. I imagine all the
men who talk to you about your books like Renata. I really don't
like Renata very much.

Bellow: Well, Renata is a delight. She's not supposed to be a
marvelous "woman," only a grand female.

Brans: What was all this stuff about her marrying death—what's
his name? Flonzaley? Why didn't Citrine get the girl? I think
Citrine should—it's American for Citrine to get the girl.

Bellow: I think it's American for a swinging girl like that to make
the best match she can.

Brans: With a mortician?

Bellow: Oh, well, that's just poking fun at poor Charlie, not at
Renata. I was not poking fun at Renata.

Brans: I like to think that Demmie is what you really think
women are. And Renata is just a sort of . . .

Bellow: Renata is the nympholeptic dream of elderly gents like
Charlie Citrine, who still want to be accepted as virile and
desirable, as a wonderful man for a beautiful woman to have.

Brans: Why couldn't you have told the story of Charlie Citrine,
say, from Demmie's point of view? I'm just asking that as a possibility. Could Demmie have told that story?

Bellow: Yes, she could. I could have done it, too.

Brans: Yes, she's a fully realized character. You could have
talked from her. There are passages in there where she speaks
. . . You know, she has the wonderful ability just suddenly to haul
off and knock Charlie in the chops.

Bellow: Yes.

Brans: But you've never tried this, really?

Bellow: No, I think I could. I know I could, as a matter of fact. All this stuff about my prejudices is just nonsense. I probably have certain prejudices. I mean, never believe what a man says about his own prejudices. But he doesn't know. That's why they're prejudices. But . . . I do have the kindliest, closest feelings to certain women. I always have had, and it just hasn't come out that way, that's all.

Brans: I think it has come out that way. I really think that people who read your books with any attention know that. It's just that you do always have this kind of Schopenhauerean female figure, standing there in all of her curves.

Bellow: Take somebody like Ramona in *Herzog*. Now Ramona is nice, an awfully nice girl. She just happens to be realistically portrayed, and this is what people can't take. She is the good-hearted (and she is good-hearted), giving, charitable, but ideological female. She is an ideologist. She makes speeches. She thinks she knows what's best for Moses.

Brans: But it seems that at the end of the book he's pretty much disposed toward her point of view. He's waiting for her, after all.

Bellow: He's going to forgive her all this ideological stuff. It is a matter of forgiving, because he has no use for it. He's gotten rid of his own. And why should he consent to listen to hers?

Brans: But her ideology is all about love, and renewing the spirit through the flesh.

Bellow: He doesn't believe that!

Brans: He doesn't? At all? Well, then he really doesn't find the solution. He's just sort of at a way station, is that the idea?

Bellow: Well, he's come to a point of rest, which is saying a lot for anybody these days.

Brans: But it won't last.

Bellow: No, he's going to have to assume roles again, and deal with people again. He's just come to a well-earned interregnum. Don't grudge poor Moses *that*.

Brans: Do you equate those two things? Assuming roles and seeing people?

Bellow: Well, you have to deal with them. You have to make allowances for them. You have to make allowances for their vanities and their weaknesses and so on, even though at bottom they're really ok. But there are so many vain struggles, and there's so much wrangling, and so much nonsense. Most of what passes between human beings, except in their finest moments, is nonsensical. And it gets more nonsensical all the time. The more books we read about conduct, self-regulation . . .

Brans: What books?

Bellow: I'm thinking about those deep books, those heavy works which tell you what to do at every moment of your life. Americans seem to be unable to live without prescriptions.

Free to Feel: Conversation with Saul Bellow

Maggie Simmons / 1979

From *Quest*, February 1979, 31–35.

Dickens once said that of all his characters his favorite "child" was David Copperfield. Do you feel a special closeness to any of your own characters?

I am attached to certain of my characters, especially those who set me free—let me out of jail. But I've been writing for so many years, and have gone through so many changes, that it's as if another person had created them. Perhaps I should say found them. They were found rather than made. But the ones that warm my heart are those that liberated me, somehow.

What restraints did you feel you had to overcome?

With my first two books [*Dangling Man* and *The Victim*], I was still learning, establishing my credentials, proving that a young man from Chicago had a right to claim the world's attention. So I was restrained, controlled, demonstrating that I could write "good." I didn't understand that if you came from the streets of Chicago, to write "good" was to write in a foreign language. So *Dangling Man* was my M.A. and *The Victim* my Ph.D.

What did you consider your first breakthrough?

The idea of writing *Augie March* fired me up. I was in Paris when it came to me, and I had been sinking into a proper depression because I was writing another proper book. I decided to let other people write the proper books. I had a wild time with the first half of *Augie;* I was stirred to the depths. Later, I recoiled from my own excesses. There were things in the depths I wasn't glad to see.

How did that affect your work?

In my next book, *Seize the Day,* I was again under good control. But even in *Seize the Day,* the liberating effects of *Augie* are apparent to me. It isn't Tommy Wilhelm, the sentimental Tommy, that

interests me but that crook and phony, Dr. Tamkin. Like most
phony phonies, he is always somewhere near the truth. When
Tamkin lectures Tommy, he has Tommy forever saying "True,
true" under his breath. But Tamkin's truths aren't really true.

So, in writing Seize the Day *you were solving a more difficult
problem than in* Augie March?
I can't say that I was solving any problems, only that I was trying
to escape from my limitations and the limitations of Augie. He is
such a blue-eyed *ingenu* and leads *such* a charmed life. Too much
the Sherwood Anderson sort of thing: "Gee whiz, what wonderful
people, what a mysterious world!" All wrong!

Who else did you feel was a liberating character?
I got a stupendous break with *Henderson the Rain King*. That
man was talking through his hat, and therefore could say whatever
he pleased. And he turned out to be a considerable rhetorician. One
of the limitations of realistic writing is that its heroes and heroines
can't sing out. They have to talk in the usual grudging, mutilated
way. The simple subject-predicate singsong.

*Can a liberating character also be an instrument for self-crit-
icism?*
Well, it was liberating to write *Herzog*. He said wonderfully
disrespectful and negative things about a class of people toward
whom I had always been deferential—the intellectuals. Like most
American writers, I felt an oppressive responsibility, that of
defending eggheads from *Boobus americanus,* the Philistine enemy.
But I am never comfortable with any party line. Thus, Herzog the
intellectual says, "I rose from humble origins to total disaster." It
dawned on Herzog, one glorious morning, that the intellectuals
themselves often proved on close examination to be Philistines. A
new variety.

Soon after Herzog, *you wrote your first play,* The Last Analysis,
*which has a comic hero named Bummidge. What new direction
did Bummidge allow you to pursue?*
The play is mostly silliness. But I thought that a rhetorical play
might be of interest. Most of our playwrights write simple declarative

sentences. Give an actor a sentence with a subordinate clause and it kills him. He gets a hernia trying to heave it across the lights.

A collection of your stories, Mosby's Memoirs, *came out in 1968. Do any of them have special significance in your development as a writer?*

I wrote *The Old System* with all the stops out. All that family feeling. It's supposed to be old hat. What's so great about the new hat?

Perhaps you could relate all this more explicitly to the story. In The Old System, *Dr. Braun reflects on the fat Tina's vengeful treatment of her brother Isaac, especially when she upbraids him as she lies on her deathbed. Braun says that humans exploit such passions, make an uproar, create a "crude circus of feelings." But then he says that with the weeping, the sorrow, comes an "intimation of understanding . . . a promise that mankind might . . . through its divine gift, comprehend why it lived." Isn't there a contradiction here in what you're saying about the expression of feelings?*

Why worry about contradiction? You'll never write about feelings if you do. As for the idea of exploitation—well, that's a fairly common idea, and you find it among the purest of pure literary intellectuals in the 20th century. Paul Valéry, for instance, asks, in effect, "What's so precious about tears? Why weep or cause others to weep? Why need writers and readers have these outbursts?" But is feeling nothing but self-indulgence? What about William Blake's belief that a tear is "an intellectual thing"?

The superintellectuals of the 20th century pride themselves on their coldness and their hardness—like Brecht the Bolshevik—their achievement in raising themselves above bourgeois morality. But that, too, is a kind of bunk. The real problem is that people now don't lead a morally expressive life. The coldness and hardness of a Valéry are directed against theatrical emotions which have been deader than nails for a century. Now we are all correct, *faute de mieux,* and expect to be congratulated for it. And it isn't even correctness, but rather the absence of a moral foundation and the atrophy of feeling.

When people release emotion, they so often feel like impostors.

By restraining themselves, they claim credit for a barren kind of honesty. In modern literature, there are not many clean and beautiful bursts of emotion or moral power. But, of course, if anyone were to let rip in the *King Lear* style, readers would feel as uncomfortable as if one were to say "Forsooth" to them. In *Humboldt's Gift,* when Citrine is beaten and abused in court, he has an impulse to speak out indignantly—citing principles, justice. But he checks himself because he realizes that it would only make matters worse for him. Nothing is gained by letting yourself go among people who hate such letting go. But in a family situation such as the one in *The Old System,* people do sound off. That is why the story is called *The Old System.* Within the family, the old dramas can be played out, and under all the emotional clamor there is a serious moral and emotional meaning.

Was Mr. Sammler's Planet *another kind of a landmark for you?*

Yes, in that I allowed myself to deal with a world subject and to do it seriously. In *Herzog,* I was still covering myself with wit, lest I be accused of pretentiousness.

Your latest novel is Humboldt's Gift. *Is it too soon for you to assess what you've learned from living with its fictional characters?*

I was peculiarly attached to Humboldt himself, to the character. But writing for me is no longer the way to liberation. I am too old. By now, I either am or am not liberated. What concerns me is if I am capable of bringing out the deepest sense I have of those about whom I write—about the spirit in them. This may not be readily apparent in *Humboldt's Gift,* because it is a funny book. I can't quite cure myself of the habit of writing funny books. Sometimes on fatal subjects. *Humboldt* is funny, I think, but it's also a death-book. I was, of course, joking about Renata and the undertaker she marries, but when Charlie tries to communicate with the dead, I don't make fun of him.

In a sense, then, Humboldt's Gift *provided the most important release, since in that book you dealt head-on with the final issues: death and the spirit's survival.*

Yes, and we modern writers are not really prepared to deal with these ultimate questions, and this is one reason why literature has been forced back, and has allowed itself to be forced back, into trivialities. A great misfortune. For once you have decided to become a writer of fiction, you have assumed responsibility even as a craftsman to determine whether you are really obliged to accept such cruel restrictions of subject, whether you are going to go on picturing reality as your trade has defined it for you. These trade definitions (every writer knows what I mean) make dull reading, I tell you that. I would rather be a computer programmer than operate in this way.

Is the process of liberation or self-discovery possible only through art?
Why, no. It should be possible through religion, metaphysics, hard thinking, independence of spirit. In fact, I don't see how we can do without these now that we've come to the end of the line—I refer to the literary line.

What in your own writing gives you satisfaction?
I'm happy when the revisions are big. I'm not speaking of stylistic revisions, but of revisions in my own understanding. This is what matters now, this is everyone's greatest need. Exceptional things must be attempted if the game is to be worth the candle.

What are these "exceptional things"?
You need only look at the dehumanization of the 20th century to answer that for yourself.

You seem to feel, then, that readers and writers fail to grasp the central issues of literature. Why is this?
Writers generally represent the reality about them quite faithfully, like it or not, pleasant or unpleasant. But the representation is also limited by their own values and interests—psychological, imaginative, metaphysical, professional. Writers of fiction will show you what is out there in the world. They are historians, and they have no choice. But with the first words of their story they have decided, they have chosen, the limits within which they will write, and it's these limits that we have to reexamine. Art has always drawn a line between what is visible and what is not, but in the past, artists ventured farther than their eyes could see. Now we stand immobi-

lized on the hither side of that line. We say we are prevented from
crossing by our "rational" or "critical" or "scientific" standards.
But if these standards are true—true, final, and eternal—we had
better forget about the arts. For more than a century now, poets
have sat on the hither side and sighed in longing for the gorgeous
kingdoms beyond. Think of T. S. Eliot, so cozy and so heartbro-
ken in the modern world.

*Do you think that in your own fiction you are going against
the stream?*
Yes. I am going against the stream. That's not an attitude.
Attitudes are foolishness. It's just that there's no use in doing
anything else, is there? I blame myself for not having gone hard
enough against it, and if I live I shall go harder.

Humor has been a major device in your fiction—certainly in
Henderson the Rain King, *but also in the later novels. Does it
come easy to you?*
Well, yes, I don't know what to do about it. There it is. You open
the funny box: Is it a hope chest or a coffin?

*In your Nobel lecture in 1976, you disputed the French novelist
Robbe-Grillet's position that the novel of characters is obsolete,
and you affirmed your own belief in the power of human beings,
their individuality, spirit, and solidarity. Why did you choose this
as your central theme?*
I suppose that a Nobel Prize tempts one into sententiousness, but
I thought that what I was saying was obviously true. One can
accept the historical account, the account which has been traditional, of the dwindling of the human being, the atrophy of his
significance, etc., etc., *ad nauseam,* or one can dismiss all of those
cultural textbook ideas and look for oneself at what is there.
When I published my second novel, *The Victim,* I confessed to
friends that it was something like a Ph.D. thesis. Now, literature
has no room for Ph.D. theses, but in Robbe-Grillet and other
intellectual writers, I see little more than high-minded Ph.D.
exercises. No ideological supervisor can define our subjects for us,
or tell us that there are persistent intimations or strongly rooted
feelings which we must, for "historical reasons," set aside. I have

been accused of being vague about certain unconscious sources
of inspiration, simply invoking them in a blah-blah manner. But
when I speak of unconscious sources, I am not thinking of any
Freudian or Jungian unconscious, but of a much-neglected metaphysical unconscious.

I am suggesting that we receive epistemological guidance of which
we are unaware and that we actually have infinitely deeper and
better ways of knowing than those we've been "educated" in. We
think we understand what we see about us, and we are, at the
conscious level, persuaded that we can understand our own behavior and that of others if we apply the "scientific" rules recom-
mended by rational teaching. But if we really tried to live by this
teaching, life would be even more absurd than it is.

Luckily for all of us, we work from deeper motives, impulses of
which we are not conscious. Among these are the moral impulses.
I have seen "cynical" men doing their duty by their children, their
wives, their friends. They reject a notion like "duty." They find
no visible conscious ground for it. But they *do* it. You see hard
drinkers who hate their jobs and yet continue to provide, and you
ask yourself how these near alcoholics explain to themselves their
solicitude for their small daughters. The human understructure is
much larger than any measure our culture gives us. Our meager
measures get us nowhere.

*In the same speech you describe Conrad as a writer who applied
the larger, truer measure to characters in his fiction. Who else do
you think belongs in that class?*

Proust, for one. He was not a man who worked in a closed
system. He did not look to "culture" for absolute guidance. He
was sensitive to those "unknown" human qualities. Joyce, on the
other hand, though a writer of great genius, seemed to have made
up his mind to accept the formulas by which we now live—advanced
formulas, but nevertheless formulas. In him a "modern consciousness" dissolves everything into itself.

*You seem to feel a great kinship with certain writers of the past.
Among the works of these authors, are there certain characters
you've always had a special affection for?*

Yes, ranging from Sairey Gamp in Dickens's *Martin Chuzzlewit*

to Odysseus, until the moment when he kills all the suitors and
hangs the girls—there he puts me off. And then there's Tolstoy.
Karenin is a marvelous character. Especially when he tries to stand
up to his humiliation. . . . What are you doing to me with these questions!

Which contemporary writers do you admire?
Well, Marquez is a wonderful writer. He certainly knows what
it's about. But when the chips are down, he's betting on some
kind of politics. Then there is the Australian novelist Christina
Stead, who is *really* marvelous. She gropes here, she gropes there,
she introduces this subject and that subject, seems to talk to no
purpose—talk and talk! Then suddenly, with a wild outburst, she
understands something. A discovery has been made. And there is
John Cheever, Wright Morris. There are many.

*Could you talk about a character from one of Christina Stead's
books whom you find especially appealing?*
I love the heroine of *The Little Hotel.* She's living with an
impossible "respectable" man who won't marry her—he's using
up her money—but she's faithful to him and good to everyone.
She's straight and takes an immense amount of abuse. She's left
at loose ends, finally, with nothing to show for herself but her
generous acts toward the crazy people around the hotel. She's a
wonderful lady—so quietly human among all the small monsters.

*You have said publicly that there are certain cultural trends
you're opposed to. What specific ones?*
That's a *Jaws* question. I can't open my mouth wide enough.
Shall we stick to literature? I object to the substitution of analysis
for imagination. Writers are trying to please an intellectual public—
have themselves become intellectuals. And this new class, so
happy with itself, is not really pleased with imagination. You pick
up a magazine like *Encounter* or *Commentary* or any of a multitude
of journals; you are impressed by the training and the brains of
many of the contributors; you are *de*pressed by their lack of style,
their jargoning, by their inability to make an argument clearly and
simply. You are soon driven to conclude that they reject the rule of
imagination and that there is no way for imagination to please them.

And they make a terrifying clatter. A large imaginative framework would create a community for them, give them points of reference, calm their nerves.

You've been talking about trends in literature. What larger cultural movements do you feel are wrongheaded?
A wonderful invitation to say what other writers are saying, and join the happy platitudinous throng. All right, we have a miniculture of highly specialized professionals. Some of them are wonderfully intelligent, but almost all of them are, in the Matthew Arnold term, Philistines.

What is the solution for the specialists?
I have no solutions for specialists. Those with hearts can search them, for starters. And it would be nice if they were just a little less pleased with themselves. I have heard great biologists talking politics. I would rather listen to a call girl taking the Elks on a nature walk.

Aren't you applying somewhat unrealistic standards?
I sure am.

Do you feel a special responsibility to speak out on these issues?
We are all special, and our main responsibility is not to throw the word "responsibility" about recklessly. I am dejected when I see what the free societies of the West are doing to themselves—when I see what occupies their minds. I read the books. I look at the pictures, and I think, is that all we can do? We're sunk if we can't do better.

What do you consider a worthwhile accomplishment?
I see you insist on keeping me honest. Or serious. Or even solemn. Here's one worthwhile accomplishment. Almost every man has been educated to think himself an object among objects in an object world. It would be worthwhile to induce him to see himself as a true subject, not some 98¢ worth of minerals which will disappear forever into a $1,500 coffin.

You have said that art can only give us glimpses of this essence of what in Conrad's words is fundamental and enduring. Are the glimpses at least longer for you now?

My mind at the moment is a mass of transitions. I'm in the midst of multiple revisions. Almost everything that I used to consider stable in life I now doubt. And much that I doubted before now seems to me stable. All I can report at this moment is that I'm hard at work and that the results may appear one of these days. It's interesting that you should mention Conrad—he was convinced that the reality behind appearances was unknowable, and that the best a man could do was to work devoutly at his trade. Not as simple as it sounds. With Conrad it is a great and bitter idea. I used to subscribe to it wholeheartedly—behind the beauty of the appearances is the unknowable.

Here again is the line to which I referred earlier. For some centuries, we have stood on the hither side, and sent only our immortal longings across the line. Modern literature has not dealt confidently with the intimations of the far side. And in recent years, the West has given up on this almost completely. In Eastern Europe, people still talk about a spiritual life and tell us that we are in decline because we have neglected it, and that we cannot lead the rest of mankind because we haven't got it. Well, it is fairly certain that we in the West haven't got it. But you can't call upon anyone to *have* it. To exhort people to have a spiritual life is at best futile, and at worst hokum. You can only look more deeply into the world and into yourself.

Is there another way to make an honest start? I think not. A writer would be a fool to tell anyone in advance what he intends to accomplish in this respect. He had better keep his mouth shut until he has a result to announce. And then he should announce it, not in a proclamation, but in some imaginative work. Anything else is public relations. Or politics. I should say both PR and politics, for the two have merged into a single monster.

The Quintessential Chicago Writer

Steve Neal / 1979

From *Chicago Tribune Magazine*, 6 September 1979, 14–16, 18–19, 22, 24. © 1979 by Chicago Tribune Company. All rights reserved. Reprinted by permission.

It is a bright summer afternoon at the University of Chicago, and the leaded glass windows sparkle in the Gothic towers along the Midway.

In his fifth-floor office, Saul Bellow is wearing slacks and a blue golf shirt. He is a slightly built man with expressive, heavy-lidded eyes, well-chiseled features, and white hair, and he projects the aura of a literary person. The small room is dominated by tall metal bookcases with foreign language editions of his works, a set of leatherbound Coleridge, a multi-volume history of Jewish literature, and a miscellany of other books.

He is an intensely private man who shuns the talk-show circuit and the trappings of celebrity.

At age 64, Bellow is recognized as America's master storyteller, a superb craftsman, one of the most gifted novelists of his generation. He has been honored—the first American writer since Steinbeck to receive the Nobel Prize. At the same time, he is a commercial property whose books are best-sellers and book-club selections.

In novel after novel he has returned to the slums and ethnic neighborhoods of Chicago, and he is now writing a nonfiction book on the city that has been home for most of his life. "I thought it was time, after so many years in Chicago, to put down my ideas and feelings about it," says Bellow, "partly my own recollections of the '20s, '30s, and part of the '40s, and the book will contain some comparisons between the old Chicago and the new."

From *Dangling Man,* his first novel, through *To Jerusalem and Back,* his most recent book, Chicago has been the setting for some of Bellow's most memorable prose. A native of Canada,

Bellow moved to Chicago when he was 9 years old. "I grew up there and consider myself a Chicagoan, out and out," he once said.

As a youngster he lived in the vibrant, multi-ethnic neighborhood of Humboldt Park, and he has drawn heavily from those formative years. His Chicago book began as an affectionate tribute to the old Chicago, but it soon evolved into a more ambitious project.

"When I set about this task," he says, "I was confident I knew the city. I soon learned how little I knew of contemporary Chicago. So much of what I thought was my knowledge of the city turned out to be inapplicable to present conditions. You have to look very closely to find the Chicago of the '20s and '30s."

He laments the passing of ethnic Chicago, the throbbing immigrant neighborhoods that gave the city a special vitality. "Chicago was a collection of small towns—German, Irish, Polish, Italian, Jewish, Czech," he says. "Where these small communities survive, they survive on a reduced scale. The suburbs have drained so much of the old Chicago. And there have been generational changes. The descendants of immigrants have given up the old trades and occupations. They have experienced what people like to call upward mobility. In the old neighborhoods, there were cabinet makers, cobblers, pastry cooks, tinsmiths, locksmiths, and blacksmiths. I doubt that many people now follow these occupations in the Old Country. Technology has put them out of business everywhere. Those locksmiths, pastry bakers, and printers of the old days have vanished."

Bellow's present neighborhood is Rogers Park, where he lives with his fourth wife, Alexandra, a Northwestern mathematics professor, in a fashionable apartment on Sheridan Road. "It's nothing like a Chicago neighborhood of the old days," he says. "What you have on the North Side is a fringe of high-rises and people in a state of semi-siege, especially the elderly, for whom shopping or simply getting about presents difficulties. Last winter during the blizzards I saw very old people trying to make their way from Sheridan Road to the shops on Broadway. Some used aluminum-frame-walkers while trying to manage their bundles. Many of them were quite frightened at having to venture out. They walked in mid-street."

Born in Lachine, Quebec, in 1915, Bellow was the youngest of four children. Until he was 9 years old, he lived in an old and impoverished Jewish neighborhood of Montreal.

As a youngster he learned four languages—English, Hebrew, Yiddish, and French—and, when he came to Chicago, quickly discovered the city's libraries and the works of Mark Twain, Poe, Dreiser, and Sherwood Anderson.

From boyhood his ambition was to make his mark as a famous writer. To school chums he confided titles of books he one day planned to write. At the Mission House in Humboldt Park, he read his work aloud to kids from the neighborhood. At the same time, Bellow was a determined athlete—a runner on the track team, swimmer, and tennis player.

"I used to go often to the Humboldt Park branch of the Chicago Public Library," he says. "It was located in a storefront on North Avenue and, later, in a storefront on California Avenue facing the park. I would combine my library visits with activities in the Association House on North Avenue, where kids of my neighborhood played basketball. So I would carry my Sherwood Anderson to the Association House, put it in my locker, then read it as I walked home.

"I was a determined athlete, but not outstanding. I was not in a class with Julius Echeles, now a criminal lawyer, who was the school's (Tuley High) basketball star. 'Lucky' was his nickname. I'd been a sickly child and was determined in adolescence not to be a convalescent adolescent. And I drove myself hard. Characteristically, I read a great deal about body building. I studied physical development books like *How to Get Strong and How to Stay So*. From the great Walter Camp I learned to carry scuttles filled with coal, holding them out at arm's length."

Bellow graduated from Tuley in 1933 and entered the University of Chicago, where he found himself restless and confined in what he termed "the dense atmosphere of learning, of cultural effort." In 1935, he transferred to Northwestern University, studying anthropology and sociology, and graduating with honors two years later. He wanted to become a graduate student in English literature but the dean of Northwestern's English department told him that it would be unwise because anti-Semitism might thwart his career.

Instead, Bellow went to the University of Wisconsin and studied anthropology but found it less than compelling. "Every time I worked on my thesis, it turned out to be a story," he said. "I disappeared for the Christmas holidays, and I never came back."

For a time he worked for the New Deal's WPA Writers Project, writing short biographies of Midwestern novelists. It was one of the most unusual cultural aid programs ever launched by a government, a massive project that gave jobs to hundreds of writers, poets, playwrights, masters and hacks, radicals and right-wingers. Among the WPA writers were John Cheever, Nelson Algren, Loren Eiseley, Richard Wright, and Ralph Ellison, and they produced hundreds of books and pamphlets including the celebrated state guide series. "We adored the project, all of us," Bellow wrote in a 1969 letter. "This was in the days before gratitude became obsolete. We had never expected anyone to have any use whatsoever for us. With no grand illusions about Roosevelt and Harry Hopkins, I believe they behaved decently and imaginatively for men without culture—which is what politicians necessarily are."

As a struggling young writer, Bellow had looked forward to making friendships with such published novelists as Nelson Algren and Jack Conroy. It didn't happen. "I rather looked up to them," said Bellow, "and they rather looked down on me."

In Depression Chicago, Bellow did his writing on yellow sheets from the five and dime. "I became attached to this coarse, yellow paper which caught the tip of your pen and absorbed too much ink," he said later. "It was used by the young men and women in Chicago who carried rolls of manuscripts in their pockets and read aloud to one another in hall bedrooms or at Thompson's or Pixley's cafeterias."

Bellow taught for several years at Pestalozzi-Froebel Teachers College and then worked on the Encyclopaedia Britannica's "Great Books" project.

In the early 1940s Bellow sensed that he was on the threshold of a writing career. He went to New York and mixed with such gifted young artists as poet Delmore Schwartz and critic Alfred Kazin. Bellow struck Kazin as witty, cultivated, supremely confident, a writer with a sense of destiny. "Bellow was the first writer of my generation," said Kazin, "who talked of Lawrence and Joyce,

Hemingway and Fitzgerald, not as books in the library but as fellow operators in the same business."

Bellow served in the Merchant Marine during World War II and wrote what would become his first published novel, *Dangling Man*. It was a remarkable book, a journal of a young Chicago man who quits his job, expecting to be drafted, but is left dangling for nearly a year. It was a powerful document, often moving, and it captured the tensions and anxieties of wartime America.

Dangling Man served notice that Bellow was a somebody, a talent to be reckoned with, a young artist of extraordinary promise. Edmund Wilson, the *New Yorker*'s renowned critic, called it a wonderful book, "one of the most honest pieces of testimony on the psychology of a whole generation who have grown up during the Depression and the war."

Soon afterward, Bellow joined *Time* magazine as a film critic. "I was young, inexperienced, and tired of knocking about," he recalled. It was a short-lived career. On Bellow's second day, *Time* senior editor Whittaker Chambers, who would win notoriety as Alger Hiss' accuser, asked what Bellow thought of Wordsworth. "What does that have to do with film reviewing?" asked Bellow. When Chambers demanded an answer, Bellow said that Wordsworth was a romantic poet. Chambers said, "There's no place for you in this organization." So Bellow went back to writing books.

Bellow's second novel, *The Victim,* came in 1947 and was also well received, but he was uncomfortable with the form. "I labored and tried to make it letter perfect," he said in a *Paris Review* interview. "In writing *The Victim* I accepted a Flaubertian standard. Not a bad standard, to be sure, but one which, in the end, I found repressive—repressive because of the circumstances of my life and because of my upbringing in Chicago as the son of immigrants. . . . A writer should be able to express himself easily, naturally, copiously in a form which frees his mind, his energies."

In his next book, Bellow chose to write directly of his own experience, of the old neighborhood, and the result was nothing less than a classic, *The Adventures of Augie March,* a long, crowded, picaresque novel that captured Jewish Chicago with a richness reminiscent of James Farrell's portrait of Irish Chicago.

"The great pleasure of the book was that it came easily," said
Bellow. "All I had to do was to be there with buckets to catch it."

Bellow started the novel in Paris and Rome while on a Guggenheim fellowship. Augie, Bellow's protagonist, the salesman, thief,
union organizer, merchant seaman, and genuine character, was
based on a kid from Humboldt Park. "When I was in Paris in the
'40s, I vividly remembered a boy who had been my playmate,"
says Bellow. "He came of just such a family as I described. I
hadn't seen him in 25 years, so the novel was a speculative biography."

His snapshots of Chicago were fresh and descriptive. "It is a city
with the bloody-rinded Saturday gloom of wind-borne ash, and
blackened forms of five-story buildings rising up to a blind Northern
dimness from the Christmas blaze of shops." He wrote with
verve of poolrooms and clipjoints and City Hall.

"Years ago, I found it was much better to write a book about
Chicago while living in Paris," Bellow says. "From abroad, the
hometown seemed a very exotic place."

Augie March earned Bellow the first of three National Book
Awards, and it made his reputation as a literary heavyweight.

Few major American writers have managed to cope with such
charmed success. When an early book is widely acclaimed, some
writers find it impossible to live up to the standard. Scott Fitzgerald
and Thomas Wolfe lost their grip, cracked up, and died years before
their time. Ernest Hemingway became so consumed by his macho
image that he committed suicide. Others, like Sinclair Lewis and
Norman Mailer, turned to producing potboilers, cashing in on
their names.

By contrast, Bellow's success has grown with each novel. He has
the longest hitting streak in American letters, an unbroken string
of first-rate books.

A 1965 Book Week poll of novelists and critics found Bellow to
have written the "most distinguished fiction of the 1945–1965
period." In the same poll, three of Bellow's books were voted
among the six "best" novels of the post-war years.

When the *Philadelphia Inquirer* recently polled readers on the
American author whose works would be read into the next century, Bellow was an overwhelming winner.

Bellow's work has staying power, for he is recognized as a serious artist with a great deal to say and, at the same time, an engaging and exciting writer. He has given us painfully moving tragedy in *The Victim* and *Seize the Day*, where the West side of New York is the setting for the fall of Tommy Wilhelm, one of Bellow's most memorable losers. He has also written very funny comedy in *Henderson the Rain King, Herzog,* and *Humboldt's Gift,* and these books are his special favorites.

In his view comedy is the bright hope of American fiction, for he contends that it is difficult for American writers to grasp the nuances and subtleties of tragedy.

"I think people in America have been spared the worst of the 20th Century," he says. "They didn't know wars as other countries knew them. They were spared the experience of totalitarianism. Even the least fortunate Americans can scarcely be compared with the Latin American or Asian poor. So either the gods have spared us or they have shown their contempt for us.

"We have not seen the worst of extremism, and this has made us less aware of what reality can be—in the way of cruelty, sadism, forced labor, mass murder. We American writers can hardly expect to compete with those who have known the worst of war in their own cities, or who have been condemned to slave labor camps.

"I think we are intimidated by those who have seen human life at its worst. But perhaps we can do in the realm of comedy what we are unable to do in the realm of terror. Totalitarianism, extremism, turn us away from the middle range of human experience and make us intolerant of life as most people know and always have known it."

In his novels, Bellow draws heavily on experiences, including some very personal ones. Herzog, for example, was twice divorced and suffered in relationships with women. Bellow went through three divorces, including a long, nasty court fight over alimony with his third wife, Susan. He is the father of three sons by his first three marriages and remains close to them.

Bellow is a city man. He plays handball at a downtown club. He is a devoted fan of the Chicago Art Institute. He is a keen observer of the local political scene. He is not, however, much of a

sports fan. A friend says that Bellow enjoys watching a game for a
few minutes to pick up color but gets bored.

In the summer he prefers more rustic surroundings, a place of
learned retreat where he can work without distraction. This
summer he and Alexandra stayed at a country home in Vermont.

Bellow's best writing is marked by its attachment to the urban
environment, particularly Chicago. He came of age during Chicago's
literary renaissance, when such writers as Dreiser, Sherwood
Anderson, and Carl Sandburg brought the city special distinction.
"When the '20s ended, so did the era of Dreiser, Anderson, Masters, Hecht, and all the rest," says Bellow. "The East drew most
of them away from Chicago, and Hollywood took the rest. Chicago
did not export as much poetry as it did pork."

That Bellow not only writes about Chicago but continues to live
here has long baffled the New York literati. "I seem to have had
an intuition long ago that it wouldn't do much good to bounce about
looking for the best place for a writer," he says. "I think that so many
American writers have a need, even a hunger, for the good great
place where they don't have to explain themselves to the neighbors, where they are surrounded by cultural riches and enjoy the
fellowship of other writers and artists.

"For American writers, there are no such conditions—never have
been. Most of our writers are solitaries. I don't mean that they
are absolutely deprived of companionship or understanding. But, as
writers or painters, they have to make it on their own.

"Some went to Paris in the '20s and some headed for San
Francisco in the '50s and '60s. But I always thought that there
was no answer to the problem of place. The only answer was to
accept it for what it was. Karl Shapiro has pointed out that nine-
tenths of American poetry in the 20th Century complains about the
unpoetic character of life in the United States. The theme is not a
rich one."

In Bellow's most-recent novel, *Humboldt's Gift,* the hero, writer
Charlie Citrine, discloses, "I came back to settle in Chicago with
the secret motive of writing a significant work."

"The main thing about Chicago," Bellow once said, "is that it's
not New York. There are no writers to talk to in New York, only
celebrities on exhibit. In Chicago, you have a city in which the most

dressed-up people are artistic, in which restaurants and shops
and wines and cheeses and parties and sexual delinquencies are all
the art life the city boasts."

Which suits Bellow very nicely. He writes for several hours each
morning in his apartment. "Sometimes the subject leaps at you
and you can write a story in a few days or a novel in several
months," he says, "But a novel generally takes years."

Bellow sets high standards for himself. When his first novel was
accepted for publication, he had second thoughts and destroyed
the manuscript. He is a meticulous craftsman who writes and re-
writes.

One of Bellow's listeners and a favorite critic is Richard Stern, a
novelist and faculty colleague at the University of Chicago. *Humboldt's Gift* was more than eight years in the making, and Bellow
signed Stern's book, "For Richard, who endured 10,000 versions
of it."

"The idea that a novel should be formally perfect is a recent one.
Novels had always been loosely written, even slovenly. Until the
period of Flaubert and his heirs, no one paid much attention to the
well-made novel. Dickens, Dostoyevski, and Victor Hugo did not
write well-made novels. Those are a 20th-Century specialty. The
well-made novel comes to us by way of Flaubert and Henry
James.

"I have sometimes written novels the form of which had to be
discovered," says Bellow. "The novel couldn't be completed until I
had succeeded in discovering its form.

"Since young writers are and should be imitative, in my first
book *(Dangling Man),* I imitated Rilke's *Journal of My Other
Self.* After all, composers would be considerably handicapped if
each had to invent the form of the sonatas for himself. No one is
or should be entirely original. Each writer has his ancestors, and he
knows perfectly well who they are. Without Mérimée (19th-Century
French writer and dramatist), who wrote *Carmen,* without Stephen
Crane, there would have been no Hemingway. I know perfectly
well to whom I owe."

Though he is the most honored American novelist of his age and
is already part of literary history, Bellow is not content to rest on his
laurels. As long as the story juices are still flowing, he will keep

writing. As Bellow looks at his career, he concludes that he has fallen short of his talents, that there are new mountains to climb.

"Some people mature very slowly," he says. "I think I had an extraordinarily long adolescence. For some reasons I held back, I *sat* on my own intelligence. I discovered how timid I had been about subjects I should have treated more boldly. Sometimes it seems I've been quite stingy with my talent, saving myself for what was to come. There's no little egotism in such a view of the future. I seem to have felt that I would live to do better."

A Talk with Saul Bellow:
On His Work and Himself

Michiko Kakutani / 1981

From the *New York Times Book Review,* 13 December 1981, 1,
28–30. © 1981 by the New York Times Company. Reprinted
by permission.

"I sometimes enjoy saying that anybody's life can be encompassed
in about 10 wonderful jokes. One of my favorites is about an
American singer who makes his debut at La Scala. He sings his first
aria to great applause. And the crowd calls 'Ancora, vita, vita.' He
sings it a second time, and again they call for an encore. Then a
third time and a fourth . . . Finally, panting and exhausted, he asks,
'How many times must I sing this aria?' Then someone tells him,
'Until you get it right.' That's how it is with me—I always feel I
haven't gotten it quite right, and so I go on singing."

Saul Bellow tells this story with great relish. Sitting down in a
black leather easy chair, he gazes out through the window of his
high-rise apartment to the dark waters of Lake Michigan beyond,
and throws his head back and laughs. His conversation, like his
books, is at once colloquial and lofty, intellectual and passionate,
filled with jokes heard on the Chicago streets and the high
seriousness of Academe. The author himself bears a certain resemblance to his own heroes: earnest, elegantly dressed and deeply
thoughtful, he too is "a hungry observer" of everything around him.

At 66, Mr. Bellow has written nine novels—the latest, *The Dean's
December,* will be published in January by Harper and Row—and
created in his work a distinctive fictional world. It is a world
animated by an acutely moral imagination and populated by
assorted cranks, con men and fast-talking salesmen of reality who
goad and challenge Mr. Bellow's now familiar heroes. Whether it is
poor, put-upon Moses Herzog or Eugene Henderson, that absurd
seeker of higher qualities, or wise old Artur Sammler or Albert
Corde in *The Dean's December,* they are men caught in the middle
of a spiritual crisis, overwhelmed by the sheer "muchness" of

the world and frightened by the stubborn fact of death. Rejecting both easy optimism and easy despair, they tend, like Corde, to wonder if their own problems are simply their share of "the big-scale insanities of the 20th century."

Like these characters who are continually searching for a way to apprehend reality, Mr. Bellow tends to regard fiction as a kind of tool for investigating the society around him; he sees the novelist as "an imaginative historian, who is able to get closer to contemporary facts than social scientists possibly can." But while the madness of the modern world, manifested in everything from sexual profligacy to random violence, has always reverberated in his characters' lives—a phenomenon that became more pronounced in *Mr. Sammler's Planet*—specific public issues have remained largely in the background. With *The Dean's December,* such matters as oppression in Eastern Europe, the plight of the American "underclass," student militancy and the deterioration of life in American cities are more directly addressed.

What brought about this heightened focus on political and social issues? For one thing, Mr. Bellow says he realized after writing *To Jerusalem and Back,* an account of his 1975 trip to Israel, that "it was as easy to write about great public matters as about private ones—all it required was more confidence and daring." The winning of the Nobel Prize in 1976 no doubt provided some of that necessary confidence, and he made plans to write a nonfiction book about Chicago. After making hundreds of pages of notes, however, he decided to abandon that approach and write a novel.

"I found a more congenial way to do it, my own way, developed over many decades," he says. "But I think I've begun to write differently—I had never really attempted anything of this sort before, though I've been all my life an amateur student of history and politics. It became clear to me that no imagination whatsoever had been applied to the problems of demoralized cities. All the approaches have been technical, financial and bureaucratic, and no one has been able to take into account the sense of these lives."

"I thought I had to cut loose with this book," he goes on. "It seems many of my contemporaries don't take many personal risks—they shoot fish in a barrel. They write about wounded adolescents—there's no problem there. Sexual adventures—there's no problem there. Wounded ethnicity. They appear occasionally to be bold, to challenge the powers that be, but they're generally pretty safe. I think I'm speaking out quite frankly about the deterioration of life in American cities [in this book], and I wouldn't be surprised if I drew some flack. But if you've told yourself all your life that you're a friend of the truth, there comes a time when you must put up or shut up. They're not going to be able to shrug this one off, though there are some very powerful shruggers around.''

By now, Mr. Bellow points out, he is somewhat accustomed to drawing flack—at least from certain quarters of the literary establishment. For all the honors he has received—a Pulitzer and three National Book Awards as well as the Nobel—he sees himself as going against the mainstream of contemporary literature. He has long rejected the fashionable nihilism of what he calls the "wastelanders," those who believe—as he put it in a 1966 speech—that it is "enlightened to expose, to disenchant, to hate and to experience disgust." He is equally skeptical of willful estheticism.

As far as Mr. Bellow is concerned, those writers who substitute analysis for imagination have estranged literature from the common world and removed one of its original and most important purposes: the raising of moral questions. Contemporary writers, he adds, are also easily tempted by the sensational, for they are faced with "the Ancient Mariner problem"—like Coleridge's seaman, "they need something to buttonhole the wedding guests with, as they go from wedding to wedding or orgy to orgy; they need something that has the power to penetrate distraction."

Such views, coupled with his attitudes toward more general social matters—most notably his skepticism about the 60's counterculture—have been delineated by Mr. Bellow in both his essays and his novels, and they have occasionally made for controversy. Touring universities in the 60's, Mr. Bellow was occasionally denounced by students during his lectures, and the critic Richard Poirier contended, in an essay written for *Partisan Review,* that *Herzog* and *Mr. Sammler's Planet* were "efforts to test out, to substantiate, to vitalize, and ultimately to propagate a kind of cultural conservatism." It is an observation Mr. Bellow rejects.

"People who stick labels on you are in the gumming business," he says by way of reply. "What good are these categories? They

mean very little, especially when the people who apply them haven't
had a new thought since they were undergraduates and now
preside over a literary establishment that lectures to dentists and
accountants who want to be filled in on the thrills. I think these are
the reptiles of the literary establishment who are grazing on the last
Mesozoic grasses of Romanticism. Americans in this respect are
quite old-fashioned: they're quite willing to embrace stale European
ideas—they should be on 10th Avenue where the rest of the old
importers used to be.

"They think they know what writers should be and what writers
should write, but who are these representatives who practice what
Poirier preaches? They're, for the most part, spiritless, etiolated,
and the liveliest of them are third-rate vaudevillians. Is this
literary life? I'd rather inspect gas mains in Chicago."

With their old-fashioned characters, their passion for big ideas
and problems of the spirit, Mr. Bellow's own books clearly belong
to a different tradition. The Old Testament, Shakespeare and the
great 19th-century Russian novels—these were the books Bellow
read as a boy, and these were the books which, in large measure,
gave him a sense of what great literature ought to do. Indeed, his
choice of vocation, he says, was animated by the traditional challenge "to account for the mysterious circumstance of being."

"I don't think I was a very sophisticated person," he says,
recalling his youth in Chicago as the son of an onion importer
who had immigrated from Russia. "Chicago is not a city that
produces sophisticated people, but it was in Chicago where this
child of Jewish immigrants got the *idée fixe* of becoming an American author, and he had to find a way to prove he wasn't halluci-
nated, that he could write English sentences and that he could hold
the attention of a reader or two. In those days, the WASP
establishment wouldn't listen till you established your credentials—
there are people even now who don't."

To establish his credentials, Mr. Bellow wrote two books that
filled what he calls "formal requirements": *Dangling Man*, the
story of a young Chicagoan awaiting induction into the war, was his
B.A.; *The Victim*, a portrait of a journalist and his importunate,
anti-Semitic alter ego, his Ph.D. Both these somber books won
modest critical acclaim, but their author, who was living in Paris

on a Guggenheim at the time, says he was already sinking "into a depression by trying to do the wrong things." In a kind of manic reaction, he began another book, a book that he would write "in a purple fever" over the next three years. The book, of course, was the exuberantly picaresque *Augie March*.

Augie March marked Mr. Bellow's discovery of his own voice. It was a supple voice, infused with the rhythms and idioms of Yiddish, a voice that was capable of articulating a moral vision and lofty philosophical speculation in the most colloquial of terms. "I loosened up," Mr. Bellow recalls, "and found I could flail my arms and express my impulses. I was unruly at first and didn't have things under control, but it was at least a kind of spontaneous event. It was my liberation."

Augie March, Mr. Bellow said at the time, came easily—all he had to do "was to be there with buckets to catch it"—and it won the National Book Award in 1953. But, in retrospect, the experience was somewhat disconcerting as well, for it revealed to Mr. Bellow certain prejudices within the literary community that would last for many years.

"I began to discover," he says, "that while I thought I was simply laying an offering on the altar like a faithful petitioner, other people thought I was trying to take over the church. It came at a strange point when I think the WASP establishment was losing confidence in itself, and it felt it was being challenged by Jews, blacks, and ethnics, and some people were saying there was a Jewish mafia, and other people, who should have had more sense, spoke of—well, they didn't use the word conspiracy, but they saw it as an unwelcome eruption. I began to talk of Malamud, Roth and me as Hart, Shaffner & Marx, and there was a pathetic absurdity under it all—all we wanted was to add ourselves to the thriving enterprise we loved; no one wanted to take over. That's a motive worthy of the Mafia, and I don't think Hart, Shaffner & Marx were Mafiosi.

"I think of myself as an American of Jewish heritage," he goes on. "When most people call someone a 'Jewish writer,' it's a way of setting you aside. They don't talk about the powers of the 'Jewish writers' who wrote the Old Testament; they say to write novels you need to know something about manners, which is something

you have to be raised in the South to know. I felt many writers
[during the 50's and early 60's] treated their Jewish colleagues with
unpardonable shabbiness, and anti-Semitism after the Holocaust
is absolutely unforgivable."

With the breakthrough in style achieved in *Augie March,* there
also came a shift in tone. Whereas the first two books shared a certain
depressive quality—underlined by the fact that their heroes did little
to resolve the condition of their alienation—*Augie March* was a
wildly extroverted work, ending with its hero looking forward to his
next adventure. Later books such as *Henderson the Rain King*
and *Herzog* would go somewhat further: each ended with its protagonist taking the first step toward an affirmation of his life, and
these books would also play, with greater facility, between what
Mr. Bellow refers to as "the two sides of my psyche"—the brooding
side and the exuberant.

"For many years," he explains, "Mozart was a kind of idol to
me—this rapturous singing for me that's always on the edge of
sadness and melancholy and disappointment and heartbreak, but
always ready for an outburst of the most delicious music. I found
Mozart temperamentally so congenial. I'm not claiming the same
range of talent, but I often feel an affinity with him."

Certainly many of Mr. Bellow's characters have shared temperamental affinities with their author—a fact that Mr. Bellow ac-
knowledges by quoting Alberto Moravia, who once told him, "Every novel is some kind of higher autobiography." In *The Dean's
December,* for instance, Albert Corde takes a trip to Bucharest to
help his wife attend her dying mother—as Mr. Bellow himself did
several years ago—and Corde shares, more or less, his creator's
age, occupation and place of residence. Like many of Mr. Bellow's
heroes, Corde is also something of a lapsed intellectual, who takes
pride and pleasure in exercising his mind, but also worries about
the inadequacy of all his theories. As Mr. Sammler puts it, "Intellectual man had become an explaining creature. Fathers to children, wives to husbands, lecturers to listeners, colleagues to colleagues, doctors to patients, man to his own soul explained. . . .
For the most part, in one ear and out the other. The soul wanted
what it wanted."

Of course, Mr. Bellow himself has curiously ambivalent attitudes

toward academia. He believes, on one hand, that "it's in the university
and only in the university that Americans can have a higher life,"
and yet he also contends that professors "are so eager to live the
life of society like everybody else that they're not always intellectually or spiritually as rigorous as they should be." By institutionalizing the avant-garde magazines and giving writers the security of
tenure, he argues, universities effectively destroyed the independent literary culture that once existed in this country.

Still, Mr. Bellow finds that an academic community provides him
with people "to talk to about the things that concern me most,"
and he has served, since 1964, on the prestigious Committee on
Social Thought at the University of Chicago. His decision to leave
New York and return to Chicago in the early 60's, he says, was
motivated, in part, by what he saw as the increased politicization
of writers in New York.

When he first arrived in New York during the 40's, a "young
hick" bent on "going to the big town and taking it," a sense of
community existed among writers associated with the *Partisan
Review*. Mr. Bellow became friends with such writers and critics
as Meyer Schapiro, Dwight Macdonald, Delmore Schwartz and
Clement Greenberg—"they were not always friendly friends, but
they were always stimulating friends"—and he enjoyed the "open
spirit of easy fraternization" that animated their discussions. Politics,
generally in the form of Marxism, tended to be mostly theoretical.

"Then," Mr. Bellow recalls, "a new generation turned up—a lot
of people out of Columbia University, a lot of students of Lionel
Trilling, who got into enterprises like *Commentary*—and suddenly
the whole atmosphere in New York became far more political
than it had been before. With the Vietnam War and other issues,
people became organized in camps, and while I was opposed to
the war, I just refused to line up with the new groups. I didn't like
it, and it seemed to me a good time to leave New York, because
I'd been drawn there in the first place by my literary interests, and
there seemed to be no room for an independent writer in New
York anymore. It became harder to find people to talk to, and it was
harder to stay out of the draft—you were always being solicited
for this cause or that, always being drafted for one thing or another.

"People have said in their memoirs that I was guarded, cautious, career-oriented, but I don't think that's so—after all, there was nothing easier in New York during those days than the life of the extremist, and that's continued to be so. I was not comfortable with the extremist life, and so I thought I might as well go back to the undiluted U.S.A., go back to Chicago. It's vulgar but it's vital and it's more American, more representative."

Indeed, Mr. Bellow finds that in Chicago he is able to keep up with his old high school friends, as well as a cross-section of society including contractors, lawyers, doctors, physicists, historians, policemen and retired social workers—some of whom surface in his fiction. "You meet people," he says. "They reveal or conceal themselves, and you read them or try. They struggle with their souls or don't. They either generate interest or not. It forms a picture for you. The people who interest me the most do concern themselves with the formation of a soul. The others are what Hollywood used to call the cast of thousands."

When he is working on a book, Mr. Bellow spends his mornings at an electric typewriter, set up by a window overlooking Lake Michigan. After nine novels, the craft has been mastered, but the magical aspect of the art remains. Mr. Bellow, in fact, has spoken in the past of "a primitive prompter or commentator within, who from earliest years has been advising us, telling us what the real world is"—a commentator not unlike Henderson's little voice that constantly cries, "I want, I want"—and he attributes his best writing to this unconscious source.

"I think a writer is on track when the door of his native and deeper intuitions is open," he says. "You write a sentence that doesn't come from that source and you can't build around it—it makes the page seem somehow false. You have a gyroscope within that tells you whether what you're doing is right or wrong. I've always felt a writer is something of a medium, and when something is really working, he has a certain clairvoyant power; he has a sense of what's going on. Whenever I've published a book that's received wide attention, I've heard from thousands of people around the world who have been thinking the same thing—as though I'd anticipated things. I didn't mean to, but I've learned one does."

Since he won the Nobel Prize for Literature in 1976, of course, those letters from readers have increased, as have the demands on Mr. Bellow's time. He is asked to deliver speeches (he recently gave the celebrated Tanner Lectures at Oxford), serve on committees and sign all manner of petitions. As far as he is concerned, these responsibilities act as distractions from his true vocation.

"I could spend the rest of my life now functioning on committees," he says, "standing up for all the right things and denouncing all the bad ones. What good this does your art, I leave to the expert guessers to guess at. I have yet to feel I've intimidated Brezhnev by signing protests.

"The Nobel changes things in different ways," he continues. "For one thing, you feel that you have more authority, and if the Academy was mistaken in giving you the prize, you try to make the best of it, and recover your balance and your normal poise and not feel oppressed by the weight of this honor. I don't intend to let this laurel wreath of heavy metal sink me. I'm treading water very successfully, thank you. I know people like John Steinbeck thought it was the kiss of death, but I've decided to choose my own death kiss. No one's going to lay it on me."

A Cry of Strength:
The Unfashionably Uncynical
Saul Bellow

Cathleen Medwick / 1982

From *Vogue,* March 1982, 368–69, 426–27. Courtesy *Vogue.* ©
1982 by The Conde Nast Publications Inc. Reprinted by permission.

Saul Bellow is sitting, professorially, behind a large desk, in a
spacious office, in front of a lavish picture window with a view.
Not a Chicago office: he is in New York City on business. The world
outside in no way resembles Chicago's ruined, resurrected inner
city, which Bellow can see from his high-rise apartment; this
window gives out on New York's rigid shadow boxes of glass and
steel. Saul Bellow, who has spent the better part of his life in
Chicago, inviting the city to shape him into its oddly native mold
of academic and street-tough (the ghost of Nelson Algren haunting
the University's ivied halls), seems, in this borrowed publishing
executive's office, particularly out of place.

On the other hand, he seems determined to belong here—having
chosen, after all, to sit behind this vacant desk (there are comfortable
armchairs and a sofa in the room), a position of some authority.
Something the streets of Chicago might teach you: seize your
turf, and hold onto it. An unnecessary precaution, one might think,
for a man of Bellow's stature in the world. But ancient habits die hard.

Saul Bellow, at sixty-six, is white-haired, keen-eyed, a gentle-
manly-looking man. The author of nine novels (his latest, *The
Dean's December,* was recently published by Harper & Row), he
has won the Nobel Prize for literature, the National Book Award
(three times), the Pulitzer Prize; and his books, venerated as they
are by the literary pundits, actually do sell. But this tremendous and
consistent success has hardly altered Bellow's view of himself. He
speaks, almost officially, as a displaced person—like one of his
fictional characters, a dangling man, an intruder on an alien planet,
disaffected, remote. Bellow's novels are stories of men (never women)

190

who more than casually resemble him. These he depicts as fast-
aging apparitions who try—usually (they feel) with small success—to
become human, to locate themselves emotionally in the world.
Distressed, damaged hearts searching, like the poet Humboldt (in
Humboldt's Gift), for "an original world, a home-world." The self-
savaging hero of *Henderson the Rain King* hunts for that world in
Africa—only to discover, like Dorothy, that Oz is no place like
home. And home is, in the final analysis, Reality City, where
even the soul's most murderous instincts can come to roost.

"John Berryman once told me," says Bellow, leaning back into
his swivel chair, "that some book reviewer was trying to 'put me
in my place.'" (Bellow's voice here rises, lilting—Olivier would
play it perfectly.) "And I said to him I'd be grateful if he could
tell me what my place was."

There are those who would argue that Saul Bellow's "place" is
Chicago—that he has claimed it the way Joyce claimed Dublin
and Edith Wharton New York: by living and writing it. Bellow
inherited his Chicago, one might say, from Dreiser, Farrell, from
those writers who drove straight at the grisly center of the American
Dream, giving it a local habitation and a name. The city belonged
then, as now, to the literary muscle men. "Algren left Chicago,"
Bellow points out, "because he said it was much too tame and no
longer resembled the Chicago of the Depression to which he had
given his heart. He felt that Paterson, New Jersey, was more
like it."

The Dean's December hovers relentlessly about Chicago, viewing
it close up, then from enormous distances—the New World seen
from the Old—revealing, in the process, the nightmare alleys of the
American Dream. Bellow has no illusions about the city. Nor is he
fashionably cynical about it.

"Yes, it is the Midwest, and yes, it is the bread-and-butter, pig-
sticking U.S.A.—that publicity poem that Carl Sandburg wrote
called 'Chicago': 'Hog butcher for the world. . . . City of the Big
Shoulders' and so on, it was a sort of advertising man's masterpiece about Chicago, I always thought.

"But that's not the Chicago that makes my nerve endings tingle.
The fact is that all these American cities were cities of immigrants,
they were exotic places—hybrid cities of hybrid populations, united

by certain ideas: The idea that you can lead a free life, that you don't need to fear the authorities. The idea that you had entered into a contract with a hundred million others, to be an American, to forget your own history and start over again.

"An old friend of mine who's now dead used to say everybody in the world should have the chance to be an American, at least for a while. It is a special state of mind. And being foreign is not so terribly important if you grew up among Poles, Germans, Swedes, Irishmen, Mexicans, Italians, and blacks, as I did."

Bellow was nine years old when his family moved to Chicago from Montreal, to which they had emigrated from Russia. They arrived in Chicago in 1924, the year of the Loeb-Leopold murder trial, which Bellow remembers following, as a child, with intense interest. His mother, by that time, had been in North America for eleven years; but she never got used to it. "She was thinking of her family in Riga all the time. And this was just a sort of exile, purgatory as far as she was concerned. It was very hard to bring up four children in so strange a place."

From the beginning, Bellow felt like an insider/outsider, "even though I went to grammar school and high school and college in Chicago, lived in the streets and knew it so well. I felt there was a kind of exoticism about the place.

"I suppose part of the feeling of strangeness came from my mother's situation, to which as the youngest child I was very sensitive. We were already exotic when we came. The trunks my parents traveled with were exotic—the taffeta petticoats, the ostrich plumes, the long gloves, the buttoned boots, and all the rest of those family treasures, you know, made me feel that I'd come from another world.

"Then I was on the streets of Chicago and playing a game called Piggie-move-up, which was a baseball game played in the street, and hanging upside down by my knees from porch railings, which was my favorite diversion in Chicago as a kid. Well, I was a street kid, although I played the violin and attended a Hebrew school. But I broke with that—the choice was between the Hebrew school and the pool room and the playground, and the pool room and the playground won out. Together with the public library."

The street kid went on to glory; the feeling of strangeness never

wore off. When Bellow won a Guggenheim fellowship in 1948, he
moved to Paris—which turned out to be an excellent place in which
to think about Chicago, to remember it. That's what Mr. Corde
(the name suggests a rope, a heart) does from his wife's native
Rumania, in *The Dean's December:* sees Chicago as clearly as if
through a crystal ball—its rackets, its rage, its inexplicably erotic
brutality. Chicago shuts Corde out. And it is only by journeying to a
remote country—a place where his strangeness is somehow more
tolerable, less unique—that he begins to discover why.

Bellow has left Chicago many times—for New York, Minnesota,
Paris; but, like his characters, he always returns. Perhaps "to
continue," as Corde says, "my education." What he returns to: the
broad Chicago lakefront, the inland sea, which offers "plenty of
emptiness, as much as you needed to define yourself against, as
American souls seem to do." The city itself, "Lying at the
southern end of the Great Lakes . . .Chicago with its gigantesque
outer life contained the whole problem of poetry and the inner life in
America. Here you could look into such things through a sort of
freshwater transparency."

Bellow returned—not to the deceptive tranquility of Chicago's
suburbs but to the city's center, its steely heart.

"I don't live in a cloistered neighborhood. I live in a high-crime
neighborhood. It's difficult. But one doesn't live anywhere for
sociological reasons. There are two ways to do it as a writer: either
to find a privileged life for yourself, or to stick to your guns."

Bellow's Chicago, where a prize-winning writer gets his Mercedes
bashed in by a sleazy character whom he, the distinguished intellectual, has stiffed in a poker game; where another gentleman, a
professor—a dean, in fact—becomes embroiled in a gruesome murder
case from which he can find, emotionally, no escape and that makes
him its ultimate victim. A city of shrewd operators, iron-fisted
magnates and fast-talking bullies. A city that grabs you by the
lapels, even if you *are* a disillusioned intellectual, and shakes you up,
at least. There's something to be said for that; and Bellow says it,
with such clarity as fever evokes. As Charles Citrine, in *Humboldt's Gift,* explains it, "Just because your soul is being torn to pieces
doesn't mean that you stop analyzing the phenomena." Violence,

among its other effects, makes you see clearly—and clear vision is
Bellow's strong suit.

Bellow's characters grab at anything that smacks of reality—
whether it is an African lion hunt or a Chicago murder trial (by
no means dissimilar events). "What a passion to be *real,*" observes
the solitary denizen of *Mr. Sammler's Planet.* "But *real* was also
brutal"—a metaphysical kick in the teeth. The men in these novels,
always self-punishing, are never more relieved than when they are
violently shocked. The Big Bang Theory, as applied to personal
life, seems to simplify matters, if only for the moment. And if
anything is axiomatic in Bellow's world, it is that every moment
counts.

"Shall I tell you something?" says Bellow with a grim smile—the
look of a street kid who just took your baseball and dares you to
take it back. He leans forward. "I'll tell you something personal.
I've observed for a long time that people are capable of being
blasé about their surroundings, as if they knew who they were, as if
they knew what they were, and where they came from, and as if
they could explain circumstances in their lives fully and had a strong
grasp of all the facts and of their history. That they could answer
all these questions.

"I never felt that way. I felt from the beginning of my life that to
exist is something of a miracle. I have never existed before; and
this existence is so engaging, so passionately interesting that I could
never stand away from it sufficiently to take a sophisticated view of it.

"Human beings don't know who or what they are—least of all in
this age of scientific education when our brains and our mouths are
full of explanations, you can't explain anything. So to avoid a city
where sophistication rules is a good idea, because it is the most
prevalent falsehood of civilized societies that people know something about what causes them to be here."

Hard to be a cynic if you feel that way.

"Well, I'm not fashionably cynical, and I don't give a damn how
people describe me. People obliterate this childishness in themselves as though it were an obstacle to survival. They substitute a
sort of cleverness for it. I'm as capable of being clever as the next
joker. I've learned all the tricks in my life. But when I write, that's

not what I write about. That's where I take myself and others seriously."

The men he writes about, the reality seekers, are trying to pluck some valid emotion from the flurry of miscellaneous sensations that make up everyday modern life.

"People become accustomed to the sharpest stimulants, and they're not happy unless there's a regular succession of events—they don't even notice the so-called insignificant events. That is, Reagan is only shot in the lung; compared with Sadat's being assassinated, that is a trifle. The Pope is shot. Two hundred years ago, since he was shot by a Muslim, that would have caused a holy war. . . . But now—it's just something that happens, and it'll be topped.

"But people say, 'Well, what are you yaking about? How are you going to grade the various horrors? The bombing of Rotterdam was not as bad as the bombing of Hamburg, and the bombing of Hamburg was not as bad as the Gulag Peninsula, and the Gulag Peninsula was not as bad as the extermination camps.' And so it goes, right? This sort of bidding of catastrophe against catastrophe.

"So then what happens to the life of a person? It is as it were price cut into insignificance. Through this kind of swelling and irritation of the public sphere, the private sphere becomes insignificant. People will say, 'Don't tell me about that, this. Why should I listen? If I want to think about suffering, I can think about infants being thrown still alive into the furnaces at Auschwitz.' "

Perhaps, Bellow speculates, people have formed a subjective callus. They are cushioned by their own existence. They respond to the sensational event but don't really care about anyone.

"This is what people mean when they say that culture is being extinguished. Because, if culture means anything, it means knowing what value to set upon a human life; it's not somebody with a mortarboard reading Greek. I know a lot of facts, history. That's not culture. Culture is the openness of the individual psyche, soul if you like, to the news of being. It's having access to your own soul also, you know.

"Three former United States Presidents attended Anwar Sadat's funeral. They seemed to me to be having the time of their lives.

The PLO's celebrating in the streets of Beirut was more real than the people who put their formal regrets on tape.

"So now," says Bellow—and the smile, the challenge, are doubly fierce, "we come to one of the themes of my book: whether people still have any power to experience. Mr. Corde got this shock: That where there is no heart, where there is no imagination, there is no capacity to experience, really. That is what this book is about in large measure."

Corde returns to Chicago—the heart's journey, as it were, a sort of medieval pilgrimage. What he found in East Europe, the Old World, was a kind of moral starvation; the political and bureaucratic red tape wound more and more tightly about the throats of the people, until memory and desire were choked. Bellow sees the effects of this strangulation in Western Europe, as well.

"Europe has changed immensely. Europeans live between the two superpowers, and it's no longer the same sort of life. There's not much happening there. What I say in *The Dean's December* is quite right: they simply decided to take a holiday from history. That history happened brutally between 1914 and 1946, and now they'd rather opt out.

"As a result, the action has passed to the United States. When I say the action, I mean the all-significant struggle that determines whether masses of people live in a condition of freedom. That's the test we're undergoing, right now: Whether a country like this which is a conglomerate and hybrid—I don't say this in a pejorative sense—can find the will to preserve itself as a free society. This is what it all means. This is what the Third World means, this is what missile confrontations mean, this is what the arms negotiations mean—that we are going to decide these questions. It seems to me that this is what puts us where the action is; whereas, in Western Europe, a large part of the population has decided that rather than face nuclear obliteration, they would make a deal."

And what is happening in America, in cities like Chicago, which, for all its bravado, its vaunted ruthlessness, still seems, compared to European cities, to have a certain brash naïveté, an innocence that may be the last vestige of the American Dream?

"I think there is a residual feeling of pride in the corruption in Chicago, and the fact that it's Toughville. You have to have guts and savvy to live there. But the sense of the old city has disappeared with the old neighborhoods. People don't even like to have nostalgic conversations anymore, because then they have to turn around and face the dangerous el platforms, the bad buses, unsafe streets, as elsewhere.

"Chicago still has a political machine; it's one of the last cities in the country still to have a political machine, and that's an old-fashioned thing. What does it signify? It signifies that they are reluctant to move, and that they accept the transformation of the city under their eyes, a transformation for which poor and unimaginative leadership is partly to blame. . . .

"What you have now in Chicago is a new form of segregation, which is owing to the abandonment of the public institutions by the white population. They send their kids to private schools. They move out, to the suburbs or the sunbelt. Do you call that the old American moxie?"

Chicago, like other cities, is succumbing to the imperatives of shopping malls, skyscrapers, the grim outline of what Bellow calls "a commercial wasteland." Still, the city fascinates him.

"There's something going on there. I don't know what it is—if I knew what it was, I would just name it and be finished. I still vibrate to it somehow. And sometimes I feel that I let myself become too uncritical. But, look, it was said long before me, and by better writers, that democracy was going to be a hybrid and that it would have its own kind of strength, its force. It would be deficient in a kind of high culture, but in compensation it would offer other opportunities to people of strong nature and intelligence. I don't know whether Chicago together with the rest of the country can face the test of this time. . . ."

You can see it in Chicago, past and present: democracy, in its rudest form, struggling to survive. Never more than now, when so many people are rallying in the name of a particularly questionable "morality."

But are Americans justified in calling themselves moral, now?

"Well, they're on their knees, but you can't be sure what they're doing. They may be looking for their marbles.

"Americans want goodness, sure. Human beings have an appetite for this, and it won't die out. But they don't seem to be very clear in their minds when they talk about it.

"I think Americans have always told themselves they were good people. And I think in many respects it is true. Americans are a generous people, especially when the going is good. They're child-like in many ways. They can't bear to think ill of themselves. They can't bear to think of themselves as international criminals and terrorists, killers of Vietnamese children—this was intolerable to them, and they did everything possible to clear themselves from that guilt. Now, in a way, that's greatly to their credit insofar as it's an impulse; but it's not to their credit as long as the impulse has an ignorant setting."

Bellow sits back in his chair and considers, then smiles.

The smile is gentle now.

"I sometimes say that virtue in America is like a ghost town. Anybody can move in and say that he's mayor. But who really lives there?"

Interview with Saul Bellow

Rockwell Gray, Harry White, and Gerald Nemanic / 1984

From *TriQuarterly*, 60 (1984), 12–34. Reprinted in *Top 20: Twenty Years of the Best Contemporary Writing and Graphics from TriQuarterly Magazine.* Spec. issue of *TriQuarterly*, 63 (1985), 632–50. © 1984 by Saul Bellow. Reprinted by permission.

The text of this interview has been prepared from the transcript of a two-hour conversation taped on March 12, 1983, in Mr. Bellow's office at the University of Chicago. Mr. Bellow subsequently emended the transcript, clarifying his replies and providing further context for them. As much as possible, the conversational quality of the dialogue has been retained.

TQ: What are your reflections on the relationship between physical place and the sense of identity sought by a writer and his characters? Would you say, for example, that a city like Chicago becomes, in fiction, more a central metaphor for self-definition than a merely reportorial or naturalistic backdrop?

Bellow: I don't really know what to make of Chicago—a mysterious place and also much maligned. When people ask whether I have roots here I say that tangled wires would be more like it than roots. One's attachment to a place is seldom understood. People always want to know for regional-patriotic reasons why I am attached to this heath, which is not my native heath. I arrived here when I was nine years old and have spent most of my life here.

Chicago has earned the right to be considered the center of American materialism—the classical center. It has cultural pretensions, of course, and has had since the great Fair of 1893. These pretensions aren't very significant. They are associated with boosterism. The rich, growing more boorish and ignorant with every decade, put up money for museums, orchestras, opera companies, art associations, arty clubs and so on. *Poetry* magazine

has had its headquarters here since the days of Harriet Monroe.
Banks and big corporations recognize art as a sort of asset, but
Chicago's wealth is not in culture. The universities have absorbed
almost everything that resembles cultural life. The newspapers have
a thousand times more pork, sex and scandal in their pages than
they do painting and literature. The pulse of culture beats thinly in
the "media." We have one fat, glossy, squalid magazine—a big
money-maker. The universities give sanctuary for delicate people
who need it. And the universities also have their sassy con-artists
and noisy promoters. I never had much use for sanctuaries. I did
need a certain amount of conversation, and that, after diligent
search, I could eventually find in the university. And from students
I could learn where the U.S.A. was heading. But I couldn't be
described as an academic. When I was younger I thought I needed
"protection." I was wrong. I wasted much time in looking for the
great good place. American artists, for more than a century were
determined to find it, traveling to Europe, dreaming of an environment friendly to writers. They were on a wild-goose chase. Certain
of them had a good time. In Paris towards the end of the last
century, from, say, the Whistler-Henry James period until the
middle of the Depression, they were very happy. They had little
to do with Paris itself. But for nearly a century France was the
center of a powerful international culture. It was hospitable to the
Picassos, Modiglianis, Rilkes, Apollinaires, Joyces, Marinettis,
Brancusis—a multitude of foreign geniuses. For political reasons
Paris, too, began to be corrupted in the thirties. The struggle of the
two totalitarianisms, reaching its climax in the Spanish Civil War,
infected Paris with a violent and dulling disease. Politics took over.
Postwar Paris was dominated by Sartre. Marxist *ratatouille* was
served to all visitors. After the Second World War all the action
seemed to be on our side of the Atlantic. No getting away from it.
Paris was no longer the home (or locus, if "home" is too sentimental
a word) of an international culture. You had to reconcile yourself
to life in commercial-technological-etc. America. Here you would
stay put, and make silk purses out of pigs' ears—or other organs.

TQ: Some of that of course you grasped right away as a boy, I
take it.

Bellow: Yes. It was possible to grasp it, but it isn't easy to

understand what your connection to this business society signifies. You can't understand when you're very young—and few understand in middle age—what the situation really is. The underlying
fact is that in the modern democracies a contract was offered to the
majority. It's plainly spelled out in many documents—in the *Federalist
Papers,* for instance. It reads as follows, in my own summary:

"We will provide for your real needs. You will be fed and
protected, you will live in peace. As for the life of the imagination,
unfortunately we can't do much for you in that respect. Scientific
imagination, yes. That must and will thrive, but as for esthetic
imagination—forget it." Bear this in mind and you can begin to
understand the isolation of the great American writers of the
nineteenth century. They were great solitaries.

TQ: The Customs House syndrome.

Bellow: Yes, the Customs House, or Edgar Allan Poe's desperate
queerness and boozing, the self-incarceration of Emily Dickinson.
Many young writers of my generation protected themselves as a
mass of sensibilities, or tics, tried to make special provision for
their special needs, took measures to armor themselves. Meaning-
less. Foolish. To the romantic French, up to and including Malraux, the artist made war on bourgeois philistinism. "Sensibility"
had political implications. This can mean very little to Americans
whose French history comes from textbooks. For Americans the
question is what can be done by writers, painters, etc., in a
country which has so little use for artists. That old devil "environment."

TQ: Achieve through feeding off it sometimes, I would take it,
by observing it carefully.

Bellow: Well, yes. It's important, though, to avoid the cliché of
artist vs. bourgeois. It's true that the rich were forever aping the
artists, looking for nicer ways to be rich, or more interesting ways
to spend money. Today the "life-style" trend has deprived the artist
of his influence. He is no longer interestingly imitable, not part of a
compact, exclusive clan attractive to people with money. To put
the whole matter briefly, it's extremely important not to be drawn
into futile struggles with the Situation, not to be in opposition on
principle, and not to try to convert hostility into friendliness—not
to think that you have to edify the unedified masses or try to

prevent them from becoming irretrievably sodden. For that's a mistake, too, one that almost everybody makes. Henry James, when he said that his business as a writer was in part the cure of souls, was making it. The "cure of souls" isn't the writer's business. The writer works, or cultivates, certain permanent human impulses and capacities. I take it for granted that such cultivation is good for the soul. To have a soul, to *be* one—that today is a revolutionary defiance of received opinion. But the cure of souls—writers as priests or would-be priests? No.

TQ: When you talk about the would-be priests, whom are you thinking of, especially?

Bellow: Most American writers of the nineteenth century were guides, teachers, counselors, spiritual advisors. Emerson and Thoreau preached. Whitman added illustration to preaching. He made it quite explicit that in a democracy it was the business of the poet to create models of manhood and womanhood. He did a wonderful job of it, although his models, when you find them today, are more degenerate than inspiring. Edification was big in England, too—the Carlyles, the Ruskins—Dickens, too, up to a point (of course he was freed from mere teacherism by his genius).

On the other side were the counter-edifiers who proclaimed that the condition was irredeemably decadent: the negative romantics, Baudelaire, Flaubert—Joyce, for that matter. Finally we reach the *Waste Land* outlook—despair over the withering of all the great things and the flourishing of all the trivial things. At this extreme, a higher edification is invoked, or hinted at, or prayed for. Democrats, naturally, were edifiers. The anti-edifiers were, as writers, more powerful. The nihilists expressed what the majority of civilized mankind thought and felt. They were more truly representative than the edifiers, hence their greater power.

TQ: You mean that the doctrines of the edifiers have worn too thin or that the current fix is simply an impossible one to address?

Bellow: Well, writers don't seem to understand the situation. Not long ago I picked up *Junkie* by William Burroughs. He states in the introduction that his purpose in writing the book is to warn people about narcotics. Well, people won't read him for the moral lesson. They want to know about dope. But one must edify. Even Burroughs accepts that rule.

TQ: You mentioned that the writer is ignored in this country. Does this help the writer insofar as he is thus unencumbered, that he doesn't have to live up to any particular standards?

Bellow: It helps if he isn't damaged, if his feelings aren't too badly crushed. One needs *some* attention. It's all or nothing in the U.S., and if you don't make the celebrity circuit you are wretchedly ignored.

TQ: The would-be edifiers as well?

Bellow: Very often. In their own way. It's very hard to escape edifying—a social duty in which everybody has been drilled. The public will say, "What are you doing for us? How do you justify your existence?" As I see it, the writer's obligation, insofar as he has one, is to liberate his imagination, to write as he lives, to live as he writes.

TQ: But the writer is praised or faulted instead for his ability to edify or not to edify. Those become the terms by which he is measured.

Bellow: Most often. Edification is part of the populist tradition. Read Carl Sandburg's collected poems and what you see as you turn the pages is one instruction after another: this is what a guy ought to be like, this is the attitude he ought to have towards personal freedom, towards children, towards standards of success. The poetry affirms certain principles. Sandburg's celebrated title sums it up: *The People, Yes*.

TQ: I was thinking of those who are in the profession of edifying, the critical establishment or the university professors. They write gobs of material measuring the artist in those terms. They want somebody whom they can submit to their own edification-mills. And they come to evaluate literature in terms of the excitement of the ideas it presents. That's the particular nature of that kind of beast.

Bellow: The nature of the beast is to turn a cognitive profit on imaginative activities. You read a poem and then you talk about its cognitive equivalents—really a kind of translation. After much travail you obtain an "intellectual" result, and such "intellectual" results enjoy the very greatest prestige. In my student days a professor might claim, "I've examined George Herbert's theology, his political background, the cultural history of his times, and

I am therefore able to tell you what his poem means.'' He would set before you an intellectual shadow, highly pleasing to all parties. We feel very much at home with what one of my profs was fond of calling "the cognitions." In my day, the ruling cognitions were those of Rousseau or Marx (Lenin), whose books had inspired revolutions. Interpretations of painting and literature followed the same revolutionary path, producing a body of doctrines (Malraux will serve as an example) whose binding power we are only now beginning to feel—when I say "we," I refer to those of us who resist the power of the victorious cognitions. Not all the conquering stereotypes are political. Freud is one of our conquerors. In many branches of thought his authority is supreme. We must reckon also with the "behavioral scientists," the philosophers (existentialists and logical positivists), historians, theologians—bands of academics, critics and pundits, creators of "schools." Taken altogether, the body of "thought" created by these "intellectuals" is a huge affliction. Its effects are deadly. Few are strong enough to ward them off. Writers can't afford to draw their premises from this stock of "ideas"—*idées reçues* is a more suitable expression. The unhappy fact is, however, that they do—even the best of them draw major premises from the cliché stockpile. "Are you an Antihumanist, Brother? Have you squared yourself with Malraux? With the Structuralists? Are you on *truly* bad terms with the prevailing *ethos*?" You couldn't be a real writer if you hadn't estranged yourself from the culture and the society of your time.

Whereas the older generation of academics were sworn edifiers, their younger successors are proud of their "estrangement." They enjoy the esthetic prestige of the "estranged" (the only real) "artist." At the same time, they control the departments (philosophy, English, etc.) in which they have tenured appointments. In the name of "deconstruction," they have taken over not only these departments, but literature itself, operating in the cockpit side by side with Shakespeare, Milton, etc., as copilots. These academics—good God! Suppose that a dwarf sitting in Shakespeare's lap were to imagine that he was piloting the great Shakespearean jet!

TQ: We came quite a way from the original question about the city as metaphor. Is there any interest in picking up that original thread, or not?

Bellow: Yes, why not? I've spent most of my life in Chicago. A glance from the window in the morning is enough to set off endless trains of associations. The weather alone will do it—sixty years of chill, darkness, rain, ice, smoke, winter blue, summer blue. Structural steel or the brick walls of six-flats send messages to me. Inevitably, you invest your vital substance in familiar surroundings. That's why they are called "familiar." Chicago is one of the larger provinces of my psychic life. I refer, of course, to the old Chicago, which is now in full decay. A new, proud, synthetic Chicago has begun to spread outwards from the Loop.

TQ: You seem to suggest that it's simply an accident that you wound up in Chicago, that although Chicago has certain associations for you there is nothing unique about it. Some kind of vitality . . . ?

Bellow: I was brought here by my parents at the age of nine. Accident? I am reluctant to speak of "my karma." Yet I do sometimes feel that I was stuck here, assigned to the place, shackled to it by one of those phantom intelligences that Thomas Hardy invokes, his "Spirits Sinister and Ironic." Mine would be a Spirit Comedic. In my late sixties I am able to share the joke with my tutelary Spirit.

TQ: I wonder if, when we see Chicago portrayed in the work of an imaginative writer, we are seeing the "real" Chicago so much as a metaphor of the city. In other words, aren't we sensing Chicago as a kind of concrete manifestation of the emotions of the writer's characters? In the novels of Dreiser, for example, are we being shown what Chicago of 1900 was really like or what Dreiser felt he had to show us?

Bellow: Dreiser was the star-struck country boy madly excited by the provincial capital. I find it very agreeable, at times truly moving, to read books like *Sister Carrie* or *Dawn*. How deeply the Hoosier kid feels the power of the great city—the purposeful energy of the crowds. Everything fascinates him—factories, horse-cars, hotel lobbies, a machine which makes keys, a hardware warehouse, luxury shops, fast women, plausible salesmen, exponents of social Darwinism and other bookish ninnies, sturdy railroad men. He's drunk with all this, thinks The Windy City the most marvelous thing that ever happened. When I read him I am

inclined to think so, too. In his Cowperwood novels the play of
power behind the scenes inspires a similar excitement. Who's got
the money? Who controls the streetcar lines, the newspapers, the
city council? What sort of women do these money titans marry,
what sort of mistresses do they keep? Dreiser loves to speak of the
animal "effrontery" of his magnates, and to theorize clumsily about
their motives, the "chemisms" that drive them. He's crammed
himself with T. H. Huxley, Herbert Spencer, Darwin and a heavy
diet of "artistry," but he's such a passionate materialist that he
carries you with him even while you are dismissing his theories
and his clumsy artiness. For he was a big man, and the humanity of
his characters was large. Dreiser's old Chicago, the Chicago of
1900, is gone; few traces of it remain. The old materialistic innocence has disappeared—florid bars, good carriage horses, substantial Victorian virtues, substantial carnality; German, Irish, Polish, Italian Chicago bursting with energy—the Protestant
businessmen, bankers and empire builders. The crass, dirty, sinful,
vulgar, rich town of politicians, merchant princes and land specula-
tors, the Chicago of Yerkes and Samuel Insull, has vanished. Suddenly the "Hog Butcher for the World" was there no longer (I've
never been able to decide whether Sandburg's "Chicago" was a
poem or an advertisingman's effusion). Vitality—I suppose that
means a passionate release of the energies which had been restricted
in the old country. Here Europeans—even New Englanders—
were able to let themselves go. And now a new population of Third
World immigrants has settled in. Also internal immigrants from the
South.

   TQ: Then you think that the new immigrants coming to the city
are having an experience significantly different from the one you
had when you came here as an immigrant?

   Bellow: Of course they are. Chicago is a far more dangerous
place now. Black politicians and white city-council crooks who
have taken over the old Daley Machine have between them divided
the city on racial lines. Has the crime rate increased? The police
fiddle with the records on orders from our mayors, so it is impossible to obtain reliable figures. Impossible also to get an accurate
breakdown of the statistics. Newspapers, when they report abomi-
nable crimes, do not refer to the race of the suspects. The public,

which understands only too well, is resigned to the imposition of
this taboo. Right-thinking liberal citizens, hoping for future improvements, recalling past injustices, counsel themselves to be patient.
"Patience" sounds better than "intimidation" or "surrender," and
nicer than "cowardice." Perhaps there are not more muggings,
knifings, shootings and murders than there used to be, but the
crimes seem to be more outlandish—committed in a more demonic
spirit. You are robbed, and locked in the trunk of your car; raped,
and also forced to go down on the rapist; or sodomized. Consider
the hazards new immigrants must now face. Different? Of course
Chicago is different! The public schools are now eighty-seven
percent Negro and Hispanic. What sort of democratic education do
you suppose such schools afford? There's no way to compare the
experience of old and new ethnic groups—the Central Americans,
Koreans, Pakistanis, Iranians come here seeking employment,
peace, stability. A refugee from the terrors of Beirut opens a grocery
store in Chicago, thrives, and then is shot in a holdup. Not an
uncommon story. The funny misfortunes and torments of *Candide*
are the literal facts of modern experience. The older "ethnics," the
Poles, Czechs, the Italians, the Irish, the Germans and the Scandi-
navians, live in heavily-defended districts, clinging to the properties
in which their parents and grandparents invested so much labor.
They organize neighborhood watch-groups, and they buy arms. But
the division into blacks and ethnics is a disaster. A second disaster is
the swift rise of the demagogues in both factions. They expose each
other's corruption and criminal connections. But the more the
public learns, the more its paralysis increases.

   TQ: Are you saying that the traditional image of Chicago from
the 1920s and 1930s—Chicago as a violent place—is rather superficial?

   Bellow: In the twenties the Capone guys shot up the O'Banion
guys. Only one innocent died in the Valentine's Day massacre.
You knew when a body was found in a sewer which gang the victim
belonged to. The circulation wars sometimes affected the newspaper guy on the corner because he might lose all his teeth if he
carried the *Examiner* instead of the *Tribune*. Most ordinary citizens—
civilians, if you like—were not greatly affected. By contrast, over a

recent Thanksgiving weekend no less than nine murders were reported.

TQ: The picture of Chicago—circa World War I—in the fiction of a writer like Sherwood Anderson emphasizes his sense of shock at the amount of violence and the press hype of this kind of activity in the city. Anderson seemed to think of Chicago as a kind of dreadful sin bin.

Bellow: Yes, but he was an artistic small-towner. He had left the provinces because his sensibilities required more culture, more ideas, conversation and refinement. In Winesburg he found only psychopathology in Freudian (sexual) forms. Anderson was characteristic of the small-town American with esthetic inclinations, circa 1910. That doesn't mean that he lacked talent, only that he was a provincial, craving big-time esthetic and cultural horizons. That Chicago should seem awful to him is easy to understand.

TQ: He simply couldn't have known enough about the city to be able to apprehend the whole of it?

Bellow: Right. And he applied to it standards of "refinement" and "art" which today make us a bit uncomfortable.

TQ: To another topic. Your fictional vision of how a genuine man comes to be appears to have much in common with European predecessors like Dostoevsky and Mann. I refer partly to the traditional form of the *Bildungsroman*—the novel of education—as it embodies the process of authentic character formation and partly to the emphasis you all (that is, yourself, Dostoevsky, and Mann) place on family influence, or lack of it, in the formation of character. The question then is: Do you feel that there is an essential difference between the way a contemporary writer needs to approach the problem, "How do I live genuinely?" and the way such earlier writers as Dostoevsky and Mann approached that problem?

Bellow: First of all, I would make a distinction between Dostoevsky and anybody else because he was the greater writer by far, a man struggling to justify his Christianity against his own skepticism and nihilism. Mann was more ready to play; rather, to make a game of examining the bourgeoisie against a background of nihilism, and to exploit the opportunities for historical painting that this offered. In *Buddenbrooks* the bourgeois order in which the family had been rooted was decaying, falling into pessimism (Schopenhauer) and decadence. My own situation was that of a person who early understood that, like it or not, he was an exotic among other exotics. The children of immigrants inherited no "bourgeois stability." This may be a little difficult to interpret. Stability, if we were to have any, must be found or created. The word for this was "Americanization." The masses that came from Europe in the great wave of immigration between 1870 and 1930 wanted to be as American as possible. I was quick to recognize how hard the immigrants were trying to be something that they were not. They had excellent reasons for making themselves over. The distortions they suffered in Americanizing themselves also charged them with a certain energy. It was this energy that built the great cities. "Traditionalists" disliked—no, despised—this, but what American cities did "tradition" build? When FDR said on the air one night during a Fireside Chat that we are all aliens here, that this was a nation of aliens, he could safely, generously, advantageously, say it because he obviously was not an alien. He was a rich country squire who belonged to a famous family, but he was picking up a lot of votes by speaking plainly about the others. Though everybody wished to be an American, everybody's secret was that he hadn't succeeded in becoming one. My friend Lillian McCall, in her forthcoming memoirs, develops this theme in an original manner. The immigrant might have changed his name and his clothing and denied his native Italian or Russian or Yiddish, but the mark of the alien was upon him—you could see it. I picked *that* up, and that's why I don't know whether a book like *The Adventures of Augie March* is so much a *Bildungsroman* as it is a piece of ethnography. And I understand now why Augie March himself was such an *ingénu:* he didn't want to acknowledge the worst; the fact is, he wanted to enjoy his situation, wanted to play the American naïf. There was a price to pay. He was unwilling to pay it.

TQ: Paying for it would have meant recognizing the unfinished quality of his world?

Bellow: Yes, and its wickedness, rawness and vulgarity. He wanted to relish it, I think. He was that kind of *ingénu*. He didn't want to be bitter about it. Sad, yes. I think he expressed what was probably very genuine just then for adolescent Americans of

immigrant background: the desire to embrace everybody, the desire
for fraternity, the wish to be the lover of experience for its own
sake, the lover of novelty. At any rate, he did not intend to be
disappointed. He was very much like the young man Dreiser
described—the one who had just arrived in Chicago, the young
Theodore of *Dawn*.

TQ: Does Augie March's desire for fraternity differ very much
from that which Dostoevsky describes in *The Brothers Karamazov*?

Bellow: Yes, because Dostoevsky's fraternity has to overcome,
first of all, a heavy dose of neurosis, and secondly, a kind of
deadly accurate sadistic insight into the motives of people. *The
Brothers Karamazov* is not brimming with lovable human beings.
Here and there, yes—a child, or an Alyosha, or a Zossima. Can
Americans swallow Father Zossima?

TQ: I was thinking about how somebody like Augie relates to his
brother Simon. It's a very difficult relationship for him, and then
when Simon reveals, at one point, his terrible hatred of the parents:
"Well, Augie, you know who our father was, don't you? He abandoned us; he wasn't even here. And you know what our mother
was like, don't you? A simpleton. The two of them craved sex, and
that's how we came to be." That's something difficult for Augie to
overcome, it would seem to me. Augie sees the power of his
brother and somewhat understands the wild suffering Simon is
undergoing. Simon's suffering, and who knows? The absent father's suffering, the mother's . . .

Bellow: Well, I think that Augie's attitude is: "Nevertheless, I
am personally free. No matter how I happened to get here."
There is a kind of light-hearted equality about the book which
is—well, inaccurate. It's not really the way it was; it's just the
way Augie wanted it to be.

TQ: But accurate in terms of the dreams that young people had
at that time?

Bellow: Right. And I think *Augie March* also reflected the spirit
of Chicago during the Depression—a feeling remarkably widespread and now gone, leaving hardly a trace. What everyone felt
then was that a terrible thing had happened—something like an
earthquake, a natural disaster. Everybody had been stricken by it.

You were called upon to pitch in and help. Then Happy Days would presently be Here Again. Never mind the disgrace; never mind that educated people were digging in the city dump, that M.D.'s and engineers had become scavengers or worked on the roads for the PWA or the WPA. Everything was going to turn right-side-up.

TQ: Are you referring now especially to the immigrant neighborhoods rather than those of the middle class?

Bellow: Many middle-class Americans felt that the Depression was a hideous disgrace, that they had fallen to the level of the immigrants. Were now indistinguishable from greenhorns.

TQ: It was the middle-class Americans who felt they had suffered dramatic reversals, who, as a consequence, sometimes took drastic actions like stepping out of high windows.

Bellow: That wasn't so common, really. I think the country then was at its best and was unified by a spirit which disappeared with World War II, when the country had a visible enemy to fight and hate. Pearl Harbor was a terrible shock. We heard songs about going out to slap "the dirty little Jap." Vile songs. Rationing made people very angry, and the black marketing made them angry. There were currents of racism which hadn't been felt before. There certainly was a surge of Jew-Hatred during the first days of the war. And the internment of the Japanese. And so on. A great deal of ill nature, just then. You heard people complaining: "We can't get tires for our cars, or meat, or Lucky Strikes." All these articles were easy enough to find on the black market.

TQ: Why would the war necessarily have brought on anti-Semitism and other forms of racism?

Bellow: While most people approved of the War in the Pacific there were those who didn't like the War in Europe. Many did not. They said, "Why should we go to war with Hitler? Let the Germans fight the Bolsheviks. It's the Jews who want us to fight Hitler."

TQ: You think the change was permanent after the war?

Bellow: No, it wasn't permanent. When the war ended, the boys were brought home. And then the country soared into a state of pig-heaven prosperity. Everybody had two cars, unskilled workers could afford campers, speed boats, Florida condominiums, trips to Hawaii.

TQ: Americans were going to hell in a hand-basket.

Bellow: Very quickly.

TQ: Wasn't that basking in prosperity an antidote to the anxiety previously brought on by the Depression and the war?

Bellow: America found itself a superpower, at the heart of world politics. Americans were understandably uneasy. They turned to money and property with a heightened intensity. Wealth in the twenties had been snobbish (Fitzgerald); in the fifties it was democratized, more widely shared, more infected with anxious disorders, more consciously or ideologically hedonistic, sexually more open and also more troubled.

TQ: Getting back to literature a bit. In your concern with the comic mode in fiction, you've been interested over the years in the role of the fool or the *schlemiel,* if the two can actually be linked. Could you comment a little for us on the continuing vitality of this figure for the fiction writer now?

Bellow: Well, I don't really know much about that.

TQ: I guess we could say about fools in general. I'm sure you know a lot about that [laughter]. No names please, but presumably real fools are the models or inspiration for literary fools.

Bellow: Well, I think that something else is going on, and it has to do with increasing literacy and the forced growth of a mental life, of cleverness. On a large scale, in modern societies, you also have a sense of reduced personal scope. Dostoevsky, in *Notes from Underground,* anticipated this in the last century. His Underground Man, a creature of resentful, impotent intelligence, is aware that the world is darkened by a metaphysical shadow, and that one can no longer easily and clearly distinguish good from evil. Existence is a minefield. Civilized consciousness is anarchic. *Schlemiels,* when their hats blow off, chase them across minefields. Your typical *schlemiel* will seldom theorize.

TQ: I was thinking, too, of some of the positive connotations that could be given to the term, in the sense of one who somehow becomes a survivor, who is bumbling almost, but he realizes that he can't cope with it, and in some way rolls with it or bounces with it—that this is one dimension of the fool.

Bellow: Your modern "Fool" has a sharply comic sense of himself. He is not a bumbler, simply. The bumbler has no pattern, no structure. Your Fool—not your *Schlemiel*—holds well-defined ideas.

TQ: Some wit?

Bellow: Some wit. He is an astute observer. He is a Cassius who will never stab his Caesar. I think of somebody like Herzog. People were frightened by *Herzog* because they thought it was a serious book. It was a funny book—

TQ: [Laughter.]

Bellow: Well, it's true—

TQ: No, no, of course. I wouldn't argue.

Bellow: It intimidated readers because it was so full of "ideas." It was really, I think, in the twentieth century, the first portrayal (naturally comic) of the American intellectual trying to come to grips with life. My *intellectual* has been educated out of his senses. He has received an utterly useless education and breaks down as soon as he faces a real crisis. Simply doesn't know what to do. He starts to drag books from the shelves to see what Aristotle advises, or what Spinoza has to say. It's a joke. To his credit, he quickly understands this. His blindness ends when he begins to write letters. By means of these letters the futility of his education is exposed. On Job's dunghill, and scraping himself with a potsherd, he recognizes (with joy!) how bad an education he has had. And this was what I was after in my book. I was investigating the so-called culture of a new powerful class—the professors. Professors did all right for themselves, but humanly they were as dumb as they come. Their ignorance doomed them to a kind of hysteria at the first touch of pain and suffering. Herzog didn't really know what to do when his wife took a lover and pushed him out of the house. He therefore played the fool. He played out all the fine roles that his education had acquainted him with—intellectual, lover, abused husband, longing father, pitiable brother, armed avenger— all of that. And finally he found himself at square one again. What is square one? Square one is the square in which you resume your first self, with its innate qualities. You recover (or almost recover) your original sense of life and your original powers of judgment return. Lucky to have a second opportunity. Herzog is thus a negative *Bildungsroman*. It goes in reverse.

TQ: That somehow must relate to the idea of the axial lines in *Augie March,* those pages late in the book having to do with rediscovering your true self again and again in your life, if you stay quiet enough.

Bellow: When the noise dies down you'll find yourself with the "I" you first knew when you came to know that you were a self—an event which occurs quite early in life. And that first self is embraced with a kind of fervor, excitement, love—and knowledge! Your formal schooling is really a denaturing of that first self.

TQ: You know that wonderful quote out of Thoreau's *Journals* where he poses the question, "What does education often do?" And he answers it by saying, "It makes a straight-cut ditch of a free, meandering brook."

Bellow: I think we would have to agree with him. In a recent article my colleague Allan Bloom has written that a modern education removes the created soul and implants an artificial one.

TQ: As you were talking I thought of Ivan Karamazov, who confesses to Alyosha before launching into his great world-denouncing diatribe, "But I love the sticky green leaves that come in the spring," as if that elemental feeling is enough, almost to say, "Well, I know this is all rubbish, but as an intellectual I feel bound to the rubbish."

Bellow: Yes, the sticky leaves—the melancholy love that your intellectual, ruled by a critical intelligence, cannot enjoy—but cannot quite forget. Ivan is a romantic intellectual. It is his fate to suffer from the development of a "higher consciousness" which separates him from the common life and leads him into hubris and madness, etc. Higher consciousness, Western-style, deprives him of his true—his Russian—identity. You cannot expect a Jewish reader, however sympathetic, to grow enthusiastic over Slavic nationalism and the anti-Semitism that goes with it. Let's descend from the heights a bit. My own temperamental preference is for comedy. To return to my book, I discovered as I was finishing it that Herzog had played out all the roles he had learnt in order to demonstrate their bankruptcy.

TQ: In what way bankrupt?

Bellow: Bankrupt because inapplicable. Bankrupt because we revere "thinking," but know so little about real thought. I was reading the other day Lord Moran's reminiscences of Winston Churchill, and Moran records a conversation with a professional soldier, a brave man who led a guerrilla group in Burma. This man tells Moran, "People like me should be teaching in the universities. I can remember my own university education, and there was nobody to teach me anything real because everybody there was trained in books and was the product of a long course of professional instruction and didn't really know anything about what matters." The brave soldier was quite right. I can remember two sociology courses in "Marriage and the Family" taught by Professor Ernest Burgess, a clear, mild, touchingly gentle bachelor. What had he to tell us about women or sexual love? We should have been instructed by someone burnt in love's fires, by a Laclos, a Casanova, a Stendhal. What had poor Burgess to tell us? From his classes we were sent directly into the lines. No, to the shooting gallery. Of the real things we learned nothing, nothing that mattered.

I realize now that I loved some of my teachers—loved them for their innocence, mainly, or for their eccentricities. For they hadn't much to tell us. Thank God for the formative affections they elicited! And I am grateful also to certain academics whose classrooms anticipated the Theater of the Absurd. Mortimer Adler had much to tell us about Aristotle's Ethics, but I had only to look at him, even as an undergraduate, to see that he had nothing useful to offer on the conduct of life. He lectured on Prudence, or Magnanimity. It was—well, tomfoolery. True, we did read Aristotle. And Mortimer Adler gave good value in his way. But we should have had Jimmy Hoffa as well. He was often at the Shoreland, within walking distance of the campus. Such, at any rate, was the liberal education we received. I wonder whether the professional schools were any better. Were there courses in the Law School on the venality of judges? Was there a bagman seminar? It was only after you had been admitted to the bar and went downtown to practice that you learned the facts of life.

TQ: You made the statement that Herzog is a reverse *Bildungs-roman* . . .

Bellow: As a matter of fact, before this interview I never thought of *Herzog* as a non-*Bildungsroman*. I see it now, thanks to you.

TQ: But doesn't he know at the end a great deal more than he knew at the beginning? You say he does go back in a sense to first things, but yet he goes back to those first things with the memory of what's gone in between.

Bellow: Well, he's learned from his false education that he didn't have an education. Maybe this is the moment at which education begins. As in *The Way of All Flesh*.

TQ: I was wondering if you chose the name Herzog because it suggests a kind of natural monarchy. You do talk of the "marvelous Herzog," a person trying to get back to a sense of being marvelous.

Bellow: Well there were lots of tough kids in Chicago called "Duke" [laughter]. And even their dogs were called "Duke."

TQ: I was thinking also about the root etymology of the word, *Herz,* and was wondering if Herzog also went back to that person who had pledged his heart in a sense.

Bellow: It may have had something to do with that.

TQ: You've talked repeatedly about the need to affirm and have suggested that the very act of writing is in itself affirmative—

Bellow: I don't know about affirmation, but if a man writes an excellent sentence, he has performed a valuable action, one which teaches you something. Even if the sentence has no direct moral application, he's done something of value. That in itself is a good thing. It increases love in some ways. It certainly increases the love of literature for anyone who has the heart to feel it. But it's not a question of resolute edification or affirmation.

TQ: But in specific terms of the novel, or any work of fiction or poetry, how can this affirmation be given without seeming, as it were, out of touch with the times or that one is edifying or prettifying?

Bellow: One has no business to be out of touch with the times. What I dislike about Augie March is that he was too often out of touch, that he selected those things that might be enjoyed, and dropped the others. He was a kind of ethical hedonist, accepting the pleasures of an ethical life, but without looking too closely at the facts.

TQ: So this complicates talking about affirmation a great deal, doesn't it? You look back on that and say it was a certain kind of error, I mean insofar as you still would hold to that feeling about what it is that moves you or moves others when they read your work. It gets pretty tricky, doesn't it, to trace how affirmation could come about?

Bellow: Yes, it gets tricky. I can remember when I wrote that book in Paris in '48 and '49, being perfectly aware that the Nazis had just left. And I knew that when I took a deep breath I was inhaling the crematorium gases still circulating in the air, and that was more immediate than my recollections of Chicago in the thirties. In Paris I enjoyed a nostalgic Chicago holiday. I didn't at all know how to cope with the more demanding modern theme. I was too American to do it. *Augie March* may be an interesting book, but it's not a true book, not fully true. I had read my Céline, and I knew what the modern theme was. But it wasn't the kind of thing that would have come naturally to a kid who had grown up in Chicago in the twenties and thirties.

TQ: When is that attitude adopted, or should I say, when does the confrontation with these modern pains begin in your works?

Bellow: It begins to begin with what I wrote immediately after *Augie March,* a novella called *Seize the Day.* In that short book I examined a man who *insisted* on having a father, who demanded that his father *be* a father to him. But Wilhelm's father had no use for the failed "father" ideology embraced by his son—the seedy *ingénu* son.

TQ: All the larkish aspects of *Augie* have collapsed in the novel.

Bellow: Right. The only "fun" in the book is to be found in the exploitations of Wilhelm the dupe by Dr. Tamkin, a clumsy charlatan.

TQ: Those feelings of wanting to get along and not being able to—do you associate those feelings with your being in Paris after the occupation and the death camps? That one couldn't get along in the world after this?

Bellow: I needed to work this matter out within an American frame of reference. I was not going to embrace European nihilism because, after all, I was in no position to do it. The only language that I use is the language of Americans, of people whose premises are very different from those of Europeans—the promises of a democratic, if not anarchic, crowd. Theirs was the mild populist anarchism of wise guys, boxing fans, bleacher-bums, glad-handers,

go-getters. Decent enough Americans (as portrayed by themselves). The "decent American" is at the heart of Wilhelm's vision
of the human average. Tamkin the "realist" says to him, "You
don't know how crazy people are, how twisted." Wilhelm protests,
"No, no, there are wonderful people of all kinds." And when Tamkin
asks where they are to be found, Wilhelm says, "Well, they're out
there, in the country." I guess you have to go further west.
[Laughter.] But Wilhelm has no evidence for his claim. And there I
move into deeper gloom. But an American writer of the fifties could
not assume the attitudes of a European. These would have been
entirely artificial.

TQ: It seems to me that you wanted to repudiate the other stuff
as you felt it being exported from France.

Bellow: Damn influential stuff, nevertheless. And as a Jew who
knew what the Final Solution was I might have done otherwise.
A kind of blindness to the greatest of evils is an important by-
product or result of Americanization. As a nation we prefer the
milder, the vaguer, view. Dreiser was a fiercer analyst than most.
He knew that your enemies would cut your throat—wouldn't flinch
from applying the knife, even plucking a few hairs from your neck
first to test the sharpness of the blade.

TQ: A kosher slit, testing the blade like the rabbis.

Bellow: But that was a Darwinist conception applied to capitalism. Anyway, Augie avoided all this. And Wilhelm, the *bon
enfant* making his last hopeless stand, cheated by Tamkin, rejected
by his father, enters a funeral parlor to have a good cry over the
death of his cherished ideals. You can get took. You can die of it, lie
in a coffin. So much for Tommy Wilhelm, who trustingly (or
lazily) surrendered his soul to the milder, vaguer view.

TQ: And is Herzog avoiding this with his imported, fashionable
despair?

Bellow: Herzog is fortunate enough to recover the power to judge
for himself. His despair is neither imported nor fashionable, but
quite genuine. He is an intelligent man and his comic gifts are
anything but superficial.

TQ: In terms of the kind of confrontation you're speaking of,
Sammler seems to be the first major figure to have actually

suffered through the war. Does he represent a further step in
that direction?

Bellow: In *Sammler* [*Mr. Sammler's Planet*], I was trying to
write about the United States from a European perspective. My
parents, my brothers, my sister were European-born. I was the first
of the American Bellows—Canadian by birth, but an American
nevertheless. And the family left—fled—St. Petersburg in 1913. I
grew up among European uncles and cousins and neighbors. And
after the war—in Paris, London, Warsaw and Rome—I met survi-
vors of the older generation who were very like Artur Sammler.

TQ: And yet Sammler doesn't appear to be as despairing a soul
as Herzog would like to be. Sammler is still interested in a utopian
like H. G. Wells.

Bellow: You are being hard on poor Herzog. Herzog's pains are
quite real. I have often wondered why readers were put off by
him. He was an *intellectual* and people felt that their education was
being tested by him; perhaps they were grinding their teeth as they
read, like students sitting for a comprehensive examination, tense
and therefore also humorless, resentful. Herzog's high earnestness was intended to be part of the fun. But let us leave that. You
ask about Sammler and H. G. Wells. Wells' utopianism went sour
towards the end of his life. His last book, *Mind at the End of its
Tether,* is relentlessly pessimistic. His final judgment on civilization is that men destroy one another like rats in a sack. Sammler
had read this book.

TQ: A few moments ago you talked, with reference to *Seize the
Day,* about going deeper into the gloom. Relating that back to the
Paris Review interview in which you spoke about earlier modern
literature as having an elegiac bent (though somehow this going into
the gloom was not intended to or does not end up repeating that
mode), I wonder, however, whether you feel some of that earlier
mode is renewed and updated in your later writing?

Bellow: Ah, T. S. Eliot, I presume.

TQ: Yes, you mentioned *The Waste Land.*

Bellow: But that was not for me. You see, I've always been
devotedly faithful to my own history, and I've never struck
attitudes that didn't suit it. I am not a WASP trained on the classics,
the stray descendant of a golden age of gentlemen lost in the modern

abysses, and all the rest of that. That's not me. I am not about to
take that viewpoint. My Jewish history gives me an entirely
different orientation. The heavens in all their glory can open up
above the ghetto sidewalk, and one doesn't need Gothic or
Renaissance churches, Harvard University, or any of these places,
in order to condemn the nihilism of the modern age from a
viewpoint sufficiently elevated. That's what I disliked about *The
Waste Land*. It was the elevation, the nostalgia for things that
probably never were, the longing for distinctions that ruled out
those who would never be eligible for them. And I knew about
those prescriptions for eligibility. I had read my Henry Adams, my
Spengler, and T. S. Eliot's *The Idea of a Christian Society;* and I
knew there would be no place for me as a Jew in that kind of
civilization. Therefore all the greater was my enthusiasm for
embracing this American democracy with all its crudities, which
nevertheless granted me an equality which I felt was mine by right. I
wasn't going to be ruled off the grounds by those WASP hotshots;
and so I rejected all of that. On the contrary, I saw "traditional-
ism" as a further descent into the nihilistic pit. "Traditionalists"
had gone deeper into the night, with their fascism and anti-Semitism.

    A writer has no choice but to be faithful to his own history. I was
not born into the American Protestant Majority. But I was never
at all persuaded to view that majority as an exclusive club. I assume
American democracy to be a cosmopolitan phenomenon. I see it
as liberation, not as decline and fall. What has my Jewish history to
do with Eliot's "classicism," "royalism," or with "tradition" as
the term is defined by those who feel that they have suffered a great
fall? My generation of students was bowled over by *The Waste
Land* and I went down together with the rest, but I was on my feet
again quite soon. I thought it an excessively "educated" poem.
Joyce's *Ulysses* has been called a "summa of its age." Behind *The
Waste Land* there is a summa, too. Despite my great admiration
of Eliot, and even more of Joyce, I have never been able to agree
with the comprehensive schemes on which they base themselves.
Dedalus as a philosopher is not convincing with his "diaphane" and
"adiaphane" and the "ineluctable modality." And behind Eliot I
always glimpse Frazer's *Golden Bough,* and other collections of

what we have now come to know as Comparative Religion.
Perhaps because I am an amateur myself, I am quite good at seeing
through other amateurs of myth. I could never for a moment take
Freud's Egyptology seriously. I read his *Moses* as a novel and was
sorry he had burdened his story with scientific baggage. Eliot
protested that he was a "classicist." To me, however, *The Waste
Land* was a work of romantic *sehnsucht*. Joyce, to his great
credit, worked painfully and honestly through the modern age,
while Eliot was horrified at the pollution of Spenser's "sweet
Thames." Perhaps the most gifted of our Environmentalists. Here
again was the romantic "far away and long ago." To turn this
against the modern age did not make him a classicist. The modern
age is our given, our crushing *donnée*. No, Eliot is not for me. I
much prefer Nietzsche. Much more strengthening to the soul—the
soul of a Jew, I should add.

TQ: Perhaps related to the question of gloom, there is a sense,
ever stronger since *Mr. Sammler's Planet,* of leave-taking from
this world, which seems to be exhibited as ever more forbidding
and hostile. There's not the sense of embracing life that one gets
in *Augie March,* not even the quiet achieved at the end of *Herzog.*
The concerns seem more otherworldly.

Bellow: No great mystery here. With everything I write I draw a
little closer to whatever it was that made me wish to be a writer.
Recently I was surprised, in reading Philip Roth's latest Zuckerman
novel, at the horrors he experiences in writing. Why, with his
great gifts, has Roth nothing but difficulties to report? Can it be
because he believes with Freud that we write in order to get
money and women? In America any clever man can make money.
As far as *getting* women!—well, Freud had no way to anticipate
how much the sexual revolution would simplify that. But isn't
writing a spiritual activity? I seem always to have assumed that it was.

TQ: I must admit to having been stumped as to what to make of
all these excursions into theosophy and Rudolf Steiner by Citrine
in *Humboldt's Gift.*

Bellow: *Humboldt's Gift,* a comic novel whose true theme is
death, seems to have thrown a good many readers. Theosophy,
by the way, is what Mme. Blavatsky and Annie Besant did. Steiner
called himself an anthroposophist. And you may be interested to

learn that the anthroposophists, with few exceptions, disapproved of the irreverence of *Humboldt's Gift*. But no disrespect was intended. Steiner was a very great man indeed. Whether he was an Initiate I am not qualified to say. Hostile critics who attacked *Humboldt* were not qualified to say, either. They had not found it necessary to read Steiner to try to learn why he had made so great an impression on Charlie Citrine. They might have discovered that he was a great visionary—they might even have been moved by his books. This, however, is not the proper place for a defense of Steiner. I can only try to explain what it was that drew Charlie Citrine to him. It was, in a word, the recognition that everything which Charlie had taken to be commonsensical, realistic, prudent, normal—his ambitions, marriage, love affairs, possessions, business relations—was a mass of idiocies. "A serious human life? This! You've got to be kidding!" And from demonic absorption in the things of this world, he turns to an invisible world in which he thinks his Being may be founded. Is there, in fact, any basis for religion other than the persistence of the supersensible? "Science" with the aid of modern philosophy—what we call the positive outlook—has driven "the invisible" into the dark night where enlightenment says it belongs. Together with it, in our simplemindedness, we drive away revelation as well, and with revelation we drive out art, also we drive out dreaming. Dreams are readmitted only through the Ellis Island of science, by officials qualified in the legitimate interpretation of dreams. Music we bootleg. We bring it across the threshold surreptitiously.

The moral law also has a precarious existence among us. Now, what is to prevent a writer from imagining that we exist without revelation, without music and poetry, without the moral law, without the Gods, *only* in our present depleted and restricted quotidian consciousness, and that in fact life-giving forces sustain us from beyond, and also from within—in sleep, in dream, through imagination, by means of intuition? That the true Unconscious is a much bigger thing than the dark, libidinal province established by Freud, which we enter with the passport of "science." Charlie Citrine does not accept being intimidated by the representatives of "scientific" respectability. I'm a bit that way myself. I can't remember going out of my way to be heterodox. But I was born into an orthodox family, and detested orthodoxy from the first.

Our Valuation of Human Life Has Become Thinner

Michael Ignatieff / 1986

From *The Listener*, 13 March 1986, 18–19. © 1986 by BBC Publications. Reprinted by permission.

The historian and writer Michael Ignatieff discusses "Modernity and its Discontents" with novelists Saul Bellow and Martin Amis

Ignatieff: The characters in Saul Bellow's novels all seem to be saying, with a mixture of horror and fascination: "What's the world coming to?" Over 40 years he's described the loss of a whole cultural tradition, not just of books and ideas but of human qualities and feelings, of community and dignity which find no echo in the contempt capitals of America. Familiar landmarks are missing in Bellow's works, but his books make clear how important those landmarks are to us, how they help to keep us human. They're part of a cultural tradition going back hundreds of years, and without those landmarks we're lost in what he calls "the moronic inferno." A younger generation is drawn precisely by this sense of the infernal in American culture. Martin Amis, better than any, conveys the fascination and weird richness of the culture of *Playboy* fantasies and space invaders in a book of essays he happens to have called *The Moronic Inferno*. This sense of the infernal in modern culture—that it's a moronic inferno—I'm wondering what you meant, Saul Bellow, when you picked up that phrase from Wyndham Lewis.

Bellow: Well, it means a chaotic state in which no one has sufficient internal organisation to resist, and in which one is overwhelmed by all kinds of powers—political, technological, military, economic and so on—which carry everything before them with a kind of heathen disorder in which we're supposed to survive with all our human qualities. Whether this is possible or not is, I suppose, the question we're addressing.

Ignatieff: What is this lack of a centre? You seem to be implying that if somehow we could have a different kind of self, a more resolute self, we could withstand this onslaught a little better.

Bellow: It doesn't need to be a different kind of self. It needs to be a self, however. That is to say, one witnesses the obliteration of true forms of individuality in this scene. And the reason why writers are writers, if they are authentic writers, is that they do confront the scene with a fairly well-organised individuality.

Amis: I think it probably comes down to the fact that our valuation of human life has along the way become thinner, or more nebulous. We don't quite give it the credit it once had. And once that goes or starts to go, then the whole nature of reality becomes something much more unreliable. The world has become much more politicised in a woolly way. Anger is allowed on to the political scene as an accepted—if not legitimate or legal—part of geopolitical life. I often thought, during the rioting recently and in 1981, that this was sort of Criminals Lib. You know: "We're just criminals—we want to be self-respecting like anyone else, we want to get on with our job, why are we being singled out for persecution by the forces of law and order?" An imbalance seems to have been struck.

Bellow: You go back to the places where you lived in earlier times and you see that they're in total decay. The reconstructed Chicago along the lake is a sort of sanctuary, in which you live under a kind of feudal protection of moats and TV surveillance and all the rest of that. You don't go out. There is no natural life of the streets any more. And that's very hard to take because—to use the American word—socialisation of that sort has stopped, except in certain protected bars and so on. But people live with it. They don't even acknowledge how terrible it's become, they internalise all of this, and they congratulate themselves for having avoided being murdered in the streets, as if that were due to some skill of theirs.

Ignatieff: Yet the Western democracies are the most institutionalised, humane societies the world has ever known. We take care of people in ways that would be the envy of the 17th and 18th centuries, and yet both of you are saying our sense of humanity is thinning out. Now, I can't sort this paradox out.

Amis: Well, there is one great underlying uncertainty. We now find ourselves having the fate of the earth in the hands of, on the one hand, an old actor, and on the other, a prison warden. I get a great sense of discrepancy from that. That is what the world has come to. And surely we are living in the most dangerous era that the human species has ever gone through. Nadezhda Mandelstam called it the "fratricidal century," but it's the suicidal century, too. It would be extraordinary if we didn't react to it in violent ways.

Bellow: It is quite true that the democratic societies of the West feel obligated to take care of the young, the sick, the needy, the aged and so on, and this is certainly a laudable thing. But of course it has no personal dimension, it's all done in a bureaucratic way. There is nothing personal about this. The effect finally of all this caring is ultimately dehumanising. One can see that with the American welfare population.

Ignatieff: Let's broaden this frame a little. We're talking about a very scary world out there. After six o'clock at night you read your newspapers and you don't go downstairs on to the street because it's a scary world. Aren't we looking here at the decay of the public realm? It seems to me there is a recurring concern in your novels for a kind of civic world in which strangers can be together in a public place in which they can act politically together. How have we lost that? Is it just so simple as saying we've got a scary underclass on the street? Surely there must be something more to the decay of the public world than that?

Bellow: I suppose there is. And I'm not so sure that the public world has altogether decayed. I think in many ways it's supplanted the private world. When people spend 50 hours a week sitting before the television set, that means that the TV set is the master of the house. It has replaced family life and family authority. Otherwise why would everybody be looking at the set? In other words, it's an impoverishment of personal resources which turns people outward.

Amis: Also, large areas of American life are organised around television: politics, religion, sports.

Ignatieff: You've written very perceptively about the television culture, Martin. I'm just wondering whether you share this view of Saul Bellow's that the public realm of television is colonising and dominating the private world and the problem is not the decay of the public world but a sense that the private world is disintegrating in the face of television. Do you see it that way?

Amis: No, I think it's at least as much a cause as a symptom. I think one thing we haven't mentioned is the embarrassing deterioration of our leaders. No longer do Cabinet meetings break up while everyone hurries home to finish their translation of the Aeneid, that doesn't happen any more. One of the embarrassing things that these characters are now wishing on us is that they are using television. Of course, America knows all about this. Our leaders are just beginning to use it. And watching Margaret Thatcher speak now in this trained way, half-acting—what is she doing? She's not reading a speech, she's not acting, she's doing something in between. I part company with someone like that, they have stepped on to different channel of reality for me. And television isn't a symptom of that—it's an agent.

Bellow: This represents a borderline or terminating condition for civilisation as a whole; the old forms of existence have worn out, so to speak, and the new ones have not yet appeared—people are prospecting, as it were, in the desert for new forms. Television is in part an expression of that. It is at the same time, however, very powerful and manipulative and the media managers have manipulative ends of their own.

Amis: I think one thing that remains very strong in people, however debased, is the idea of art, even in the form of self-mutilation or self-decoration. If you look at the punks, you see that they are people who have, as it were, sprayed themselves with graffiti. They've vandalised themselves. But nonetheless it's all done with an idea of making something attractive or interesting.

Bellow: I recently read an account of a new survey of television-watching. It was fascinating because among other things it said that kids no longer watched a programme through. They had the clicker in their hands and they were channel-hopping, and so they were interested only in fragments of programmes. And their chief interest was in the special effects. They didn't care about the story. They didn't care about the characters. They were interested in the special effects, especially the noise effects. And this means that all coherence has gone. This is a systematic destruction of coherence. Nothing is consecutive, everything is inconsequent,

everything jumps out from strange corners. And really what this
may create in the child, or the adult too, is a sense of overwhelming sovereignty. "I am the person whom all this serves and I am the
one who makes all these decisions." You know, the old Everyman
edition used to have a thing on the frontispiece saying: "A tale to
hold old men from the chimney corner and children from their
play." That's not what holds them any more. What holds them is
the scrambler.

Amis: And this, of course, will be market research, which is
another great moronic instrument, I think. Is everyone in America
a market researcher now? It sometimes seems that way. But they
will look at this survey and they won't worry about the loss of the
narrative line in human life, they will produce ten-minute programmes full of special effects geared to the short attention span.

Ignatieff: One of the things you said, Saul Bellow, in an essay
written in 1967, was: "We long for enchantment, but we're too
skeptical." I'm just wondering what you meant.

Bellow: Literature has always referred to a world beyond the
threshold of the world that I know and see. I wouldn't want to
say that it always had a religious foundation, it didn't always. But
the more what we call "enlightenment" spreads, the more the disenchantment increases. Shakespeare's thoroughly enlightened genius:
he is himself skeptical about all these things, but of course he's
always referring as a poet to the gods and the heavens and all the
rest of that. Well, that shrinks down in modern times. That
becomes forbidden territory more and more, until we find ourselves
standing on a thoroughly shrunken ground. Now what does one
do about that? Does one say all of that was myth and religion and
of no importance to us now, we've got to find something else? Or
does one say this is a different kind of delusion? What I'm saying
really is that the transcendent has been kicked out of modern
literature on all sorts of grounds, and I think we presume too much
when we do that. It's not right. And we're not being faithful to our
own intuitions when we take it upon ourselves to say "It's finished." It's only finished in textbooks.

Amis: You're a splendid anachronism in this way. I mean, Saul
Bellow writes in a style—the high style—that has been kicked upstairs, as it were, in modern literature. In the textbooks it's all

228 Conversations with Saul Bellow

pretty plain that literature used to be about gods, then it was about kings, then it was about heroes, then it was about you and me. And now it's about them. We live in the ironic age—even rock-bottom realism is considered impossibly exotic and grand for the 20th century.

Bellow: I think that's a very apt description of how it happened.

Ignatieff: Metaphysics is one of the great embarrassments of modern life, isn't it? You can't talk about this stuff without sounding like a lunatic.

Bellow: As long as it's a separate category of discourse, there's no point in talking about it. The words for it were used up a long time ago. So the only foundation for it is in actual experience, in one's own felt life. And if that isn't there, then there is really no point in sounding off about it in an abstract sense. That's exactly the difference between literature and other kinds of discourse. And that's why it's very hard for me to read books in which there's no personal sense of what really happens within the human being. I used to feel that intellectuals knew what they were talking about. It took me a long time to find out that some small number of them did know what they were talking about but most of them were terribly misleading. In the meantime, I had gone through behaviourism and I'd gone through Marxism and I'd gone through psychoanalysis and I'd gone through existentialism and I'd gone through structuralism, and all of them evaporated.

Amis: You're saying, too, aren't you, why should a concern about what it is to be a human being be considered transcendental? The ground must have shrunk very low if that scene is very high It is *the* concern. It is what all writers should be addressing. And in fact one looks, sounds, feels like a crank the minute you bring it up.

Ignatieff: One of the things you said a long time ago, Saul Bellow, is that "ignorance of death is destroying us."

Bellow: If you don't observe the unconscious power that death has over the way people manage their lives, then you're not seeing what's happening at all.

Amis: You say elsewhere that death is the dark backing a mirror needs before it can give off a reflection, that everything has to be seen in the context of death. Death has been made available to use more generously in this era than ever before. I wonder, do you mean it as part of one's own journey through life, that death is always there as the dark backing, or that it's the sinister black vein in life?

Bellow: I don't think that it's sinister, I think it's a natural thing and I think what they used to call the *timor mortis,* the fear of death, is also very natural. What's unnatural is to blank it out altogether and to dismiss it from your life in the gay whirl.

Amis: And just as we don't think about personal death, we don't think about global death.

Ignatieff: How is it that a writer remains engaged with this question of what is going on out there in a world which is, in lots of ways that we've described, very repellent and very frightening? The reflex of a kind of hatred for it is very easy, and it seems to me a reflex that you've both resisted admirably. I'm just wondering how you sustain that engagement, why do you care about it?

Bellow: I don't know why I care about it, that's one of these questions that lead you into theology. But I do. And what a writer like me is apt to feel is that there is some loss of the power to experience life. People are really, in a sense, deprived of it now. Now it's all jargon, it's all nonsense, it's all slogans. It's all false descriptions and it's all fabrications. And, of course, one resists that.

Amis: I think also that you're disqualified from real pessimism by being a writer. I think even the blackest writers, the Célines, genuine haters of the modern world, still love it because it is interesting. What it doesn't lose is interest. It may lose everything else but it still has that.

Bellow's Real Gift

Susan Crosland / 1987

From the *London Sunday Times*, 18 October, 1987, 57. © 1987
by The London Sunday Times. Reprinted by permission.

"Why is it," he said, "that people's interest is so easily exhausted
when they live together? Familiarity breeds contempt? Pets don't
do that to you. Why is it that only human beings do that to
one another?

"I have the sense, not the conviction, that it's because we view
each other with a physical literalness—principally for sexual
purposes. Television and other media have made the demand for
novelty greater than it used to be. All of this goes against deeper
development with another human being.

"It's idle to talk about love as long as we define it externally: it's
a kind of death if what we care about is a woman's legs and
breasts," he said.

"And you?" I asked.

"Everybody is liable to the same infection," he replied. "You
use up the other person just like any other commodity, and
neither of you has got your soul's desire. So there is rejection and
eventually hatred."

We were in the flagstoned kitchen of Saul Bellow's Vermont
retreat, a fire burning on the hearth, I, at the big table, scribbling
on my enormous lined pad, he, dapper in his mushroom-coloured
corduroy trousers and emerald green shirt, standing gracefully against
the sink as he waits for the coffee to finish percolating.

At 72 he is lithe and handsome—arched black brows, straight
nose with flared nostrils, sensual mouth. Though I was to feel
quite done in at the end of our four hours, his energies stayed
unstinting, the hooded molten eyes watching me.

America's greatest modern writer is a courteous man: once he
agreed to the interview, he helped me. True, I had to make my way
to this beautiful hinterland—by three aircraft of diminishing size
and a hired car—but he'd booked me into a comfortable inn

beside an 18th century meeting house, and he fetched me in his new Range Rover for the final rugged lap through scarlet maples and golden hickory trees to the mountainside farmhouse where he spends half the year. He designed it, Janis says, combining what he liked best in other houses that he has loved.

Janis is one of his postgraduate students at the University of Chicago where during term he teaches in the afternoons. A Canadian, she has restored domestic happiness to his life after the desolation of his fourth divorce. Saul Bellow hates living alone. And he likes women.

Yet in the US his new book, *More Die of Heartbreak,* to be published here next week, has met with the charge of misogyny. Unlike the grim picture of life in the west—particularly Chicago— depicted in *The Dean's December,* this novel is an exuberant send-up of 1980s Americans, both sexes mocked mordantly.

"I had the temerity to include women in the human species," he says. "I describe them in the same manner that I describe men. 'Misogynist' really means that we are expected in every novel to redress the injustices of history. I grant you it is a bad history. I'm not guilty of all of it myself." He adds: "It's only fair to point out that women often give as good as they get." When he smiles after one of his dry asides, the central gap between the big white teeth makes the whole face humorous.

The misogynist charge came from male reviewers. "It's their way of currying favour with the feminist public. I really dislike the McCarthy style of this criticism"—he mimes Joe McCarthy brandishing his list of names—"labelling me without having to prove anything. A woman is more likely to see the truth of what I've said. Women are the ones—strangers—who write me their views. On the whole they read more than men and therefore with more sensitivity."

I say that I found the novel's principal woman, Matilda, rather touching in her innocent awfulness.

"I thought so, too. She is following the lines set for her by her breeding."

But Bellow denies that he is a pessimist. "I've removed myself from that scale altogether. I take a high view of human nature and a low view."

His major concern is that our ever-increasing specialisation is
turning humans into machines. "You are struck by the effectiveness of lawyers, surgeons, engineers, and the shabbiness, nullity of
their personal lives because they have no inner cultivation.
They've shut off access to their own souls.

"Since the soul has been rather universally rejected by modern
thought, you have to be a bold man to talk about it." He is and
he does. "Where there is no correspondence between inner life and
outer, you're a barbarian. You may look civilised, but you're
not."

"I don't wish to be impertinent," I say, "but your marriage
record is bound to raise the question of your own inner life."

"I'm not projecting from my personal life. It's from observation."

"But *does* it apply to you?"

"In some measure. St. Augustine had a mistress and then turned
around and achieved sainthood. I have no claim to be St. Augustine." He gives his light laugh. "But the claim I can make for myself
is that I'm conscious of the correspondence between the inner
and outer life."

"Can you get them together?"

"I think I do when I write. An important state of self-education
is to realise you're never going to achieve the great synthesis.
Hence the comedy in the effort—one of my specialties as a writer."

When you read a Bellow novel—*Humboldt's Gift* a flamboyant
example—you learn which escalator the author is riding in his
domestic life. Some scenes are lifted straight—grist to the mill—but
he says: "I wouldn't acknowledge that the books are mainly
autobiographical. Very hard to do. Perhaps even St. Augustine
didn't succeed: one doesn't have the benefit of disinterestedness." Again the soft laugh.

"If you write a work of fiction," he explains, "you have to make
the parts harmonise. The facts of your life don't. On the first page
you set your musical key, and you can't get out of that as you
would have to if you were going to make a totally clean breast.
The book is informed by your life, but not your life."

Born in Canada, the youngest child of Russian immigrants, he
was nine when his family moved to Chicago. Bellow claims,
proudly, that despite the protection of the closed Jewish commu-

nity, he soon found the pull of the street so strong that he broke out. Educated at the University of Chicago and Northwestern, in the Merchant Marine during the second world war, he was still in his twenties when *Dangling Man* was published. Twelve books have followed, winning manifold prizes, including the 1976 Nobel Prize for Literature.

He married when he was 22. He has one son by each of his first three wives. As is usual with a genius, Bellow cannot work if there is a distraction. His unbroken morning writing routine is seen by friends as exceptionally disciplined, but I daresay a wife didn't find it easy to keep an infant quiet between 7am and 1pm.

Though his writing has made him rich, he won't employ domestic help because of the intrusion. He points out, however, that he likes cooking and helps with it. Sometimes he is easy to accommodate, forgetting his orthodox upbringing, other times furious that you haven't remembered he doesn't eat ham: you never know. If his work has gone well, he becomes the most engaging of companions. If he's had a bad day, he is sorry for himself: everything is wrong.

His prickliness emerges briefly when, after he has extolled the culture of his immigrant parents—"their devotion to one another and their children seems almost abnormal nowadays"—I say: "Yet you didn't raise your own?"

"I don't disown my children. I had them every year for a good part of the time. I brought them up very carefully." (His friends confirm this). "I was summoned in every emergency. The connection with my sons has endured. They're now 40, 30, 23.

"Each child saw me with my various wives. They feel sorry for me when a marriage breaks up—it usually prostrates me for a year or two. They try to help me out."

He adds: "If I'd been a real philanderer, no one would have had anything to say against me. By marrying, I'm convicted of being a bad character."

In the 1960s Bellow moved to Chicago because he thought New York had become sterile for writers. While rightish, he is essentially apolitical. "Vietnam, civil rights meant writers were 'pressed'—if not quite in the old sense—to line up with the Mailer group, or *Commentary* group, lashed into one ideological column

or another. I got tired of having my arm twisted to sign statements
insulting Lyndon Johnson and so on. I got out. Chicago is openly
philistine, instead of culturally philistine.'' Bellow always inserts
his shafts deftly.

After the 1964 publication of *Herzog,* he no longer needed a
university salary. (There are considerable demands, however. He
is not a mean man. After *Herzog* his second ex-wife went straight
to the courts to get more.) He continued to teach—Chicago University
is famous for being *engagé*—because the city itself, he says, has no
mental life. At the same time, he denounces the university system
for its corruption: "The extreme specialisation turns out graduates
who know only one thing. Their human possibilities are corrupted
by the neglect of history, culture, morals, ethics."

He believes America's underclass has no hope as long as liberals
and minorities with vested interests refuse to acknowledge what is
happening. "The crime rate is out of *sight* in Chicago. And police
fiddle the statistics because a black administration doesn't want
the crime rate known lest it be given a racial interpretation. I don't
belong to the community of the blind."

Refusing to move to the suburbs like most liberals, he still lives
downtown. "I don't want to escape from the sordid streets of
Chicago." Always watching.

Through PEN he is tireless in helping disenfranchised writers.
But he resents having his own bleak observation of his native
land coupled with Solzhenitsyn's blanket condemnation of America.
"His views are the result not of personal knowledge but of
doctrine when he was a Soviet citizen. He's had nothing to do with
this country. He has shut himself away in Vermont. Odd to
dismiss 250m people as beyond redemption. I suffer for my American contemporaries. He simply turns his back on them."

"OK. But does it make any difference to America's plight?"

"I haven't been asked to take charge of my country!"

"*Yet,*" says Janis, laughing. She has joined us over the delicious
and largely homegrown lunch she has produced.

"I hope," Bellow answers my question, "that Americans will
learn something about their lives and the country from books
written by one of *them*."

When he and I settle down again in the simple, spacious sitting room, he talks about "the ordeal of desire" that is starving the western world. Women, as well as men, invite the death of love by the literalness of their imagination. In *More Die of Heartbreak*, Matilda wants "a little Muhammad Ali for straight sex, some of Kissinger for savvy, Cary Grant for looks, Jack Nicholson for entertainment, plus André Malraux or some Jew for brains. Commonest fantasy there is."

Bellow says to me: "How can an average man satisfy this fantasy? So they hold it against him."

He says that like his father before him, he needs help and support from a wife. "But in every case I found that they had married me for reasons of their own—legitimate for them, but not suitable for me. Matilda is a pretty fair example of what I mean.

"I'm describing a readily observable condition. It's not misogyny: it's a lamentation—for all parties."

The novel's title comes from Benn, the main character and world-famous botanist with whom Bellow identifies most. Benn is asked about the harmful effect of increasing radiation. "It's terribly serious, of course," he replies, "but I think more people die of heartbreak than of radiation."

A Conversation with Saul Bellow

Sybil S. Steinberg / 1989

From *Publishers Weekly*, 3 March 1989, 59–60. © 1989 by *Publishers Weekly*. Reprinted by permission.

If people in and out of the book industry are speculating about Saul Bellow's decision to publish his latest work as an original trade paperback, the author does not seem to mind. In fact, in the course of a talk with him, one detects that the Nobel Laureate, never shy about promulgating his opinions through his fictional characters, rather enjoys the chance to explain the motivation behind this month's appearance of *A Theft* between jaunty orange paperback covers bearing the Penguin logo and a $6.95 price.

It is 9 a.m. in Chicago when we talk to Bellow on the phone. For a man who has a reputation of not chatting overmuch with the press, he is affable, generally forthcoming (except when he is being arch) and not excessively modest. If he is conscious of his position as elder statesman of contemporary American literature, he is also aware that *noblesse* requires *oblige*. He takes a verbal swipe or two at various uncultured, uncouth or untalented individuals or institutions, not bothering to hide his glee at this chance to air some grievances. He is not so much disdainful as self-assured; he is Bellow, and he has earned the right to do things his way.

The idea for paperback publication was his alone, Bellow says, after *A Theft* was turned down by two national magazines. No, he won't mention their names: "I decided if I do the chivalrous thing they'll feel much worse." A great gust of laughter conveys his healthy malice. "I was miffed," he continues. "I was not in too much doubt as to the quality of the story and in this I was later confirmed by Peter Mayer at Viking Penguin, who is no slouch. I did not know for what mysterious reasons *A Theft* had been rejected. In one case, I was simply told that it was a matter of its length and the amount of space it would take up. . . . Then I thought, why not put this out as a paperback? It certainly is an evening's read—but it is too short to be published as a novel.''

Bellow says he approached his longtime agent Harriet Wasserman "very timidly. To my surprise she agreed—I say to my surprise because she is an infallible expert on these matters.'' The deal with Viking Penguin consummated, no less than Peter Mayer himself was Bellow's editor, "although at this stage in my development I don't really have much need for an editor.'' His spirits rose when he was even consulted about the format and the cover. "For the first time I participated actively in making these decisions. I think they did a marvelous job.''

He insists that from its inception he thought of the 30,000-word narrative not as a longish short story but clearly as a novella, "a form that has a very good pedigree. In Europe, people are used to this genre and in America, there used to be some excellent writers who wrote at that length—from Henry James to Willa Cather to Hemingway.'' The intermediate length would be "useful" published as a paperback; it would have a wider readership, and it would "make available shorter works of fiction of a category that most people don't get to see any more. It would be accessible, affordable, cheaper than a movie ticket or an appetizer in a fancy restaurant. I don't want to characterize myself as a statesman doing this for the readership of the United States, but I really did think I would have a wider readership for a work of this length in paperback. I also thought it might remind the magazines that they are in violation of their own constitutional principles. They are supposed to be doing this for the public and they're not doing it.''

Nor is this a one-time gamble on Bellow's part, a solution to the problem of a particular story. If all goes well, he says, Viking Penguin will publish another novella—already written—next fall. "There's a whole series on deck. I'm working on a third. There may be a fourth and a fifth.''

Not surprisingly for a man of strong opinions, Bellow has a point of view about the state of contemporary fiction that he is eager to express. "A good many writers are having trouble placing longer fiction in the magazines. I think the magazines have failed the public badly in this respect. They've gone political; they've gone social; they've dealt with health and with sex and with sports,

and really they have no patience for fiction. They ration it now;
even the very best magazine will have one small story in every
issue. They run a token poem or story—if it's minimalist it's even
better, because it takes up less space. If I had written a journalis-
tic piece of the same length I would have had no trouble placing it.''

   The kind of fiction he writes, says Bellow, should have wider
currency. He believes his stories "give an independent view of
human reality different from the prevailing contemporary view. A
significant portion of the public needs and craves these stories
because the prevailing version of human reality that they are getting
[from some sources] is thin and shallow. And I can tell from the early
reception of a story like this by my contemporaries that I have given
a new view. Non-money writers like me—not by choice, because
I have accepted all the money I could make—don't really think in
terms of big sales. It's true that I've acquired a certain amount of
accidental prestige, so publishers are willing to take a chance on
something like this with me.''

   Although he concedes that the real money in publishing these
days is in the sale of paperback rights after hardcover publication,
Bellow shrugs off the penalty, claiming that sale of the book to
QPBC has erased any financial risks he might have run. He can
count on a certain level of paperback sales—with or without reviews, he says, in response to our comment that at one time
anyone who published initially in paper took the chance of being
ignored by the review media. "I really see this partly as a rescue
operation. I think the kind of fiction that I write is being swamped
out by the titanic bestsellers. Public taste is being formed now
only by books of that kind.''

   Asked if he feels he will be reaching a new, different audience in
trade paper, Bellow is hopeful. "Every writer wants as many
readers as possible, although he may be an avant-garde writer as I
was. It's not because he despises the great public; the great public
has made other choices. Besides, in a country of 250 million people
I do feel that at least a million people will be interested in the real
thing. And I think that what I'm doing is the real thing.'' Warming
to the numbers he envisions, his voice just a bit acidulous, Bellow
comments: "There are maybe 50 million BAs in this country; some
of them have *some* education in literature, learned *something* in

college, read *some* good books. I wouldn't be surprised if they have an appetite for this kind of thing."

Into this somewhat utopian vision we intrude a mundane question: Is there any special significance to the fact that *A Theft* has a feminine protagonist? And that this heroine, Clara Velde, is on her fourth marriage (like her several-times-wed author)? A deep chuckle prefaces his reply. "Maybe one benefit of aging is that I'm mellower. I think it's just an uninformed detraction of me to say that I've never had important ladies in my stories. I refer you to one called 'Leaving the Old Yellow House.' As for Clara, given that 40% of marriages these days go on the rocks, you can't blame a lady for trying again and again."

Then is this a "lighter" book than, say, *Henderson the Rain King* or *Herzog*? "I consider it a more straightforward story. I think I've now done all the thinking that I'm going to do. All my life long I have been seriously pondering certain problems and I'll probably continue to do that, but I'm now in a position to use this pondering as a background for the story, and not intrude it so much into the narrative."

In *A Theft*, Bellow's protagonist muses: "Literature [is] the tragedy or comedy of private lives, while superliterature [is] about the possible end of the world." Refusing initially to classify his own books in these two categories, Bellow mentions Arthur Koestler, George Orwell and André Malraux as writers whose works qualify as superliterature, because their real concern was the destiny of Western civilization. The characters in their novels were generally not individualized, since they were subservient to broader historical and social questions: "whether a revolution was necessary; whether it would succeed; whether the West was in the final stage of decline; whether there was enough substance to individual human beings to make stories really interesting."

When pressed, Bellow agrees that at least one of his novels falls into the category of superliterature. "*The Dean's December* . . . is concerned with the real state of Eastern Europe and the real state of middle America, although they are not disassociated from real persons. The question a writer asks himself is, 'To whom are all these terrible things happening?' You can say they're happening to communities and they're happening to nations, but the real component is ourselves."

Writers themselves, Bellow thinks, are casualties of the changing climate in the publishing community. "I don't think writers are very close to each other in this country any more. They used to be more so in my younger days. Nowadays, they live solitary lives in various corners of the country. When I was in my 30s and 40s, a publishing house like Viking used to be a meeting place for all kinds of writers. You'd run into people like Gene Fowler or John Steinbeck and you'd sit down and have a chat. Now publishing houses belong to conglomerates and there are none of those colorful old editors to attract the writers to the publishing house itself. Editors are just middle-level executives in a big corporation."

Bellow concedes, however, that he's happy to be back at Viking, where he was published for 30 years, from 1948 to 1978. When the house was sold and his editor Harvey Ginsberg left, Bellow, too, moved on. Another factor was his annoyance over the way *Humboldt's Gift* was done. "The books were just falling apart; they were badly printed on inferior paper and badly bound. I loved that book and was indignant on behalf of the book itself." Harper & Row published his next two books, but the prickly author says, "Harper and I didn't really agree very well." When Ginsberg moved on again, to Morrow, so did Bellow, and *More Die of Heartbreak* was published there. Now, with his two-book contract with Viking, he has come full circle.

In his quest for the perfect publisher, Bellow is pursuing the author's perennial wish to reach a wide audience. "Every writer's assumption is that he is as other human beings are, and they are more or less as he is. There's a principle of psychic unity. [Writing] was not meant to be an occult operation; it was not meant to be an esoteric secret." And his current book, whatever its unorthodox birthing, comes from the conviction he brings to all of his works: "Stories are very important—and not just to me. They give a kind of illumination that you don't get in any other way."

Saul Bellow: Made in America

Keith Botsford / 1990

From *The Independent Weekend*, 10 February 1990, 29. Reprinted by permission of Keith Botsford.

When I first met him, in the early 1950s, Saul Bellow had just published the book that made his literary reputation in the United States, *The Adventures of Augie March.* At the time he rode about the campus of Bard College in the rural Hudson valley, upstate New York, knock-knee'd on a kid's bike. He had just married a second time, to the Anglophile daughter of a Russian painter who appears in *Herzog,* his great novel of betrayal, and he was already clearly a considerable figure in the world of American letters.

His career subsequently did nothing but ascend, until it culminated, in 1976, with the Nobel Prize for Literature. On his way to Stockholm, we sat in Brown's, his favourite London hotel, and went through his acceptance speech. It was not a moment he savoured, being a private man in a public world.

Bellow will be 75 this year. The uncrowned king of American letters, a sage and dapper literary lion for whose blood younger knives are out—Jewish knives because he failed to address the Holocaust, other knives because of his increasingly powerful stance in favour of High Culture over Low, and especially because of his defence of the great classical works against the inroads of lesser work. Increasingly beleaguered and isolated, he said ruefully: "They understand me better in Europe." On the other hand, "When a Zulu writes a great novel I'll read it," was not a remark calculated to make many friends in ethnic or liberal America.

His status may be too lofty for him to be entirely dislodged from his throne, but when I saw him in Chicago last week he was distinctly uneasy about his own future. A thoroughly unauthorised and probably meretricious biography which would, in the latest fashion, reveal his lifetime of amours, was about to appear; the condition of the world of culture in which he has long lived and

which he cares about passionately, seemed under attack from
all sides.

Bellow's books, however, are probably the best paradigm we
have of America from the Thirties to the present. One takes into
account that he is a Jewish writer; one also knows that Jewish
intellectuals are the ones who buy books. But beyond that, he is
clearly the most original and most American of writers. Being a Jew
is part of himself and therefore compassable, but America, one feels,
remains a mystery. And that is as it should be, for all truly
interesting things are mysteries.

"We are all here on strange contingencies," he said. "We don't
know how we got here or what meaning our being really has. All
the explanations we get fail to account for the strangeness. Systems
fall away one by one, and you tick them off as you pass by.

"Revising my life, I see with satisfaction the escape from certain
tyrants, Marx, Lenin, Freud. These philosophers and writers were
the source of powerful metaphors which took a grip on one. It took
decades to escape."

In a few characteristic sentences, Bellow was outlining some
lifelong concerns, some long blind alleys. Nearly as potent as the
myths which illuminated his childhood and his progression from the
son of Russian Jewish immigrants of some grandeur, to his
progressive Americanisation in the Chicago to which he moved,
aged eight, from Montreal.

To the boy who grew up in a cohesive home and whose head was
stuffed with religion—"God as the primal parent and the Patriarchs as members of my family"—Chicago was an event of a very
specific gravity:

"Chicago was different, it was a frontier. Matter there seemed to
be cruder: as if its molecules were bigger or coarser. My father
was violent, strong, authoritarian; he seemed to us children an angel
of strength, beauty and punishment. His affections were strong; he
was a passionate man. But Americanisation was what counted for
him, whereas the family was divided. My eldest brother pulled
strongly for assimilation. He didn't want to be known as one of
those back-street immigrant types: he made a beeline for the
loot."

And the America Bellow was growing up in, haunted by religion, drawn towards the secular, was a different America:

"Chicago was the melting pot that didn't melt," he says. "It was a place where you were free to run yourself into the ground or to improve yourself. The religious vein was very strong and lasted until I was old enough to make a choice between Jewish life and street life. The power of street life asserted itself."

Also, there have been curious transformations in the nation: "There were no apologetics back then," he remarks. "Everything was out in the open. The absence of an idea of defamation was liberating. Nobody was immune. We took abuse in return for freedom of opinion. It is a far less open society since ethnic protection came in."

The boy who had survived a six-month illness in a Montreal Hospital and had his own long flirtation with death, had excused his own fate. "As Chicago gamblers of the day used to say, I was 'playing on velvet', I was ahead of the game. A kind of mental book-keeping took place. I owed something to some entity for the privilege of surviving, I've kept such a feeling: of being overjoyed, being full of a welling vitality."

What he regrets is the absence of such major mysteries:

"We've ceased to marvel at things we can't explain. We've had introductory courses in everything, and therefore we have persuaded ourselves that we can explain anything, we don't have to, but if we wanted to, we could. We are in the position of savage men who have been educated into believing there are no mysteries."

All his major novels—*Augie March, Herzog, Henderson the Rain King, Humboldt's Gift, Seize the Day*—are elaborations, through the eyes of memory, of these themes. And they are conspicuous and lasting for three principal reasons: the huge vitality of life with which language invests them, their sheer physicality, and their prodigious cross-relations between personal memory and ideas. The language is evident, and undiminished, even as he talks and surveys, from his eleventh-floor window, the blitzed and frightening surrounds of Chicago University, where his course on masterpieces of literature (which he also gives at Boston University) attracts students from all over. "It is Bellow telling you how Flaubert wrote *Madame Bovary*," one student told me.

The physical reality is often overwhelming, and I remember once asking him in Puerto Rico, how he pulled it off. "Reality," he said calmly, "is what I put in afterwards." More accurate would be his description of himself as a "pair of eyes":

"Even in childhood, it wasn't just what people said that counted as much as the look of them. Their gestures told me as much as their words. A nose was a speaking member; so was the way hair grew and the set of ears, the condition of teeth, the emanations of the body. It wasn't entirely voluntary."

He may be considered largely a novelist of ideas, but in fact his art is far simpler—and more complex. It is as though all history, everyone he has ever known or read, coexists in his mind and works its way out on to the page. "If you opened up a modern mind with a saw," he says, "things would tumble out in every direction. You pitch yourself headlong into mental chaos and make your own way from there." As for memory, it has always been totally accessible: "It's like turning around and walking back up a street."

It would be nearer the truth to say that Bellow's novels are exorcisms of stages on his own life's way or memorialisations of vast, labyrinthine personages who are extensions of himself. Valentine Gersbach, in *Herzog,* with his "gondolier's" walk, in reality had a club foot and also stole Bellow's second wife, Sandra Chekbassov. Henderson is built in part on John Jay Chapman, Jr., whose house, a Hudson River mansion, was near both of ours, but its African setting has to do with the imagination—it was later that he travelled the Nile with Saul Steinberg. I cut a figure in *Humboldt* (its principal figure is a composite of various intellectuals close to Bellow), and he said he hoped I wouldn't be offended. I wasn't. A tiny part of me had been transformed magically, into a character in a novel, enlarged upon, recreated.

Because of this proximity to reality, many of his books seethe with suppressed angers: at the disorders of civilization, the condition of modern man. Wife number three, the Picassoesque Susan, seized his day, his books, his money. Wife number four, the Romanian mathematician Alexandra, is apotheosized in *The Dean's December.*

Two other themes play prominent parts in Bellow's mental structure. One is the Marxism of the *Partisan Review,* that pillar of US
literary life in the Forties, where he published most often. It was a
congeries of influences and personal affections: Philip Rahv,
Dwight MacDonald, Isaac Rosenfeld, Clement Greenberg. "They
were a special group of cranks which knew a little history and some
Marxist doctrine," he says. "They discussed matters on an elevated
plane." Disenchanted with their adherence to Marxism, Bellow began
drifting away from them at the time of the Finnish war.

"Some of them I liked greatly," he says. "They had a sway on
my mind because they were cosmopolitan. They may have had
the mentality of Sixth Avenue cigar importers, but they were importing a good thing, European culture. But I couldn't belong to
anything; I wouldn't join any group. I was the cat who walked
by himself."

The enchantment with the left is at its best in the Mexican section
of *Augie;* the consequent disenchantment was most severe when
he first went to Europe—England, Spain, France, Italy and Aus-
tria—after the war. "Europe opened my eyes," he says. "People
like Sartre understood less about left-wing politics than I had in
high school; I suspected they thought the West would fall to
communism and that they would be advantageously placed when
this happened."

The other dominant theme is the tenuous existence of intelligence
in modern life. There is no doubting the purity of Bellow's mind.
It is a living organism that captures the faintest nuance from the
world without: the politics of the city, the politics of marriage,
the attractions of greed, the dangers of celebrity. All of them are
rendered in outsized characters possessed with fierce monomanias
and diverse languages that stray independently and impudently from
the author of their being. He is probably the most knowing man I
know, the most jealous and jealously guarded, the least envious,
the wittiest.

But all this mix in one man is no doubt not easy for some to take.
It is not easy, either, for himself. For one thing, he believes profoundly
in literature. To partake in that high art is to have a "trained
sensibility." And that you can't have "unless you take certain

masterpieces into yourself; as if you were swallowing a communion wafer. If masterpieces don't have a decisive part in your existence, all you have is a show of culture. It has no reality.''

He is deeply involved in the development of his own mind: "I'm still in that educational self-wrestling process. I correct, correct, correct continually. But the more isolated you are, the more you develop a terrible dependency on books. One protects oneself from what one thinks of as vulgarity and squalor by becoming a fortress of high-mindedness. It's really bad stuff. I've used books like an addict. *Je m'accuse*. Whereas silence is enriching. The more you keep your mouth shut, the more fertile you become.''

I think he sees himself in part as the rabbinical student in a story his father told him. The student has married the daughter of a rich merchant, a coarse and unlettered man, but one who could be expected to support him as a scholar deserves. None the less, after five years the young scholar could stand life in a little village no longer. He left it for Warsaw without a penny. Happened what one might expect, Bellow relates:

"After he had slept on a park bench for some weeks, eating his meal in a soup kitchen, he wrote his father-in-law a letter, asking to come back. The merchant couldn't read, so he went to the synagogue to get help. But there was nobody there but the cantor, a basso profundo. No sooner had the cantor read the opening line, 'Dear Father-in-Law,' than the merchant said. 'Stop there. He's full of pride, pumped up with himself he's still got his nose full of flies. Let him stew in Warsaw a little longer and come to his senses.'

"The young man waited for his reply. None came, so he wrote a second letter. This time the only person the merchant could find in the synagogue was a boy soprano. 'Ah,' said the merchant, 'he's changed his tune. Let him come home. He's learned his lesson.'

"My father, who is telling this story, says, 'If you don't know how to read, you're at the mercy of vulgar interpretations'.''

Bellow's is a basso profundo past. His life has been [spent] in learning to read. The process is hardly complete. "There are so many things I've not been able to incorporate," he says, "things that got away from me, the Holocaust, for instance. I may even have been partly sealed against it, because somehow I couldn't tear myself away from my American life. Jewish criticism is hard on

me on this score. I'm supposed to have saved my best colours to
paint America with, as if to say that what happened in Europe
happened because Europe is corrupt and faulty."

And then there is the new life, with a new wife, Janis, a life spent
between the rigorous demands of fame, travel, teaching, writing,
a house in Vermont, Chicago, Boston, his much-loved England. He
married first when he was 22. As he says: "I didn't know what to
do with my affective life in those days. I knew I had emotional
capacities, but I hadn't been able to transmit them as such. I used
my charisma to scatter all sorts of indifferent matter. I felt more
emotional about Mexican towns than about human beings. But I
had reserves of emotion. By the time I reached my forties, I could
write with tears in my eyes. Before that, it was nine-tenths virtuosity
and one-tenth suppressed feeling."

A Half Life: An Autobiography in Ideas

Bostonia / 1990

From *Bostonia,* November/December 1990, 37–47. © Saul Bellow. Used by permission of *Bostonia* magazine.

At seventy-five, Saul Bellow is the only one of America's living Nobel laureates in literature who writes in English (I.B. Singer writes in Yiddish). He is also, as the flow of stories and novellas he has published in the past year demonstrates, a writer and social and cultural critic still at the height of his powers.

We are pleased to publish here the first "Half Life" of his intellectual autobiography. The second half life will be published in the January-February issue.

Bellow has never before granted this kind of interview; nor does he, in his own words, plan to write an autobiography. "I don't think," he says, "I should be my own haruspex." Meaning, he doesn't think he should be examining his own entrails. In short, this autobiographical interview is unique.

The first half of the interview was conducted in Bellow's Chicago apartment, hard by the university. Its terms were simple: an examination, in question and answer form, of Bellow's intellectual formation—how he came by his ideas, and how those ideas influenced his life.

Bostonia: Ideas come in two different ways—conscious ideas acquired through education and reading, and things that pop into your head willy-nilly. When were you first conscious of having an idea hit you—an idea that went beyond "let's go down and get bubble gum."

Bellow: I certainly wasn't conscious of ideas as such before I was ten. I did have ideas of some sort earlier, but they were the sort of primitive metaphysical ideas a small child has.

Bostonia: Such as?

Bellow: Sitting on the curbstone looking at the sky thinking,

248

"Where did it all come from?" "Why was I here?"—
epistemological questions. Of course that's how many philosophers
nowadays would like to handle such questions: essentially as
childlike epistemology.

Bostonia: Were ideas much batted about in your early childhood?

Bellow: I don't know that they were batted about. They were just
present. At the age of about four we began to study Hebrew and
read the Old Testament, but we didn't necessarily consider the idea
of creation and the present, nor where the world had come from
and the explanation for its existence. I felt very cozy with God and
with the primal parent and by the time I was up to the Patriarchs
(I was five or six years old) I felt they were very much like members
of my family. I couldn't readily distinguish between a parent and
the heroic ancestors . . . Abraham, Isaac, and Jacob, and the sons
of Jacob, especially Joseph.

Bostonia: So shul played a part . . .

Bellow: It wasn't so much shul as the Torah.

Bostonia: In the first stages, did you feel you were challenging
these ideas, or were you largely accepting?

Bellow: No, it never occurred to me that reality could be anything
but what I was being offered. Not then.

Bostonia: When did that notion strike you?

Bellow: Well, I had a great shock at about eight. I was hospitalized for a half-year or so. A missionary lady came and gave me a
New Testament for children. I read that. I was very moved by the
life of Jesus and I recognized him as a fellow Jew. I think the
hospital drove a lot of that home to me. Because I'd never been
away from my parents before.

Bostonia: But had you felt the fragility of life? Did you then?

Bellow: Oh yes. Death was something very familiar from an early
age. During the great flu epidemic my brother Sam and I used to
sit in the front window watching the procession of funerals.

Bostonia: This was in Montreal?

Bellow: Yes. I can remember the *corbillard* [hearse—ed.], the
bands, the funeral marches, and the *cortege* with its black horses.

Bostonia: So memory is part of the way we form ideas, isn't it?
Much of our thinking does spring from remembering very specific things.

Bellow: I have to think whether what I've learned is true. It never occurred to me it was ever anything but true. Then it was brought home to me that other approaches were possible. I had to struggle with the charge against the Jews that they had been responsible for the crucifixion.

Bostonia: But that wasn't implicit in the New Testament. How did you come to that?

Bellow: Oh yes, because there were these passages in which the Pharisees especially were prominent as the enemies of Jesus.

Bostonia: But in Jewish terms, Jesus was another Jew. Consequently it wasn't antisemitic in the modern sense of the word. It wasn't anti-Jewish.

Bellow: Yes it was. It threw great blame on the Jews, which was supported by my treatment in the hospital. For the first time I was in a hospital was the first time I was aware I'd left my street and my family. I couldn't see my parents. I was allowed one visitor a week. My mother and father had to alternate weeks. They couldn't both come at the same time. This was the Royal Victoria Hospital in Montreal. The Children's Ward. Ward H. It was a Protestant hospital.

Bostonia: But restrictive. Was it an infectious thing? Or were they just obeying the rules? Did you read much when you were in the hospital, besides the New Testament?

Bellow: I read everything I could get my hands on. There were very few books except the New Testament. Mostly there were funny papers. Which were stacked beside the kids' beds. Piles of funny papers. Characters that disappeared long ago like Slim Jim, Happy Hooligan, and in addition, the Katzenjammer Kids.

Bostonia: You were growing up in a culture, in and around Montreal, that was very French. Did that create any sense of difference?

Bellow: I was aware of being *un juif*. That was driven home quite early. I don't know if it was bad, really. I got some light on it when I read the New Testament. I think it was a children's New Testament.

Bostonia: So in essence, as with many people, the first ideas are religious, eschatological?

Bellow: Yes, and they were very keen. They were driven home very sharply. My isolation first of all, then by the fact that I knew I was in danger of death. My reading was not so bad for a child of eight—my reading ability. I got out of bed occasionally—they used to hang your chart at the foot of the bed—I would read my chart and I knew it was very unpromising.

Bostonia: So in a sense, you are a survivor. You have a feeling of that?

Bellow: It's fundamental, I think, with me. I felt forever after that I had been excused from death and that I was, as gamblers in Chicago used to say in those days, when I was ten or so, playing on velvet—ahead of the game.

Bostonia: One does feel strongly about survival as a child; election is added to what one is likely to have gone through, and that causes a special concentration in the mind, doesn't it?

Bellow: Anyone who's faced death at that age is likely to remember something of what I felt—that it was a triumph, that I had gotten away with it. Not only was I ahead of the game, I was privileged. And there was some kind of bookkeeping going on. I did my own mental bookkeeping. I thought I owed something to some entity for the privilege of surviving.

Bostonia: So there was a debt as well? A debt that had to be paid off?

Bellow: A duty that came with survival. Those are the primitive facts.

Bostonia: How did you describe that debt to yourself?

Bellow: That I'd better make it worth the while of whoever it was that authorized all this. I've always had some such feeling. Overjoyed. Full of welling vitality and perhaps that I've gotten away with something but that it had been by permission of some high authority. Occasionally I talk to others about this and I find they are dead on the subject. That they didn't have this sense for themselves. Some kind of central connection . . . in the telephonic sense.

Bostonia: So one comes out of surviving one's childhood with a sense of being privileged; then one goes home and finds the reality—one is back in a family that has proceeded without you and quite well? Did you have this feeling of imagining one's death and the tragedy it would cause to the world? Imagining your funeral and your parents weeping?

Bellow: No, but what I did see was a great many kids dying in the ward. This happened regularly. A lot of fussing in the night

and a screen around the kid's bed and nurses running back and
forth with flashlights. And in the morning an empty bed. You just saw
the bed made up for another kid. Before long there was a kid in it.
You understood very well what had happened, but it wasn't
discussed or explained.

Bostonia: So you're back home, aware you have caused grief,
suffering, and anxiety to your parents. Your brothers are there.
How do they behave?

Bellow: At first they were sympathetic, but that wore off. Then I
was just an obnoxious kid soaking up all the attention and affection
and concern of the family and I was greatly resented by my
brothers. One of them was four years and the other eight years
my senior. The brother who was four years older had in the
meantime used and broken such toys as I had. Especially my sled.

Bostonia: And then came the move to Chicago?

Bellow: Then my father moved. I didn't go back to school. It was
nearly summer when I rejoined the family.

Bostonia: Did you view the world differently?

Bellow: I must have. Of course there's no such thing as thinking
this through, but I certainly made decisions based on my condition. I had to decide, for instance, whether I would accept the role
of convalescent sickly child or whether I would beef myself up. I
decided on course two. I set myself on a very hard course of
exercise. I ran a great deal.

Bostonia: So this is an idea in its very primitive form. I have
survived, I must survive, I should survive. And the way to
survive, to pay this debt, is to become good or better. When did
this notion of "better" come into your life?

Bellow: By the time we got to Chicago I was a confirmed reader
and so I picked up all sorts of self-improvement, self-development
books, especially physical self-improvement at the public library.
There was a famous football coach named Walter Camp and
books like *How to Get Fit and How to Stay So*. This involved
carrying coal scuttles at arm's length and I did that because we
had coal in the shed (this was in Chicago) and one of my jobs which
I was glad to do was to go up and down the stairs. Up with the
coal and down with the ashes. So I became quite fanatical.

Bostonia: So in surviving, the mind's not really what you think about it. It is the body which carries the structure of the mind. Without it, you're not going to have a mind. Had you not lived, you wouldn't have been able to develop any form of betterment, so you decide you are going to protect it in some way?

Bellow: My alternatives were to remain weak and be coddled.

Bostonia: A delightful state for some children. . . . Look at Marcel Proust, he got a cold and it lasted a lifetime. Most people would probably think that the family which could have produced you would have been one of argumentation, dispute, rational analysis, logic, order, and violence, mental and other kinds. A picture that corresponds in any way?

Bellow: Well, some of the elements are there. My father was violent, strong, authoritarian. He seemed to us as children an angel of strength, beauty, and punishment. His affections were strong too. He was a passionate person. My mother was that way also. Within the family, Jewish life is very different from life outward, facing the world. You saw your parents in two separate connections. One the domestic and internal; and the other meeting external handicaps.

Bostonia: Is this an idea that's formed? Is that part of the formation of an idea? The sort of double role?

Bellow: I suppose so, because it was translated later in life. The contrast between strength, the strength that I felt inwardly, and the absurdity of my trying to express that strength outwardly.

Bostonia: There are two distinct aspects to life: One is the one in which you cope with everyone else's world and the other you cultivate within yourself. Was there a degree of concealment involved in this?

Bellow: Not concealment so much as a deep sense of strangeness in what I was doing. First I translated from the Old Testament into my inner life, then I translated from books I read at the public library, again into the inner life. In the first instance this had the approval of Judaism, that is, mainly from my family. In the second form it could only be fantasy. You had to be wary of what was in truth both stirring and ennobling but at the same time dangerous to reveal.

Bostonia: Do you remember any of the fantasies? Did any of them approximate what you've become?

Bellow: No. At first they were fairly obvious fantasies. Pioneers,

frontiersmen, independent men. Going into the wilderness with
your axe and gun (and your smarts) was very important.

Bostonia: When you arrived there, Chicago was not yet in any
sense a sophisticated city—the frontier was not that far off.

Bellow: No it wasn't. We lived on an unpaved street, a dirt street
with horses. Cars were few and far between. Kids used to throw
themselves on the ground under a car to see if it had four-wheel
brakes.

Bostonia: Was America talked about as a subject? As such? After
all, back then, Montreal must have had its own flavor.

Bellow: Yes, we did talk about the change. Montreal—that is
Eastern Canada—was very European. I didn't realize until later
that the Eastern seaboard is very different from the Midwest. I had
a strong sense of that difference as a child. Matter seemed to me
to be cruder: as if Chicago molecules were bigger or coarser. The
very soil seemed different. The trees were certainly different. Chicago's trees were elms, cottonwoods. Montreal trees were bigger. The
ferocious winters, boiling summers.

Bostonia: Did you talk about politics?

Bellow: Very much so. Because my parents were following the
Russian Revolution. They had a very specific interest in it. Their
parents and brothers and sisters were still there. I was born in 1915.
Before I was three the Russian Revolution was fully under way.

Bostonia: Were you aware of it? You knew about it? That must
have had an effect on your ideas.

Bellow: I knew all about Lenin and Trotsky. I didn't know what
the Revolution as such meant. My mother's relatives were Mensheviks. I suppose I was too young to remember that during the
Kerensky period the Mensheviks and the Bolsheviks were nip
and tuck.

Bostonia: Since it later came to have considerable meaning for
you, do you recall any effect it had on your ideas back then?

Bellow: I remember as quite a small kid being in the street with
my father. We met a young man called Lyova walking down the
street. Lyova told my father he was going back to Russia. Lyova's
father was our Hebrew teacher and his mother, Mary, a fat lady
with a huge hat, was my mother's friend. My father said, "That's a
foolish thing you are doing. Don't go." He was counseling Lyova

not to go, but Lyova must have had some kind of politics. He couldn't have been older than eighteen or nineteen. But things like that happened every day. Lyova went back and vanished.

Bostonia: How about the structure of politics. Did you have any idea how American politics were put together, how they differed from Russian or European?

Bellow: In those early days my political ideas came from the papers. Al Smith was a Catholic candidate for the presidency. Newspapers were very important. There was no radio of course. Everybody took positions based on the paper he read, whether it was the Hearst paper or the McCormick paper in Chicago. There were two Hearst papers: the *Herald Examiner* and the *Evening American,* long since gone. And there was the Republican McCormick *Tribune.* And that was daily drama. The Leopold and Loeb case, for instance. In the early twenties we were already reading about Clarence Darrow and the Leopold and Loeb murder.

Bostonia: Did your fantasies ever involve such things as politics or law as ideas? Did you think about them in terms of eternal justice?

Bellow: No, not really. We didn't think that way. More important to the family was Americanization and assimilation. The family was divided on this. My eldest brother pulled for total Americanization; he was ashamed of being an immigrant. He didn't want at all to be known as one of these back-street immigrant types. He made a beeline for the loot.

Bostonia: How did you react?

Bellow: I was just keenly interested. I didn't have any position. It was hard not to observe my eldest brother. His histrionics had a dramatizing power on our feelings and the fact that he was physically impressive—big and stout, aggressive, clever—simply added to the effect. He was eight years older than I was. By the time we got to Chicago he was a high-school senior and I was in the third grade.

Bostonia: Were there ideas as such in the schools of those days?

Bellow: "Americanism" was very strong and there was a core program of literary patriotism. Overwhelming. Terribly important. Endless strings of immigrant societies. We were in sort of a Polish-Ukrainian-Scandinavian enclave and across Chicago Ave-

nue (there was usually some car line that intervened) were Italians.
There were also Germans, Irish, Greeks.

Bostonia: The "I am an American Chicago-born" with which *The Adventures of Augie March* begins is a recrudescence of that in you, isn't it? You have a cosmopolitan and Catholic mind, yet by far the strongest streak in you is the American.

Bellow: Well, cosmopolitanism found its point of exit from local confinement in the direction of the melting pot. But it wasn't a melting pot. It didn't melt. If you played with Polish children in the streets you didn't also go to school with them. They went to parochial schools where they were taught in Polish. And even until recently, the descendants of Polish immigrants, succeeding generations, spoke with an accent, a recognizable, identifiable touch of Polish.

Bostonia: What ideas surfaced in your mind that most subtracted from or most supported that notion of Americanism?

Bellow: My father was all for Americanism. At the table he would tell us, this really *is* the land of opportunity; you're free to do whatever you like, within the law, and you're free either to run yourself into the ground or improve your chances. The gospel of improvement came through my father whose English was not very good, as yet.

Bostonia: But you also felt that virtually from the time you came on the scene. The notion of progress was already built into you; it's part of your nineteenth-century heritage, Comte's idea of progress.

Bellow: Comte wouldn't have liked the religious elements. The idea of the Author of your Life (and I'm not speaking of my father here) was very powerful and received continual support from the bible. It was a strange mixture, not an easy blending one. Let's say you went to an American school, you played baseball in cinderlots, and then you went to Hebrew school at three in the afternoon. Until five, you were studying the first five books of Moses and learning to write Yiddish in Hebrew characters—and all the rest of it. So there it was. I didn't go to a parochial school, but the religious vein was very strong and lasted until I was old enough to make a choice between Jewish life and street life. The power of street life made itself felt.

Bostonia: Conventionally, the next stage in the formation of

ideas would be puberty, schooling, reading, making oneself different
from other kids, creating an identity for oneself. By then one is
really conscious of ideas. You were well-read? Long past Natty
Bumppo?

Bellow: By the time I was in high school I was reading Dreiser,
Sherwood Anderson, Mencken. Dreiser was fresh stuff, active and of
the moment, right up to date. You could understand Clyde Griffiths
in the *American Tragedy* if you were a kid of religious background
on his way up. Full of lusts and longings.

Bostonia: Did greed constitute something of an idea?

Bellow: There was enough social Darwinism in the air to justify
greed and a lot of other things short of murder. It wasn't just the
writers I named who had that influence, but also people like Jack
London and Upton Sinclair. Those two socialist apostles, who
were also at the same time Darwinists, taught the struggle for
survival. Victory to the strong.

Bostonia: Two striking things about your childhood compared to
most: the first is common to Jewish, Catholic, or any good
religious education in general—that enormous insistence on the
power of memory, on the fact that you actually had to know and
be able to reproduce that. Second, you didn't read any junk.

Bellow: But there *was* a certain amount of junk. And my Americanizing brother brought the *Saturday Evening Post* and *Collier's*
into the house. Fanny Hurst, Edna Ferber, Peter B. Kyne, James
Oliver Curwood. You read all those as well. Of course philosophi-
cally they were usually in the Jack London vein. I imagine that even
Dreiser had a good deal of it. And there were also the Horatio
Alger books.

Bostonia: That business of memory—the retentiveness of it. How
do you get it in childhood?

Bellow: I didn't even think of it as memory. I always had an open
channel to the past. It was accessible from the first. It was like
turning around and going backward down the street. You were
always looking behind while advancing.

Bostonia: Kids on the whole are not great retrospectors. They
are prospectors.

Bellow: Well maybe the retrospective was strong in me because
of my parents. They were both full of the notion that they were falling,

falling. They had been prosperous cosmopolitans in St. Petersburg. My mother never stopped talking about the family dacha, her privileged life, and how all of that was now gone. She was working in the kitchen. Cooking, washing, mending for a family of four children. There had been servants in Russia.

Bostonia: A sense of aristocracy, of a fallen aristocracy in there?

Bellow: Max Weber says the Jews are aristocratic pariahs, pariahs with a patrician streak. I suppose it's true that Jews are naturally inclined to think of themselves as such.

Bostonia: Surely the Jewish "aristocracy" in that sense is rather religious than social. It's not personal, it doesn't belong to the individual.

Bellow: But you could always transpose from your humiliating condition with the help of a sort of embittered irony. Sufferance is the badge of all our tribe, we read at school. *The Merchant of Venice* went pretty deep. We didn't have apologetics when we did Shakespeare as high-school sophomores. That's one of the curious features of American society. Everything was out in the open in those days. And while prejudice and chauvinism were almost as ugly as in Europe, they were ineffectual too. The absence of an idea of defamation was very liberating. Everybody was exposed in the same way. Nobody could claim any protection. Of course, the respectable WASPs were somehow out of it, but even they came under attack. Nobody was immune. Not Jews, not Italians, not Greeks, not Germans, not blacks. Everything was out in the open. Which gave an opening to freedom of opinion. Everybody took abuse. This is what's disappeared since then. Without any increase in liberty.

Bostonia: And certainly no increase in communication, because by papering over differences with pieties about how people differ from one another, in aptitudes and in myriad other ways, one simply reinforces prejudice. People who pretend that difference doesn't exist make a fundamental error. If you marry, you quickly realize that.

Bellow: That's happened to me quite a few times. I think it's an important point to make. It's true there were unpleasant comic strips like Abie Kabibble with pudgy hook-nosed Jews and all the rest of that. But nobody was immune. People did strike back. But there was a kind of openness for everybody. It was a far more open society than before ethnic protectionism began.

Bostonia: In literature it had this grand effect, didn't it, that it allowed the writer's imagination to create characters who were larger than life. Their characteristics were so accentuated and out in the open that to be called a Jew or a Catholic or whatever, just exaggerated that aspect of your life. You could write a whole book about being that. By now it's reduced to our being all absolutely identical gray specks.

Bellow: Except just over the border in the first band of the unconscious, where you know perfectly well that this isn't so. But that particular band of the unconscious somewhere in the primitive part of the brain has taken a lot of punishment.

Bostonia: So at thirteen or fourteen you were already aware of being in possession of unconscious feelings?

Bellow: We were passing Freud from hand to hand at school. And Marx and Lenin. By the time I was fifteen the Depression was already upon us and everybody was suffering from it. On the other hand, there was what I now recognize as an unconquerable and spontaneous adolescent spirit which didn't recognize any such things as Depressions. Depression was a social fact, but it was certainly not much of a personal fact.

Bostonia: How does the Depression make its appearance as an idea?

Bellow: It was the first time capitalism was under direct attack for its failures.

Bostonia: Was that the way you put it as an adolescent?

Bellow: By the time I was fifteen, certainly. That was 1930. It was impossible to avoid this, you see, because the reactionary press itself introduced these terms. "We don't want any Russian revolutions here" and all the rest of that. So when they fell on their faces, they had already prepared the vocabulary of accusation themselves. And of course immigrants were filled with revolutionary hopes, because 1917 was . . . well, so glorious.

Bostonia: Was there any notion in your adolescence, again as an idea, of a difference between the intelligentsia and rest of the world?

Bellow: Yes, there was that definitely. You could see it. You could go into the main Jewish streets and see people who described

themselves as intelligentsia. They dressed differently. They wore
pince-nez. They smoked with curious gestures; they had a different vocabulary. They talked about evolution; they talked about
Tolstoy. All these things were very important in my adolescence.
I met a new sort of people on the main streets of the community. In
making the distinction between the back streets on which you lived as
a boy and the main streets on which you lived as an intellectual
semi-adult, you became a grown-up. In my case it was Division
Street, which was a mixture of Polish, Jewish, Ukrainian, Russian.
Scandinavian elements. . . .

Bostonia: Did you class yourself at that time as an intellectual?

Bellow: It never occurred to me that I was any such thing. I was
just a pair of eyes.

Bostonia: But it must have been somewhere back then that you
began to see yourself as a writer, an observer. Can you remember
any one moment, or was writing just part of the training of the eye?
The point is, you're such a physical writer, the emanations of
people, their effluvia, mean so much to you.

Bellow: I don't know whether it was training at all. I think it was
just spontaneous. I think that when I was a very small child it
wasn't only what people said, the content of what they said, so
much as the look of them and their gestures, which spoke to me. That
is, a nose was also a speaking member, and so were a pair of eyes.
And so was the way your hair grew and the set of your ears, the
condition of your teeth, the emanations of the body. All of that. Of
which I seemed to have a natural grasp. That is to say, this is the
way things are seen by me when they are most visible. I couldn't
help but do the kind of observation that I've always done. It
wasn't entirely voluntary. It wasn't based on ideas, primarily.

Bostonia: But the physicality of someone or something is surely
an idea. . . .

Bellow: Right. It's the abstraction of a speculative principle. The
abstraction came later. Actual life was always first.

Bostonia: What better foundation for ideas?

Bellow: If you go back to the Greeks, or the Greeks *and* the
Elizabethans, you may come to feel that conceptualization is a weak
substitute for this sort of feeling for things and beings as they are in
the flesh.

Bostonia: Things are visceral. Things are real. One lives in a real world in which one sees phenomena. You have a powerful affinity to such elements. As in Michelet. That comes across in his *History of the French Revolution* with such power. He understood that there are emanations from the body. And when one talks of the body politic, it really is a body; in Michelet it isn't some metaphor of what a state should be.

Bellow: I grew up to appreciate abstraction in some forms. I was thinking about this lately because I came across a passage from a book on Kafka in which Kafka says (I'm sure I'm right in this paraphrase) that he couldn't bear to read Balzac because Balzac's novels contained too many characters. He's asked: aren't you interested in characters? And he says, no, I'm only interested in symbols. And I could see that as a source of dramatic power. Especially when I was growing up, I found that a "personality" could also be constructed of something artificial. Something of conceptual origin. On the other hand, the number of types and roles were really limited: they soon became tiresome because they were derivative. This was confirmed when I began to go to Europe. I was already quite grown up. I soon began to understand that national character had been shaped by the classic writers. In Paris you could identify your Balzacian or Molieresque characters in clerks and shopkeepers, in your concierge, and all the way up the scale to the intellectual and revolutionary elites. Similarly, in London, with people being Dickensian or Trollopian, or whatever it was, I began to see that modern man's character is also derivative from literature or history. Or the movies, which are our equivalent of those old fictions. I won't mention television, because the psychology of that medium is of no interest whatever.

Bostonia: And what conclusion did you draw from Kafka's remark?

Bellow: I understood it in myself. I understood that I had both tendencies in me. On the one hand I could always count on my innate reactions to people. Baudelaire's advice: in any difficulty, recall what you were at the age of ten. On the other hand, those innate or early reactions weren't going to get me very far if I weren't also prepared to think about what I was looking at.

Bostonia: Perhaps this goes back to the days you spent at univer-

sity and afterwards, and to your choice of anthropology. That
was a somewhat peculiar one for you, really.

Bellow: The idea of anthropology is at heart a very democratic
idea. Everybody is entitled to equal time. They have their culture
and we have ours and we should not get carried away by our
ethnocentrism. The latter is a purely Western idea. It never entered
the mind of almost anybody else. It never occurred to an Iranian to
think his perspective distorted by ethnocentrism.

Bostonia: On the contrary, he'd find it nefarious, as an American
Indian would. It's funny that these very ancient civilizations really
didn't feel their ethnocentrism as in any way slanting their vision of
the world. New ones might.

Bellow: I think the idea is that real culture is blinding. Because
you're completely possessed by it. You don't have to think, with
great difficulty and some unnatural adjustments, that the stranger
coming toward you is black or white, male, female, safe, dangerous, etcetera. It isn't you the liberal democrat or *bien pensant*
making these judgments. It's that real, sometimes embarrassingly ugly
entity, your own self. Culture is prejudice in its basic (or, if you
prefer, lower) forms.

Bostonia: The catalogue of ideas one looks back on in the years
between puberty and serious study, which is universitarian, would
consist of what? It's as though you drew up a mental list of what
sorts of things you thought Raskolnikov had in his brain when he
decided to become a murderer. What was in yours? What strange
melange?

Bellow: Of course it was a melange. It's as if the head of a
modern person were sawed open and things were tumbling in
from every direction. So you had the Bible and the Patriarchs cheek
by jowl with Russian novelists and German philosophers and
revolutionary activists and all the rest. Your mind was very much
like the barrel of books at Walgreens where you could pick up a
classic for 19¢. I still have a copy of the *The World as Will and Idea*
by Schopenhauer which I bought for two dimes and read when I
was a high-school junior—or tried to read. I think I grasped it fairly
well. Those books would pass from hand to hand and the notes in
that Schopenhauer were made by my late friend Sydney Harris, a
high-school chum of mine. All kinds of mad scribbles in the

margin. But we did read those things. On the one hand, Schopenhauer and Nietzsche and on the other, Marx and Lenin. And then
again John B. Watson, and then again Theodore Dreiser and Dostoyevsky and Balzac and all those other people. You were really
pitched headlong into a kind of mental chaos and you had to make
your way.

Bostonia: What the hell has happened to our adolescents today
that this is a rare occurrence?

Bellow: Well, they have their music and sex and drugs instead.
And privilege. Privilege compared to what we had.

Bostonia: It's not underprivileged to have a mind filled with
books.

Bellow: No, but it does create a terrible disorder and you'd better
make sense of it because the premise of the whole thing is your
autonomy. You are going to govern yourself. And you don't realize
what the cost of it will be. At first it fills you with pride and a
sense of purpose and power and then you begin to see that you are
incapable of making the finer adjustments by yourself and life is
going to be a mass of errors, that clarity is to be found only in
spotting the mistakes.

Bostonia: Whereas today?

Bellow: I suppose the objectives are simpler today. You want
pleasure, you want money, you want to get ahead in the world.
You want to lead a full American life.

Bostonia: But you don't really want anything. Everything is available, which cuts down on desire.

Bellow: That's true. There's been a decline of desire. Besides,
you can no longer read a contemporary book about chaste girls
and wonder about the outcome as you did then. You used to know
how impossible it was for her to choose between rival attractions.
Meanwhile, the girl was thinking, "Which suitor shall I marry?"
That doesn't happen anymore.

Bostonia: Hence, the utter impossibility of a celibate clergy for
instance, just to mention one side effect. When bishops sit around
discussing whether homosexuality is acceptable, sacramentally,
you know there's something screwy going on.

Bellow: Oh, yes, all these things have run out. When I say I had
to decide between Schopenhauer and the rest, that was a sign of

those times. Some or many of these burning questions have run
their brief course and are no more. It's all gone. The last to be
generally discredited, except in the Third World, and the American
universities, is Marxism. I was filled with it. You couldn't read
the Communist Manifesto when you were young without being
swept away by the power of the analysis.

Bostonia: The studies are there, the mind is slowly filled and
there enters a strange concept in the world of ideas, which is
one's own originality, one's own sense of one's difference from the
stock. How does that occur to you? How does the personage Bellow
emerge from this maelstrom?

Bellow: He begins to see his life as a process of revision, of the
correction of errors. At last you have the satisfaction of having
escaped from certain tyrants. Let me make clear what I mean. I
mentioned Marx—Marx and Lenin. I might have mentioned
Freud. These philosophers and writers were the source of powerful
metaphors which had such a grip on you that you couldn't escape
them for decades. It's not easy to get rid of the idea of history as an
expression of class struggle. Nor is it easy to cast off the idea of
the Oedipus complex. Those are metaphors that will have their way
with you for a long time.

Bostonia: Yet at the same time you're working in a perfectly real
world. These ideas dominate a part of your mind, but the operative
part is full of its own pizzazz and ultimately goes its own way. It
takes these ideas but it moves somewhere centrally. Didn't you
feel that in your pre-university, late adolescence?

Bellow: I suppose that more powerful than any of the books I
read was my inner conviction that we were all here on a very
strange contingency plan, that we didn't know how we had gotten
here, nor what meaning our being here really had. I read all these
books in the hope of making some discovery of truth about these
persistent intimations. At bottom the feeling was always very strange
and would never be anything but strange. All of these explanations
you got failed to account for the strangeness. The systems fall
away one by one and you tick them off as you pass them. *Au revoir.*
Existentialism. But you never actually finish with this demand
that you account for your being here.

Bostonia: One book after another of yours expresses the same question in different terms.

Bellow: I suppose this is the highest point a modern man can hope to achieve. What do you see when you start reading Shakespeare? You begin with the early plays and you end with *The Tempest* and find just that. In Lear you are told "ripeness is all." We must abide our going hence even as our coming hither and all the rest of that. . . . You know, this sense of the mystery, the radical mystery of your being, everybody's being. The nature of the phenomena has changed somewhat. You're not just surrounded by nature's world, you're surrounded even more by technology's world. You don't understand it any better for having been educated. Because no matter how extensive your education, you still can't explain what happens when you step on a jet. You sit there, open your book, and all of these strange mechanisms of which you haven't the remotest conception, really, carry you in a matter of hours to New York and you know how long it used to take on a Greyhound bus. And even the bus was a technological advance. There's something that remains barbarous in educated people and lately I've more and more had the feeling we are non-wondering primitives and why is it that we don't marvel at these technological miracles any more? They've become the external facts of every life. We've all been to the university; we've had introductory courses in everything, and therefore we have persuaded ourselves that if we had the time to apply ourselves to these scientific marvels, we would understand them. But of course that's an illusion. It couldn't happen. Even among people who have had careers in science. They know no more about how it all works than we do. So we are in the position of savage men who, however, have been educated into believing that they are capable of understanding everything. Not that we do understand everything, but that we have the capacity. Since all of these objects are man-made and we are men, we should be able to decipher the ultimate or even the proximate mysteries.

Bostonia: You're saying the sweet mystery of life is gone. And yet that particular sort of speculative Jewish upbringing must have been one of the greatest of all gifts. It taught you that there were miracles, that the mysterious existed—for a Catholic, the

central act of worship was something you could not understand
even if you tried, because your capacity was not equal to God's.

Bellow: Now the mysterium has passed to high tech. However,
we have all been brought up to believe that we *can* understand these
things because we are "enlightened." But in fact, we haven't a
clue. We have to be satisfied with a vocabulary, with terms like
"metabolism" or "space-time." It's a funny conjunction . . .

Bostonia: Yet we remain dismissive of mystery. We think mystery
is an archaism. Only in the Dark Ages did people wonder. There
are no modern mystics except those who are spaced out: and they
don't know it.

Bellow: What I am really trying to say is that we've been misled
by our education into believing there are no mysteries, and yet . . .

Bostonia: But forgive me, you weren't misled by your education.
Why not?

Bellow: I suppose I had a radical Jewish skepticism about all the
claims that were made.

Bostonia: Did anthropology assume that sense of mystery in
any way?

Bellow: Yes it did. But I soon realized that I was really getting a
version of primitive life produced by other people educated as I
had been, giving me nothing any newer about the Trobriand Islanders than would have been the case if I had never heard of them.
Simply because you read Malinowski and Co. didn't mean that you
now knew the Trobriand Islanders. What you knew was the
version of an educated civilized European. And I guess there was a
kind of buried arrogance in the whole idea of the anthropologist:
in the idea that because these people are simpler their depths can
be plumbed. Definitely. With simple peoples we can nail down
the meaning of life.

Bostonia: Surely Malinowski understood that. That's what's good
about him.

Bellow: I chose one of the very best to criticize. You might have
some doubts in the case of Malinowski or Radcliffe-Brown, but
you would have no confidence at all in many other cases. You knew
when you met these scholars that they would never understand
what they had been seeing in the field. To me they were suspect in
part because they had no literary abilities. They wrote books, but

they were not real writers. They were deficient in trained sensibilities. They brought what they called "science" to human matters, matters of human judgment, but their "science" could never replace a trained sensibility.

Bostonia: Which brings us back to you.

Bellow: Which was what I acquired without even knowing it.

Bostonia: But there is no way to acquire a trained sensibility.

Bellow: Not unless you take certain masterpieces into yourself as if they were communion wafers.

Bostonia: The Eucharist of world literature.

Bellow: In a way it is that. If you don't give literature a decisive part to play in your existence, then you haven't got anything but a show of culture. It has no reality whatever. It's an acceptable challenge to internalize all of these great things, all of this marvelous poetry. When you've done that, you've been shaped from within by these books and these writers.

Bostonia: While you're absorbing all of this, there's one part you extract from the people you read. You extract Tolstoy's ideas, or Shakespeare's ideas. Then there's another part which is inextricable from the way they express those ideas, that is incarnate in their style, their narrative, the characters they create. Was that distinction clear to you at university level?

Bellow: It began to be clear, yes. For instance, I read all of Tolstoy when I was in college. I can agree with Natasha or with Ivan Nikolaevich even when I can't agree with Tolstoy's views of Christianity, man and nature. So I know the difference, and so did he, evidently.

Bostonia: Though he would have denied it and said only "the parables are at the heart of what I am."

Bellow: Of course there is this double, triple, or multi-dimensional ply in the great hawsers that attach you to life. That's why you can read Dostoyevsky without being particularly fazed by the antisemitism, because you know there's something at a deeper level, there's much more power at work, though many of his opinions may be trashy.

Bostonia: What did you make of your university education as a whole? By then you were becoming critical.

Bellow: At Chicago we were educated by Hutchins, really, or by

the spirit of Hutchins in which the place was saturated. You were
there for four years or for less if you were good at passing examina-
tions. You followed at your own pace. But if you met all the requirements you would graduate knowing everything there was to know
about the physical sciences, the biological sciences, the humanities, and the social sciences. Everything. You would then be fit to
stand with anybody on an equal footing and hold your own. Do
more than hold your own. There was a kind of crazy, cockeyed
arrogance in all of this, which really appealed to young Jews from
the West Side. But when I went over to Northwestern, I met just a
lot of agreeable, old-fashioned WASP English professors who
were eccentric, limited. They made no claims, no universal claims.

    Bostonia: What governed the choice? Why did you go to North-
western?

    Bellow: I was tired of marching with three or four hundred other
students to vast lecture halls, where four days a week nobody in
particular was talking to you. And on the fifth day you had a quiz
section where you actually got to see your quiz instructor for an hour
and you would go over the lectures with your master-tutors. And
they were masters. Very good people gave those general courses.
But you never got to know anybody and nobody ever knew you. I
got tired of this anonymity. I wanted a chance to distinguish
myself. You took a comprehensive examination and even if you got
a good mark, you were still answering multiple choice questions,
you weren't being asked to write any essays. I was in shallow
waters here. So I shifted over to the other place. I suppose I
wanted attention.

    Bostonia: And got it, no doubt. Had the writing begun then?

    Bellow: Yes, I was already writing.

    Bostonia: When did that fundamental idea of all writers, that this
is what you are going to do with yourself, write, first strike you?
In what form did it come?

    Bellow: It came early in my high-school years when I began to
realize that I thought of myself all along as a writer. God knows
there were plenty like me, so we formed a society of people with
literary ambitions.

    Bostonia: Did you think of these early texts as literary or did you
think of them as vehicles for ideas?

Bellow: There were wonderful magazines available in those days. You could give yourself quite a case of ambition-poisoning.

Bostonia: What magazines were you reading back then?

Bellow: The *American Mercury*, first of all, and then *The New Republic, The Nation*, the *Times Literary Supplement*, the *Manchester Guardian*. You could go downtown to Monroe Street and buy all these things. There were these great shops where you could get all the English papers, and French, too, if you knew how to read them. And German and Spanish.

Bostonia: Did you detect a visible difference between what they produced and what your local papers produced, for instance?

Bellow: In Chicago there were newspapers like the *Evening Journal* and even the *Daily News*, with people like Ben Hecht on the staff. Their book departments were flourishing and there were people around like Burton Rascoe, and quite good book reviewers. And Harriet Monroe was still around at *Poetry* magazine. You did get some sense that Chicago had been a literary center. It was already coming apart when I was in high school. But there were still Edgar Lee Masters who lived in Chicago and Vachel Lindsay who was in Springfield and Carl Sandburg. And Sherwood Anderson had lived in Chicago for so long. And Dreiser had been there and quite a few more. And the Hull House lady, Jane Addams, and Robert Morss Lovett and Thornton Wilder. Lots of people who had made the national literary scene. You felt this to be accessible in Chicago.

Bostonia: Did literature seem a career?

Bellow: I never thought of it as that. I never worried about it as a career. I never thought how will I live by it? Or how does one make a living? It never entered my mind that this was a problem. That's why I was the despair of my father.

Bostonia: You finished university, went to New York and basically put together the makings of a literary career.

Bellow: I reviewed books and lived from hand to mouth and was very happy. I was on the Writers' Project, the Federal Writers' Project. My special assignment was to cover Illinois writers. I suppose that on the WPA I was not very different.

Bostonia: That excursus took us away from New York just before the war. You are leading the life of poverty and literary grandeur. The idea floating about that this is an unlimited universe: possibility and total potentiality is everywhere. What did the war bring into your life in the way of ideas?

Bellow: I misunderstood the war completely. I was so much under the influence of Marxism—I took it at first to be just another imperialist war.

Bostonia: Had you done your *Partisan Review* by then? Had you started?

Bellow: No, the war started in '39. I wasn't published in *Partisan* until the '40s. I stood by that junky old doctrine, the Leninist line: the main enemy is at home, it's an imperialist war. I was still at that time officially sold on Marxism and revolution, but I sobered up when France fell.

Bostonia: You knew nothing of what was really going on in Germany then?

Bellow: I began to have an idea when the Germans got to Warsaw in 1939 and began to attack Jews in the streets.

Bostonia: But the *Kristallnacht* had made no real impression?

Bellow: Well, it had. I considered it a very evil and dangerous thing. I began to have my first strong doubts when the Russians invaded Finland. But I was still in the grip of left-wing ideology. And the Trotskyists (because I was closer to the Trotskyists than any other Marxist group). The Trotsky line was that a workers' state, no matter how degenerate, could not wage an imperialist war. He also argued that though it was degenerate it would neverthe-less advance the historical cause of socialism by bringing the forms of organization of a more advanced development into Finland: its lands would be nationalized, cooperatives would be estab-lished, soviets or workers' councils set up and so on. Although Stalin had done his best to emasculate the revolution, it was still a revolution, and Trotsky told his followers they must not oppose this war because it was a war against the whitest of white regimes, a white guard, antirevolutionary regime. But when the Germans reached Warsaw, I began to feel differently about things. When Paris fell, of course it was devastating.

Bostonia: It didn't affect most Americans.

Bellow: But I wasn't most Americans. I belonged to a special group of cranks that knew a little history and some Marxist doctrine and used to discuss matters on an "elevated plane."

Bostonia: Would you say that historical ideas played a major part, that history played a role in your development at the time?

Bellow: Something like the knowledge of history. We thought that the French communist party was in part to blame for the defeat of France in 1940. The armies had been demoralized by the communist line. So the word went around. *La France est pourrie.* That wasn't really enough of an explanation, no substitute for understanding. But still the people around the *Partisan Review,* who then had considerable influence with me, stuck to that Marxist view. The P.R. people were the best we could do in the cosmopolitan line. They thrilled us by importing the best European writers and familiarizing the American literary public with them. Where else would you find Malraux, Silone, Koestler and company but in the *Partisan Review?* It's true that some of them had the mentality of Sixth Avenue cigar store proprietors, but they were importing good things. Some of them I liked very much. They were not only mentally influential, they charmed me personally. People like Dwight Macdonald and Philip Rahv, Delmore Schwartz and Will Barrett and Clem Greenberg. But Clem and Dwight were obstinately, rigorously orthodox in their Marxism and kept saying, "Don't kid yourself, this is just another imperialist war. Don't be seduced by propaganda as people were in World War I."

Bostonia: Did you feel that you were, as a young litterateur, easily influenced?

Bellow: I wouldn't belong to anything. I wouldn't join any group. I was never institutionally connected with any of these people. I was the cat who walked by himself.

Bostonia: You look frightfully intense in the pictures of the day.

Bellow: There were sexual reasons for this intense look. Then too the politics and literature of the period laid you under great pressure. I had read all of these never-again war writers like Barbusse and Remarque. There was the revolutionary myth that the masses had taken things into their own hands in 1917 and destroyed the power of capitalist imperialism. It took me a long time to get over that. It was probably the most potent political mixture in the twentieth century.

Bostonia: What caused the myth to collapse?

Bellow: Stalin himself did a great deal to discredit it. I knew

about the purges. I knew the Moscow trials were a put-on and a
hoax. All of that was quite clear. And like everybody else who
invests in doctrines at a young age, I couldn't give them up.

Bostonia: Does the adult Bellow criticize himself for this?

Bellow: No, I don't see how I can. To avoid every temptation of
modern life, every pitfall, one would need a distinct genius. No
one could be so many kinds of genius.

Bostonia: At what point does it become impossible to forgive
people for holding ideas that are patently false?

Bellow: It depends on the weight of the evidence available. People
who clung to Stalinism after the Hitler-Stalin pact deserve harsh
criticism of course. But then most people somehow failed to—they
were reluctant to—grasp the meaning of the camps, both the
German and the Russian kind.

Bostonia: Could you tell us something about your circle of affinities, about close friends like Isaac Rosenfeld or Delmore Schwartz
and John Berryman? The forming of ideas with one's close friends
at a critical age between eighteen and thirty is absolutely fundamental. What was the energy flow of those ideas and how would
you describe the people and the ideas they represented?

Bellow: After some years full of love and admiration, I began to
suspect Isaac of having a weakness for orthodoxies. He was in
many ways an orthodox left-winger. Which I found curious. He
couldn't relinquish some of these things. But even some of the
best people I knew, and I include Isaac among the best, were unable
to divest themselves of their Marxism.

Bostonia: Did you know anybody contrary to that flow?

Bellow: Jewish friends who had a more American orientation,
yes. They didn't go leftwards. Mostly schoolmates of mine here
in Chicago. I use the word intellectual nowadays in a much more
pejorative sense. I never did like the idea of being an intellectual
because I felt that these intellectuals had no power to resist the
great orthodoxies and were very easily caught up in Marxism
and Stalinism.

Bostonia: Did they lack the penetration or did they fall for the romance?

Bellow: They were intellectuals. I think they saw there was an
advantage for them in following a certain line. One of the things

that was very clear to me when I went to Paris on a Guggenheim grant was that *Temps Modernes* understood less about Marxism and left-wing politics than I had understood as a high-school boy. I strongly suspected they expected the West to fall to Communism and they would be advantageously placed when this happened. I don't know how else to explain some of Sartre's positions and those of the people around *Temps Modernes.* Why was it they were unable to criticize the Russians in 1956? To behave as they did, you have to be attracted by more than doctrine. You had to have some idea of possible advantages. One saw so much of this, especially in France and Italy.

Bostonia: What were you doing during the war?

Bellow: When I was called up I was rejected because I had a hernia. Immediately I went into the hospital to have surgery. The operation was not successful. I didn't recover for about a year and a half. By that time the war in Europe was ending. So I went into the Merchant Marine. I was in Merchant Marine training when the bomb fell on Hiroshima. By then I had recognized Hitler for what he was. I knew most of the story and I felt that not only were my Jewish Marxist friends wrong in theory, but I was horrified by the positions they—we—had taken. That was the end of that. And I felt that I should do something in the war.

Bostonia: Did the break with these people hurt?

Bellow: No, by this time I was estranged from them. I was still going through an educational self-wrestling routine. I do it all the time. Trying continually to correct, correct, correct. And I also find that the more isolated you are, the more you develop a terrible book-dependency; you begin to see how you protected yourself from what you thought to be brutal, vulgar, and squalid. Building a fortress of high-mindedness. Really bad stuff. I don't mean to say books are bad, I mean to say that I have used them like a dope addict. I still catch myself doing that. I'm not accusing myself of anything. I'm just saying that this has been the case. Zola wrote *J'accuse* over the Dreyfus case, but our mighty book is *Je m'accuse.* On the other hand, silence is enriching. The more you keep your mouth shut, the more fertile you become.

Bostonia: Would you say you had any mentors between eighteen and thirty? Did they play a role in the formation of ideas?

Bellow: I would like to have had some, and some people came
forward in that role; but I had trouble accepting them. In fact I was
always looking for guidance. A leading art critic of the day offered
to take me in hand. He was strangely persuaded that a young man
needed to be formed by an older woman, or preferably a European
woman, who would civilize him, teach him something about sex
and introduce him to a higher social sphere—smooth his rough
edges. Somehow I didn't take to that, especially not when I saw
whom he had in mind for me, his castoffs. Another senior intellectual who took an interest in me was Dwight Macdonald, but he was
himself nervous and unfocused. I suppose Isaac had really a great
influence on me. After Isaac, Delmore Schwartz was really an
important guide and, later, John Berryman. But these were friends,
not shapers of my character.

Bostonia: When did you first know Berryman?

Bellow: In the Village around *Partisan Review* and then I went
down to Princeton for one year when Delmore and I replaced
Blackmur. That was about 1952.

Bostonia: Tell us something about your first contact with Europe.

Bellow: My first trip over (to Spain) was in 1947 when I was in
charge of a student group from the University of Minnesota. I was an
assistant professor there in 1946. *That* promotion came thanks to
Red Warren, because I was brought in as an instructor and he
twisted Joseph Warren Beach's arm and got him to advance me. He
rescued me from freshman comp papers. Madrid in 1947 was a
great eye-opener for me. In Spain I felt as if I was returning to some
kind of ancestral homeland. I felt that I was among people very
much like myself and I even had notions that in an earlier incarna-
tion I might have been in the Mediterranean. I was absolutely
charmed by it, by everything. The air seemed to be different.
Something especially nourishing. And then of course I had followed the Spanish Civil War and knew as much about what had
gone on in Spain between 1936–38 as a young American of that time
could learn.

The place was still shot up. Virtually as it had been during the
war. The buildings were all pockmarked. Madrid itself was like a
throwback to a much earlier time. The trolleys, for instance, were
strictly Toonerville trolleys. I wrote a piece about all this in the

Partisan Review. I met a great many Spaniards; it was my first
prolonged contact with Europeans and the European intelligentsia. At least the members of a *tertullia* in the café near my pension,
which was in the middle of Puerta del Sol. I had a letter to some
people—Germans, who had been journalists during the Civil War.
They received me and introduced me to people like Jimenez
Caballero, who was a fascist, a literary man in the Cortes, with
whom I had a few dinners. People were curious. They hadn't seen
many Americans. Spain had been quite thoroughly sealed off for
years. They felt so isolated that even a trivial instructor from
Minnesota was readily taken up by them.

I met the Papal Nuncio in Madrid. Since when does a kid from
Chicago get to meet a Papal Nuncio? And had dinner at the
Nunciatura. And had one of his assistants say to me that these
Spaniards are not Europeans, *son moros,* they are Moors. They
don't really belong to the European community. I also spent a lot
of time in the Prado which was then empty and soiled looking. I spent
a lot of time looking at Goya and Velasquez and Bosch. I did a little
traveling around Spain. I went to Málaga. We had come by way of
Paris so I spent a preliminary week there and, on the way out, a
second week. London in '47 was absolutely miserable. All those
vacant lots, flowers growing everywhere among the weeds. There
was nothing to eat in the restaurants and you strongly suspected they
were serving you horse meat.

Bostonia: When did you finally hit the heart of the matter, Germany, and what had happened there?

Bellow: I went to Salzburg in 1949 and then to Vienna. The
Russians were still in occupation. I had been invited to the
Salzburg Seminar, but I took a trip to Vienna. I was fascinated of
course, I went to see the monuments. I didn't like Vienna much.
I knew a lot of Central European literature. My favorites were
Kafka and Rilke. In Rilke, the poetry meant less to me than the
Brigge book which I loved. It had a great effect on me. Thomas
Mann I always viewed with some mistrust.

Bostonia: You are then in your early thirties. You are on the verge
of writing *The Adventures of Augie March.* Would you have called
yourself a formed man by then? Or is this really a half life that
doesn't conclude?

Bellow: No, I don't really think I was formed. There were lots of things I hadn't been able to incorporate. Things that got away from me. The Holocaust for one. I was really very incompletely informed. I may even have been partly sealed off from it because I had certainly met lots of people in Paris when I lived there who had been through it. I understood what had happened. Somehow I couldn't tear myself away from my American life.

That's what I see now when I look back at the writing of *The Adventures of Augie March*. That I was still focused on the American portion of my life. Jewish criticism has been harsh on this score. People charge me with being an assimilationist in that book. They say I was really still showing how the Jews might make it and that I saved my best colors to paint America. As if I were arguing that what happened in Europe happened because Europe was corrupt and faulty. Thus clearing the U.S.A. of all blame.

Bostonia: For a Jew to say that is like saying to be a Jew is to be condemned.

Bellow: That's right. That's as much as to say the West has nothing to offer Jews. But I wasn't considering that question when I wrote the book. I wasn't thinking about it at all. There's no shadow of it in *The Adventures of Augie March*. It was later when I myself went to Auschwitz in 1959 that the Holocaust landed its full weight on me. I never considered it a duty to write about the fate of the Jews. I didn't need to make that my obligation. I felt no obligation except to write—what I was really moved to write. It is nevertheless quite extraordinary that I was still so absorbed by my American life that I couldn't turn away from it. I wasn't ready to think about Jewish history. I don't know why. There it is.

Bostonia: Perhaps your mind didn't want to be limited.

Bellow: Perhaps. At the same time I can't interpret it creditably to myself. I'm still wondering at it. I lost close relatives.

Bostonia: Perhaps such things can only become central at an appropriate time. The time wasn't yet.

Bellow: Yes, but even then, what would writing about it have altered? You wouldn't know when you're reading Kafka's letters that a world war was raging in France and in the East. There's no mention of war in *Ulysses*, which was written in the worst hours of World War I. Proust took it in, but that's because Proust accepted his assignment as a historian of French life. He knew how to combine the aesthetic question with the historical one. This doesn't often happen. Very few writers are able to keep the balance because they feel they have to create a special aesthetic condition for themselves which allows only as much present actuality as they can reconcile with their art. So Proust was not destroyed by the Dreyfus case and the war; he mastered them aesthetically. A great thing.

Bostonia: You said the Holocaust was missing. What else do you feel was missing in your formation?

Bellow: Somehow I managed to miss the significance of some very great events. I didn't take hold of them as I now see I might have done. Not until *The Bellarosa Connection*. So I have lived long enough to satisfy certain significant demands.

This is the first of a two-part interview. The remainder, which covers Mr. Bellow's life from age 34 to the present, will be published in the January/February issue.

A Second Half Life: An Autobiography in Ideas, Part II
Bostonia / 1991

From *Bostonia*, January/February 1991, 35–39. © Saul Bellow.
Used by permission of *Bostonia* magazine.

Reading this second and concluding interview—much material is left over and no doubt use will be made of it at some
other point—what comes over most clearly is the particular
voice of a writer who, though beleaguered (petty attacks are
the daily diet of major figures), retains clarity, sanity, and
wit. The voice is like the writer: sharp, a touch gravelly,
tentative in the search for the right word, the clearest expression of an idea, honest, and not seldom bursting into open
laughter—at follies, whether his own or those of others. The
concentration, throughout, is exemplary. It comes over not
just in the speaking voice, which is always retained in the
written. The final text is the transcript of conversations,
together with exfoliations, marginal explorations, emendations, double emendations, and endless refinement. An ex-
ploration of one's own life and ideas, of one's development,
is plainly not a task to be taken lightly; Bellow did not.

Bostonia: We left you in New York. We pick you up at Princeton.
What part does the Academy play in your life?

Bellow: At first Princeton was just a relief from hack writing. I
had had such difficulty supporting a wife and small child. I took a
few jobs at NYU, teaching evening courses in creative writing and
literature. This was an amusing interlude. I was living in Queens
then, and I was glad of the opportunity to bum around the Village.
The Village was jumping at the time. The jumpers who attracted
me were Isaac Rosenfeld, Harold Rosenberg, Clem Greenberg,
Delmore Schwartz, Philip Rahv, Dwight Macdonald, William
Barrett.

Bostonia: So, the intellectual life in New York is where we
were . . .

Bellow: . . . Entrenched . . . ? I wasn't entrenched.

Bostonia: . . . and you just got into the *Partisan Review* office; the critics were taking over and . . .

Bellow: Oh, they were well-entrenched.

Bostonia: Why is that?

Bellow: The critics, the "thinkers" were the organizers and promoters. *Partisan Review* in those days brought current European intellectual life to the literate American university public. Rahv and Phillips were successful entrepreneurs in this line. As well as they could, they followed the example of *The Dial,* a magazine with a much higher literary standard. Of course, *The Dial* was not interested in the political crises of the twenties. The people attracted by the *Partisan Review* were radicals who had been associated until the mid-thirties with the Communist movement. They had literary tastes. They were, however, operators. Naturally they cleaned up on both sides of the Atlantic. But they also performed an important cultural service here.

The European stars of those decades were glad to contribute to an American magazine: George Orwell, Arthur Koestler, T.S. Eliot, Ignazio Silone, André Malraux, and so on. If you were an American, a putative writer, you were lucky to be published in the *Partisan Review*. You appeared in very good company. It was terribly exciting for a boy of twenty-three or four, who had only seen Eliot, Silone, and André Gide on library tables. During the Spanish Civil War, even Picasso appeared in *Partisan Review*. Mighty exciting to sophomoric Midwesterners.

Bostonia: Whence came the despite of what neither of us likes to call the "creative" figure? What turned people against creation, against literature?

Bellow: Well, the editors were interested in creative figures only insofar as they had some political interest. *Partisan Review* wanted the political glamor that surrounded these writers.

Bostonia: Did they think that you were a potential political figure?

Bellow: They thought that I was a kid from the sticks, from Chicago, who showed some promise and might develop into something. They were very encouraging, especially Philip Rahv. I don't think William Phillips had high expectations . . .

Bostonia: Was *Dangling Man* the first manuscript of fiction that they had of yours?

Bellow: No, I had published some things earlier in *Partisan Review*. Sketches . . .

Bostonia: So you became one of their stable . . .

Bellow: Yes, a young snorting midwestern Jew.

Bostonia: Did you enjoy your first serious teaching?

Bellow: By "serious" do you refer to my year of teaching at Princeton? I met my classes and taught my pupils. Some of them were extremely likeable. I wasn't overwhelmed by the Ivy League. I was curious about it. I had heard of these ivy compounds for class and privilege. I didn't assume a posture of slum-bred disaffection. Princeton was partly entertaining, partly touching, partly a scene of gloomy bravado. The Fitzgeraldian boozing was not associated with literary distinction. Except in the case of John Berryman, whose talent was genuine and powerful. Booze was not a primer of geniuses. Delmore became my friend there. R.P. Blackmur was and was not around. He was absent for most of that year. I never got to know him at all well. I observed that he liked to have an entourage sitting on the floor listening to his drunken undertones. I listed him as a brilliant court-holder.

Many people were attracted by the gathering of intellectuals and writers at Princeton in 1952. Ted Roethke turned up, and Ralph Ellison came down regularly to attend our parties. I had reviewed Ralph's *Invisible Man* for *Commentary* in 1949 or '50, but Ralph was not satisfied with my highly favorable review. He gently complained that I had failed to find the mythic substructure of his people. I took Ralph very seriously. He had the subject, the rhetoric—all the gifts.

I lived in Princeton with a man named Thomas Riggs, an assistant professor of English, whom I loved dearly. He was a heavy drinker—multiple personal defeats, a despairing character. He died in the next year—the year following—when I was no longer at Princeton. I was laid low by his death—by the circumstances of his life, which I knew well. In his big Princeton flat, he threw great parties in the old-fashioned Greenwich Village style, parties in which people in large numbers tramped in and out, noisily eating and drinking and smoking, coquetting, putting on the make, and

gabbing. R.W.B. Lewis lived across the hall from Riggs. In Riggs'
apartment I slept on a cot, stuffed bookcases towering over me.

Edmund Wilson was absolutely delighted by this Village revival;
he adored the parties. For old times' sake. He said of those
somehow dark, riotous gatherings that this was just what the Village
had been like in the twenties—a nostalgic exaggeration. Wilson
was wonderful, if you could interest him. If you failed to interest,
you didn't exist. You were wiped out—nothing. He was always in
pursuit of particular items of knowledge. When he discovered that
I knew some Hebrew, he was enthusiastic. He would come to my
office with hard texts. And when I was stumped and said that I
needed a Hebrew dictionary, he was off and away. He was a bit
like Mister Magoo. I don't mean that he was literally shortsighted,
but that he had eyes only for what was useful to a man with
projects. He also had the same gruff, Magoo strained way of
speaking. Partly colloquial, partly highbrow.

Bostonia: Was he the representative intellectual for those times?

Bellow: He was one of those that everyone admired. The promi-
nent were invariably put down in those circles. But those who
rose above the rest enjoyed a celestial status. Like Matthew Arnold
on Shakespeare: "Others abide our question. Thou art free."
There were certain people who were above criticism, like Wilson.
Meyer Schapiro was another such. Sidney Hook, too, though
Sidney confined himself entirely to politics. No literature for Sidney
Hook. Lionel Trilling, in those days, had made himself into an
Olympian. That was beautifully done. And you wanted to be one of
those people no one could lay a glove on. Some contrive this.
Wilson was one who did not. He didn't have to.

Bostonia: Were you one of the unassailables?

Bellow: Me? Oh no! I was boundlessly assailable!

Bostonia: But not often assailed.

Bellow: I made no great impression on the *Partisan Review*
heavy hitters.

Bostonia: Not all of the people were really seriously at work,
were they?

Bellow: Schwartz was and Berryman was. William Barrett was
mastering Existentialism—about to begin his book on the subject.

In the early fifties Berryman was writing the *Bradstreet* poem. I was finishing *The Adventures of Augie March.*

Bostonia: Where had the writing of that started?

Bellow: I began it in Paris. I was on a Guggenheim grant. You leave the U.S.A. and then you think of nothing else. I wrote in Paris, and later in Rome, at the Casino Valadier, in the Borghese Gardens. I went every morning with a notebook, drank endless cups of coffee and poured out the words. Around noon my friend Paolo Milano would appear, would mosey up. We'd descend to the Caffé Greco—for more coffee.

Bostonia: Did you stay in Princeton?

Bellow: I went up to New York as often as I could. I had an apartment in Forest Hills and kept a room in Macdougal Alley. In those days you could rent one for three or four dollars a week.

Bostonia: You must have felt on writing *Augie* that you were on some quite major departure?

Bellow: I knew it was major for me. I couldn't judge whether it might be major for anybody else. What was major for me was the relief of turning away from mandarin English and putting my own accents into the language. My earlier books had been straight mandarin. I had hoped that my offering would be acceptable to H.W. Fowler. In *Augie March* I wanted to invent a new sort of American sentence. Something like a fusion of colloquialism and elegance. What you find in the best English writing of the twentieth century—in Joyce or e.e. cummings. Street language combined with a high style. I don't today take rhetorical effects so seriously, but at the time I was driven by a passion to *invent.*

I felt that American writing had enslaved itself without sufficient reason to English models—everybody trying to meet the dominant English standard. This was undoubtedly very attractive, but it wasn't enough. It meant that your own habits of speech, daily speech, were abandoned. Leading the "correct" grammatical forces was *The New Yorker.* I used to say about Shawn and *The New Yorker* that he had traded the Talmud for Fowler's *Modern English Usage.* . . . I'd like to mention, before we leave the subject of Princeton, that in 1952 Bill Arrowsmith was there, finishing his degree in Classics, I was very happy in his company. I had met him in Minneapolis when he was a G.I. studying Japanese. He's even splendider now than he was then.

Bostonia: This use of language you were talking about in Augie? It always seemed an inner necessity.

Bellow: In Paris in 1948, in a dun fog (Paris was depressed; I was depressed), I became aware that the book I had come here to write had taken a crippling stranglehold on me. Then I became aware one morning, that I might break its grip, outwit depression, by writing about something for which I had a great deal of feeling, namely, life in Chicago as I had known it in earlier years. And there was only one way to do that—reckless spontaneity.

Bostonia: Didn't the book take off once you decided to do that?

Bellow: It did. I *took* the opening I had found, and immediately fell into an enthusiastic state. I began to write in all places, in all postures, at all times of the day and night. It rushed out of me. I was turned on like a hydrant in summer. The simile is not entirely satisfactory. Hydrants are not sexually excited. I was wildly stimulated in those first months.

(Externally) I led the life of a *bon bourgeois* in those days. Once, I ran into Arthur Koestler on the Boulevard St. Germain. I was leading my small son by the hand—Koestler and I had met briefly in Chicago. He said, "Is this your *child*?" I said, "Yes." I was then reprimanded: a writer has no business to beget children. Hostages to fortune—the whole bit. I said, "Well, he's *here*." It wasn't that I didn't admire Koestler. I did. But he was as well-furnished with platitudes as the next man, evidently.

Bostonia: The one thing that really shines out is your sheer prodigious energy.

Bellow: I hadn't read Blake then. I read him later. Coming upon "energy is delight," I remembered how I had overcome the Parisian spleen of 1948. *That* spoke to me.

Bostonia: When did it become fashionable that there should be an etiolation of this energy?

Bellow: Writers in the 1950s arranged themselves, it seems to me, along the lines laid down by Yeats: the worst were full of passionate intensity. And so they were. The Célines had the passionate intensity. The demonic figures on the Right were all energy. The *bien pensants* were pallid. *La vie quotidienne* was something that

prostrated and exhausted "good men," "men of good will." It
put you in an honorific category to be able to display the ravages of
this wasting disease of civilization. There was a nasty mournful-
ness in books written by the well-intentioned and the "ideologically
correct" in the fifties. On the left, Sartre had great energy to dispose
of, but he was even more depressing than the *bien pensants*. I
thought when he wrote his sponsoring essay on Frantz Fanon,
that Sartre was trying to do on the left what Céline had been doing
on the right—Kill! Kill! Kill! With all his desperate outlawry,
Sartre made me think of Peck's Bad Boy.

Bostonia: Your inner nature is basically optimistic.

Bellow: Well, what you call optimism may be nothing more than
a mismanaged, misunderstood vitality.

Bostonia: We arrive at Annandale-on-Hudson and Bard College.
A really curious place. It had already been celebrated in a novel
by the then-wife of a rather famous husband.

Bellow: Mary McCarthy and *The Groves of Academe*. There was
also Randall Jarrell's *Pictures From an Institution,* which I
thought much more amusing. Mary was unquestionably a witty
writer, but she had a taste for low sadism. She would brutally
work over people who weren't really worth attacking. She was by
temperament combative and pugnacious. She was a curiosity to
us because she was, in her earlier years, a most beautiful woman,
terribly attractive and apparently the repository of great sexual
gifts. I never dreamed of sampling those—you might as well have
been looking at sweets in Rumpelmayer's window. But nonetheless, there they were. I can remember her at *Partisan Review*
parties. She was very elegant, the only elegant woman present.
Her face was done up in a kind of porcelain makeup. Her look was
dark . . . arched brows, a clear skin under the makeup. You'd run into
her on the street as Nicola Chiaromonte once told me he did—she
was blooming, he said, and he asked, 'Why are you looking so
well, Mary?' She said, 'I just finished a piece against so-and-so and
now I'm writing another about such-and-such. Next I'm going to
tear you-know-who to pieces.' She was our tiger-lady.

Bostonia: What brought you to Bard?

Bellow: Princeton had only given me a one-year contract. I
needed a place to lay my head. At the time the Bard job sounded

easy. I'd be on an exiguous salary, but the country air and pleasant surroundings would compensate me. I could entertain my little boy there—take him out of the city, keep him with me on holidays and long weekends. Much nicer than dragging him around to museums and zoos in New York. Nothing is more killing. The zoo can be a Via Crucis.

But then I've had more metamorphoses than I can count. It was a time of plunging into things, attractive-looking things, which quickly became unattractive. I went through a period of psychiatry. Everybody was immersed in "personal" difficulties. Later, all this would fall away and you would feel you'd squandered your time in "relationships" and that there was no way in which you could understand your contemporaries or their ideas. You hunted for clues, looked them over, cast them aside. I would read up on a subject, discard it, and try again. I let myself in for a course of Reichian therapy: curious. A violent attack upon the physical symptoms of your character neuroses.

Bostonia: To what degree was *Henderson* underway then?

Bellow: I started to write *Henderson* after I left Bard, when I bought the house in Tivoli, New York, a few miles north of Bard. I poured my life's blood into that place; hammering and sawing, scraping, and painting, digging and planting and weeding until I felt like a caretaker in my own cemetery. So that as I mowed the grass I would think, here I will be buried by the fall. At this rate. Under that tree. But Bard wasn't entirely a negative experience. I learned certain things there. Don't forget I'd gone from an Ivy League environment to a progressive one, to Bard where there were numerous castaways from ships that had foundered en route to Harvard or characters who had fallen from grace at Yale. People still refining the airs they had acquired in the great Ivy League centers. Bard was like Greenwich Village-in-the-pines. The students came from small, wealthy, New York families. Many of the kids were troubled, some were being psychoanalyzed. Then, there were the "great" families of the locality. It was useful to get to know them. Not at first hand because they wouldn't invite me for drinks. Indirectly, however, I learned a lot about them.

My neighbors and acquaintances were Dick Rovere, Fred Dupee, Gore Vidal. My colleagues, *some* of them friends, were Keith

Botsford, Ted Hoffman, made up to resemble a cocky Brechtian, and Tony Hecht. I loved the company of Heinrich Blücher. Occasionally, I met his wife, Hannah Arendt, in New York and she would set me straight about William Faulkner—tell me what I needed to know about American literature. All that in red dancing shoes.

Bostonia: There wasn't that much humility in the Bellow of that period. That was understandable. You had made it. Most of them hadn't.

Bellow: I was speaking down to people (the nobs) who believed I looked up to them. My lack of humility was aggravated by the rejections I met or expected to meet. Those were part of my education. Five minutes of friendly clarity would have spared me this, but there was no one to assist my poor, slow mind. At that time, I was under tremendous emotional pressure. I had married into a New York bohemian family, and before long my wife began to say that my mind had been formed in the Middle Ages. She might have gone back even further—to antiquity, to the Patriarchs. My childhood lay under the radiance (or gloom) of the archaic family, the family of which God is the ultimate father, and your own father the representative of divinity. An American (immigrant plus WASP) version of the most ancient of myths: the creation, the garden, the fall, Genesis, Exodus, Joshua, Judges. These became part of your life, if you had that kind of upbringing. Imagine how well this fundamentalism would equip you to face the world I was entering—bohemianism, avant-garde art, the sexual revolution.

My wife's father was a painter, a Marxian-Freudian-Jungian theorist and the genius of a group of disciples to whom he was *the* artist. My wife had *had* it with artists . . . This flamboyant Svengali circle was fun—in a hateful way. But my young wife and I should have agreed to jettison all "formative experiences" and, to the extent possible, make a new start, shelve our respective fathers. . . .

I had an additional burden—my "higher education." That counts for a great deal. When that higher education was put to the test, it didn't work. I began to understand the irrelevancy of it, to recoil in disappointment from it. And then I saw the comedy of it. When Herzog says, "What are you proposing to do when your wife takes a lover? Pull Spinoza from the shelf and look into what he says about adultery? About human bondage?'' You discover, in other words, the inapplicability of your higher learning, the absurdity of your spray-can culture. True devotion to Spinoza et al has left you no time for neurotic attachments and bad marriages. *That* would have been a way out for you.

What the above argues is not that higher education is a bad thing, but that our conception of higher education is wrong.

One of the things you have to learn, which is never clear to you until an advanced age, is how many of the people you have to deal with are cut off from their first soul. This is in itself a revelation. And it never ceases to be a surprise to you that other people have a personal history so very different from your own. And have completely lost sight of that first soul, if indeed it ever existed for them. They may have turned away from it at a young age. In the earlier Greenwich Village generation, there was still some memory of it, even among the most anarchic and revolutionary. A person like Paul Goodman had a grip on it—on that first soul of his, as curious as it was—and as disfigured by psychoanalytic examination and the elaborate, eccentric ideas he fabricated. Still, it was there somewhere, a core of the self from first to last. It need not be—often it is not—a good or desirable core.

To many, the notion of an original center is alien and preposterous. Experience shows us more reproductions than originals. Zarathustra on the Last Man is hard for us to take. But Nietzsche didn't describe the Last Man *for* Last Men, any more than Marx described the alienated proletarian *for* proletarians. Marx was certainly addressing a new historical protagonist who was expected to survive the grinding forces of depersonalization. But who can deny that we are confronted daily with artificially constructed mass egos? And even relatively enlightened people prefer a Fabergé to a real egg.

Bostonia: Why would one marry a Fabergé?

Bellow: Because of the attraction of art. And because you may feel (or wish to feel) that somewhere within the Fabergé you see before you there is a real egg with a rich yolk, a hidden residual first soul. Remember the E.T.A. Hoffmann story of the woman of springs, cushions and wires invented by a mad Italian, and of the inflammable student who falls in love with her. She comes apart in his arms. In short, your own passion in some cases makes you think the power to reciprocate is there. And then we are not dealing with out-and-out automata—the object of your affections may know what it is that you want and have the talent to simulate it. A marvelous skill in deception often lies within "constructed" personalities.

To learn all this requires time, and you must wait long before you are ready to deal with human nature *telle qu'elle est*. Finally, we are unwilling for ideological reasons to think such things. They do not suit the liberal vision of human nature instilled by our *bien pensant* education. We shrink from cruelty and sadism. We hate to discover scheming, cunning sharp practice. The ideology referred to is our middle-class legacy.

The high comedy of the intellectual in the never-never land of the "heart." I refer to men and women who love painting or poetry or philosophy and who are surrounded and nurtured by fictions. Perhaps they rely on crisis, war, revolution to bring them to "reality" again. Hitler, Stalin, death camps, terrorist operations—these are the "real life" antidote to the "fiction" opiates.

Bostonia: We apparently have concentration camps of our own: in neighborhoods that are a vision of some future hell.

Bellow: The actual urban environment of fear and caution. What I like to call the Fort Dearborn complex.

Bostonia: Except the cavalry is not riding up. . . .

Bellow: The cavalry is not riding up and your comrades inside the fort have no intention of fighting the Indians.

Bostonia: The Nobel Prize seemed as much of a burden as a pleasure.

Bellow: Yes, I didn't really like the volume of attention it brought. I wanted *some* recognition, of course, but I didn't need, or expect, super certification.

Bostonia: The tone of your acceptance speech seemed to indicate that the times were slipping into a posture antagonistic to serious thought, anti-intellectual; literature was taking a beating; it was no longer taken seriously.

Bellow: Literature in my early days was still something you lived by, you absorbed it, you took it into your system. Not as a connois-

seur, aesthete, lover of literature. No, it was something on which
you formed your life, which you ingested, so that it became part
of your substance, your path to liberation and full freedom. All that
began to disappear . . . was already disappearing when I was young.

Bostonia: Under the influence of politics?

Bellow: Partly under the influence of the world crisis, yes. I often
try to fathom the feelings, attitudes, and strategies of a Joyce
during the Great War when he concentrated on the writing of
Ulysses. Could the fury of such a war be ignored? There's hardly a
trace of it in *Ulysses*. But it claimed the attention of most of
mankind. Like the army mule struck between the eyes: an infallible way to get the critter's attention. I understand that Rilke, sick
at heart, wrote almost nothing between 1914 and 1918.

Bostonia: In the first interview, you acknowledged that you con-
sistently ignored certain major events.

Bellow: I was late catching up. It wasn't that I wasn't interested.
I was deafened by imperious noises close by.

Bostonia: American culture can isolate, it can muffle . . .

Bellow: The immediate American surroundings are so absorbing,
so overwhelming. Because our minds are all over the place, we
tend to forget that America, like Russia, is not a country, merely,
but a world unto itself.

It has always been difficult for us to imagine life on premises
different from our own. We take foreigners to be incomplete
Americans—convinced that we must help and hasten their evolution.

Bostonia: But if literature is something to be lived and absorbed,
Americans generally represented that as "ego."

Bellow: Important American writing after the Great War was
avant-garde writing. Young Americans took as their models the
great figures of Symbolist and postwar European literature. That
was, after all, small public literature. It was not meant to be
offered broadly to a democratic public.

It was something of a paradox for writers whose background,
whose vital substance, was American to adopt these imported
attitudes. The truth is that they weren't entirely imported. You had
here a great public utterly devoid of interest in your literary plans.
And, in fact, you didn't wish to approach this public on *its* terms.

Wyndham Lewis, in a book called *Rude Assignment,* his intellectual biography, examines this question with exemplary clarity.
He makes a distinction between small public art and great public art. The great public writers of the nineteenth century were the Victor Hugos, the Dickenses, the Tolstoys, the Balzacs. They wrote for a national public. With the appearance of a Baudelaire, a Flaubert, you had an art which was intended for a limited public of connoisseurs. As the indifference of the great public to this firelight art increased, it became, perhaps from defiance, less and less accessible to the generality of readers.

I think this happened on both sides of the Atlantic. The Americans, of course, closely following the best European models, produced their own kind of small public art. It was one of the achievements of Hemingway to reach a vast public with small public stories and novels. What you had in America subsequently was a generation of writers who, with an esoteric outlook, presented themselves to a large public.

Bostonia: A doomed enterprise.

Bellow: An odd one at best. Also, increasingly associated with the universities, which gave shelter to small public artists.

Bostonia: Did you feel it yourself?

Bellow: Of course I felt it myself. I was schooled, as others were, in this art of choice means. Or refined instruments. I think *The Adventures of Augie March* represented a rebellion against small public art and the inhibitions it imposed. My real desire was to reach "everybody." I had found—or believed I had found—a new way to *flow.* For better or for worse, this set me apart. Or so I wished to think. It may not have been a good thing to stand apart, but my character demanded it. It was inevitable—and the best way to treat the inevitable is to regard it as a good thing.

Bostonia: That might account for some of the petty rancor the American literary establishment does feel towards you at times: that you've tried to occupy a stage, take literature seriously, and deal with public issues. They really don't like that, do they?

Bellow: They don't take it kindly. But let's remove me from this for the moment. The question has a wider interest, which ought to be addressed.

I think the mood of enthusiasm and love for literature, widespread in the twenties, began to evaporate in the thirties. Not only in America, but in England, France, and Italy. Not in the Soviet Union. There, the Stalin dictatorship generated a spiritual need for it. In the United States, and even in France, it became nugatory. In the United States you had a brand of intellectuals who presented themselves at the beginning of their careers as literary people. But they quickly abandoned literature. Didn't really much care for it. They made their reputations on the ground between literature and politics, with diminishing attention to literature. Not large-scale politics, because they were ineffectual there. They were literary highbrows who continued the work of Orwell and Koestler. They moved from literature to political journalism. The "literary" screen, a stage property, was hoisted away.

Here's my recollection of a conversation between William Phillips and Philip Rahv. I heard it in the Astor Place office of the *Partisan Review* nearly fifty years ago.

I have come to deliver the manuscript of a story. Rahv enters and asks Phillips, "Has anything for the next number come in?" Phillips says, "None of the important stuff (i.e. political, critical, academic) is here yet."

Though half of his preoccupations were political, Rahv was genuinely a literary man. But the repositories of vast power in my day never were art lovers. Stalin telephoned Pasternak to get a reference for Mandelstam: not because he was thinking of reading his poems but because he had Mandelstam on his hit list. Party leaders, heads of state, generalissimos, board chairmen, etc.—down to junk-bond scammers—have no time for belles lettres. Nor do the once literary intellectuals who buzz about them as (largely unheeded) advisors, rooters and *besserwissers* [know-betters].

These intellectuals, now totally political, have gone over to junk culture. High-level junk culture to be sure, but junk is what they genuinely prefer. After a day of unremitting crisis they want pleasant entertainment. They're not rushing home to read Act Three of *The Tempest* or to get in a few pages of Proust before bedtime, are they? And much of junk culture has a core of crisis—shoot-outs, conflagrations, bodies weltering in blood, naked embracers or rapist-stranglers. Junk culture is heard over a ground bass of extremism. Our entertainments swarm with spectres of world crisis. Nothing moderate can have any claim to our attention.

The prospect of his hanging will concentrate a man's thoughts wonderfully, Doctor Johnson has told us: For us, perhaps, thrillers are aids to such concentration, and help us to stay braced through the night. Nothing "normal" holds the slightest interest. Spare us the maiden joys of Tolstoy's Natasha. Give us only his spinning minié balls about to explode. We use the greater suffering to expel the lesser. The top ratings are permanently assigned to Auschwitz, Treblinka, and the Gulag. The Vélo d'Hiver is somewhat lower. Famine makes Ethiopia eligible. Now North America, if you except Mexico, isn't even in it.

This continent is the Kingdom of Frivolity, while all the "towering figures" are in Eastern Europe. This is how literary-political intellectuals view the present world. It isn't contemporary literature alone that is threatened by this. The classics themselves are shooting, not drifting, Lethewards. We may lose everything at this rate.

Bostonia: Is this a note of despair I hear?

Bellow: Do I look or sound despairing? My spirits are as high as ever. Not despair—anger. Contempt and rage. For this latest and longest betrayal by puffy-headed academics and intellectuals.

Mr. Bellow's Planet

David Remnick / 1994

From "The Talk of the Town" section of *The New Yorker*, May 23, 1994. © 1994 The New Yorker Magazine, Inc.

Saul Bellow was in town the other day, to deliver a lecture on anti-Semitism, and, truth be told, he seemed out of sorts. On the morning we met him, at the Lotos Club, on the Upper East Side, he looked fit (he is seventy-eight), and was outfitted like a moderate dandy. But he was glum all the same. Recently, he and his wife, Janis, moved from Chicago to Boston, where he is a professor of literature at Boston University. It seems something of a mystery even to him why he made the move. A little more than a decade ago, Mr. Bellow had described himself as one of the faithful "who have never abandoned Chicago."

So why *did* he leave?

"I was testing my youthful plasticity," he said now, over breakfast.

And how was it going in Boston?

"Not so hot," Mr. Bellow said, his brilliant, buggy eyes widening. "I feel the rupture. Janis does, too. I felt that I had given Chicago the best years of my life, as they say in divorce court."

Besides Chicago, the other familiar ground for Mr. Bellow, in fact and in his fiction, is New York—in particular, the Upper West Side, where Artur Sammler, "with his bushy eye," rode the buses and negotiated Broadway. And now this locale, too, was—well, not so hot. "I still enjoy the Upper West Side," Mr. Bellow said, "except walking up and down Broadway is like strolling through some foreign writer's invention of an American slum. It doesn't necessarily scare me, but it's disgusting. To have known Broadway in the days when those neat little trolley cars zipped up and down! The most exotic thing about Broadway in those days was the piña-colada stands. There's an obvious drug scene now, the hustle of the homeless. I can understand why liberal principles are so potent. The real feelings are very quickly worn out. After one block,

293

you've gone through your emotional repertory. You just don't
have any more feelings to give out. So you try to take an over-all
view of the thing that is more elevated, benevolent. But the fact is,
you resent it and you think it's degrading.''

In recent years, Mr. Bellow's political reputation has taken on a
more conservative cast—his decline-of-the-West funk seemingly
gloomier, the world-weariness of his fictive heroes more frequently
read now as autobiographical. Mr. Bellow does not call himself a
conservative, though. ''I consider myself some sort of liberal, but I
don't like where liberalism has gone in this country in the last
twenty years,'' he said. ''It's become mindless—medallion-wearing
and placard-bearing. I have very little use for it. It's a cover also
for a great deal of resentment and hatred, these terrible outbursts
from people whose principles are affronted when you disagree with
them. It's a bad moment in the history of the country.''

He went on to say, ''P.C. is really a serious threat to political
health, because where there is free speech without any debate
what you have is a corruption of free speech, which very quickly
becomes demagogy. People in general in this country have lost
the habit of debating questions. TV does it for them. People hold
opinions, but the opinions are not derived from either thought or
discussion. They are just acquired, as an adjunct, a confirmation of
the progressive status of the person who holds these opinions—as an
ornament, a decoration. It's like those Russian generals, their
chests covered with medals. People wear these opinions like medals.''

Mr. Bellow said he thought that the roots of P.C. were in the
debates of his prime, the supercharged battles between anti-
Communists and anti-anti-Communists. ''Liberal people felt they
were being dragooned, especially by Republican Administrations, into
the Cold War and they were being forced to line up, and they hated
that, they resented it very deeply,'' he said. ''I think there was
enough Stalinist influence in general to account for this in part,
especially in a city like New York. It was transformed—it changed
into liberal fanaticism after it had been Stalinism. This was the great
ideological divide in the civilized world. It really did train people
in attitudes of mind which have remained into the present and color
the way we think about social problems in the United States.''

The phenomenon of Louis Farrakhan—a figure Mr. Bellow had

been watching in Chicago for many years—was also very much
on his mind. "I think Farrakhan has a real appeal to the black
population and in a way that expresses its inclinations," he said.
"I don't know how deep the anti-Semitism runs among blacks, but
it is certainly conspicuous. There is this sort of attitude among
the blacks: Whatever else we may be, whatever handicaps we may
labor under, we are, nevertheless, not Jews."

Mr. Bellow continued, "There was a black columnist, a very
good one, many years ago, named George Schuyler. Schuyler wrote
a notable piece describing the black as the mudsill of the other
immigrant groups—the mudsill being a primitve step in front of a
shack—and everybody steps on the black in order to rise higher. I
think this is pretty much a conviction among blacks, and sometimes seemed to have a foundation, because all the other immigrant
groups were rising and the blacks remained where they were,
under this handicap. But that was not necessarily a Jewish conspiracy. The blacks have always been convinced that they have
remained inert and passive while everybody else rose in life and
used them as a stepping stone. That resentment has remained. I
see it also as a result—an unfortunate result—of the civil-rights
movement, that the first consequence of the civil-rights movement
was the development of black anti-Semitism. It seems a very strange
thing indeed."

When we had first asked Mr. Bellow about today's racial politics,
he had winced, saying he hoped we could find "an undangerous
way" to talk about it all. "There seems to be such a taboo on open
discussion that no habits of discussion have developed, no vocabulary for discussion, no allowance made for intellectual differences,
because you are immediately labelled a racist," he said. "There
are certainly many blacks with whom you can talk openly. And
they do the same. There's none of this poisonous stuff. With
Ralph Ellison you could say anything, just speak freely, as he did.
Or Stanley Crouch now, who is clear on all these questions, or
William Julius Wilson, at the University of Chicago. But there are
very few people in general who don't respond to the taboo."

Are things so much different from the way they were twenty
years ago?

"There's a certain tangible, palpable fear of putting your foot in it now," Mr. Bellow said.

And has the new atmosphere affected his writing? Would he hesitate for fear of attack?

"The writing is independent," Mr. Bellow said. "It's autonomous by this time. I write as I write. If I'm going to take heat because of it—well, that's the name of the game."

Index

A

Abel, Lionel, 35
Academic life, 20, 114–15, 141, 187, 200, 203–04, 215, 278
Adams, Henry, 220
Addams, Jane, 269
Adler, Alfred, 142
Adler, Mortimer, 215
After the Banquet, 22
Aleichem, Sholom, 13
Alger, Horatio, 257
Algren, Nelson, 49, 51, 106, 128, 174, 190
American Mercury (magazine), 269
Amis, Martin, *The Moronic Inferno*, 223
Anderson, Sherwood, 29, 104, 162, 173, 178, 208, 257, 269
Apollinaire, Guillaume, 200
Aquinas, Thomas, 147
Arendt, Hannah, 286
Aristotle, *Ethics*, 215
Arnold, Matthew, 169, 281
Arrowsmith, Bill, 282
Art, 92, 112–13
Auerbach, Erich, 47

B

Baldwin, James, 47
Balzac, Honoré de, 60, 102, 118, 261, 263, 290
Barbusse, Henri, 271
Bard College, 4, 241, 284–85
Barfield, Owen, *Saving the Appearances*, 129–30
Barrett, William, 271, 278
Barth, John, 93, 100
Baudelaire, Charles-Pierre, 202, 261, 290
Beach, Joseph Warren, 274
Beckett, Samuel, 134
Bellow, Abraham (father), 3, 13, 29, 80, 246, 256
Bellow, Alexandra Ionescu Tulcea (fourth wife), 128, 144, 172, 178
Bellow, Daniel (son), 57

Bellow, Janis Freedman (fifth wife), 231, 234, 247, 293
Bellow, Liza (mother), 29, 192, 250, 258
Bellow, Sandra Chekbassov (second wife), 244
Bellow, Saul: autobiographical elements in writing, 3, 236, 249, 293; biography, 3–4, 11–15, 86, 110, 127–28, 174–79, 187–95, 222, 236–37, 252–60, 272; family of, 80, 153, 233;
Works: *The Adventures of Augie March* (novel), 3–5, 7, 12, 15–16, 19–21, 25, 28, 30, 34, 49, 54, 63, 75, 79, 89–90, 161, 175–76, 185–86, 209–10, 216–18, 221, 241, 243, 245, 256, 275–76, 290; *The Bellarosa Connection* (novel), 277; *The Dangling Man* (novel), 4, 7, 14–15, 25, 28, 63, 68, 89, 171, 179, 233, 280; *The Dean's December* (novel), 181–82, 186, 190–91, 193, 196, 239–49; "A Half Life" (intellectual biography), 248; *Henderson the Rain King* (novel), 7, 17, 19, 21, 25, 28, 34, 64, 68–69, 80, 84, 89, 177, 186, 239, 243–44, 285; *Herzog* (novel), 7, 19, 24–26, 28, 33–34, 37–40, 42, 49, 52, 57, 59, 64–66, 68, 73–74, 80, 86, 93–98, 145–47, 113–14, 123–24, 132, 136, 155, 173, 177, 179, 182, 239, 285; *Humboldt's Gift* (novel), 123–24, 126, 140, 151–52, 158, 164–65, 177–79, 191, 193, 221–22, 232, 240, 243–44; *The Last Analysis* (play), 19, 25, 28, 32, 56–57, 158–59; "Leaving the Old Yellow House" (story), 239; *More Die of Heartbreak* (novel), 231–32, 235; *Mosby's Memoirs and Other Stories* (collected stories), 163; *Mr. Sammler's Planet* (novel), 78, 84–87, 93, 96–97, 99, 156, 164, 182, 183, 194, 219, 221; *Seize the Day* (novel), 7–8, 17, 21, 25, 28, 89, 97, 217, 243; *The Victim* (novel), 4, 7, 15, 25, 28, 63, 68, 89–90, 175, 184; "Who's Got the Story: Writing after Joyce" (lecture), 93; "The Writer as Moralist in American Society" (lecture), 19

297

Printed in the United States
51284LVS00003B/20